LANCASHIRE DIARISTS

Lancashire Diarists

THREE CENTURIES OF LANCASHIRE LIVES

by

J. J. BAGLEY

Phillimore

1975

Published by
PHILLIMORE & CO., LTD.,
London and Chichester
Head Office: Shopwyke Hall,.
Chichester, Sussex, England

ISBN 0 85033 197 8

L000028118

Text set in 11/12pt Journal
Made and printed in Great Britain by
Unwin Brothers, Ltd., Old Woking, Surrey

Dedication

For BESS—herself an indifferent diarist,
but a letter-writer extraordinary.

CONTENTS

LIST OF PLATES

(*between pp. 118 and 119*)

ACKNOWLEDGEMENTS FOR ILLUSTRATIONS

Frontispiece: Lord Clitheroe (Photo, N. Duerden); Plate 1, Mrs Whitlock-Blundell (Photo, F. Tyrer); Plate 2, W.J. Smith, Esq; Plate 3, Dr. J. Marshall; Plate 4, Society of Friends; Plate 5, Mrs Whitlock-Blundell (Photo, F. Tyrer); Plate 6, Lancashire Record Office; Plate 7, Photo Mrs C.F. Barber; Plate 8, W.J. Smith, Esq; Plate 9, Blackburn Diocesan Board of Finance; Plate 10, Manchester Libraries Committee; Plate 11, R.N. Dore, Esq; Plate 12, Society of Friends; Plate 13, F. Tyrer, Esq; Plate 14, Lancashire Life; Plate 15, Photo, Douglas Birch; Plate 16, Photo, Mrs C.F. Barber; Plate 17, Drawn by Douglas Birch; Plate 18, Manchester Libraries Committee.

The ASSHETONS of GREAT LEVER, WHALLEY, DOWNHAM, and CUERDALE

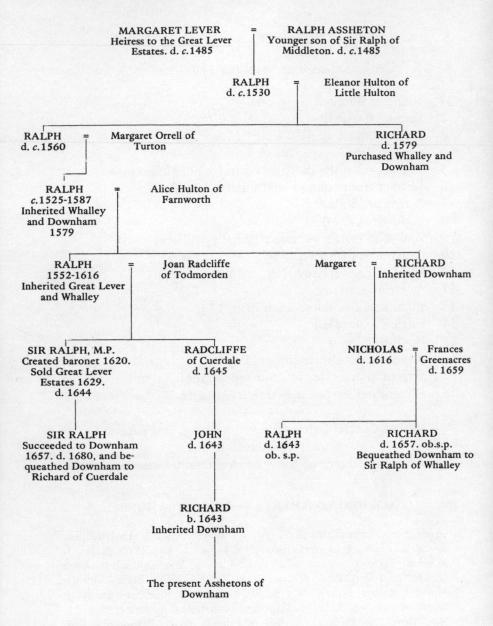

MARGARET LEVER
Heiress to the Great Lever
Estates. d. *c*.1485
=
RALPH ASSHETON
Younger son of Sir Ralph of
Middleton. d. *c*.1485

RALPH
d. *c*.1530
=
Eleanor Hulton of
Little Hulton

RALPH
d. *c*.1560
=
Margaret Orrell of
Turton

RICHARD
d. 1579
Purchased Whalley and
Downham

RALPH
c.1525-1587
Inherited Whalley
and Downham
1579
=
Alice Hulton of
Farnworth

RALPH
1552-1616
Inherited Great Lever
and Whalley
=
Joan Radcliffe
of Todmorden

Margaret
=
RICHARD
Inherited Downham

SIR RALPH, M.P.
Created baronet 1620.
Sold Great Lever
Estates 1629.
d. 1644

RADCLIFFE
of Cuerdale
d. 1645

NICHOLAS
d. 1616
=
Frances
Greenacres
d. 1659

SIR RALPH
Succeeded to Downham
1657. d. 1680, and be-
queathed Downham to
Richard of Cuerdale

JOHN
d. 1643

RALPH
d. 1643
ob. s.p.

RICHARD
d. 1657. ob.s.p.
Bequeathed Downham to
Sir Ralph of Whalley

RICHARD
b. 1643
Inherited Downham

The present Asshetons of
Downham

PREFACE

For most of us the voyage from the cradle to the grave is
full of incidents, some sad, and some gay. We all have to
navigate the narrows of childhood and the turbulent
waters of adolescence before we can sail across the wide
seas of adult life, but no two voyages are ever the same.
Each human being sets out with his own peculiar assets
and liabilities, and, guided partly by uncontrollable circumstances and partly by deliberate personal decisions,
steers his singular course through the difficulties and
delights that lie ahead.

Just because each voyager encounters different dangers
and enjoys or endures personal experiences and adventures,
we all have a natural interest in other people's life-stories.
However different in time and social status their circumstances may be, common experience of life enables us to
identify with them at least in part. We can 'rejoice with
them that do rejoice, and weep with them that weep'
because we have rejoiced and wept on similar occasions
in our own life. For ourselves, we cannot see far ahead.
We sail into the mists of the future hoping that unseen
hazards will not compel us to abandon or modify our
chosen course. In the logs of earlier voyagers we search
for instruction and encouragement as well as for entertainment. At best, these records strengthen our resolution,
bolster our courage, and help us count our blessings.
Those that fall short of such virtue cannot help but
enlighten us a little about the social and economic background against which previous generations lived their
lives, and reassure us that we and our contemporaries
comprise nothing more than the latest wave of a vast
armada making the same voyage across life's ocean.

The personal records of individuals are of special interest
to historians. Today, few scholars would be so dogmatic
as Thomas Carlyle, who once defined History as 'the
biography of great men'. Historians now study the past
more comprehensively than Carlyle did. As far as the
extant records allow them to do so, they concern themselves as much with lesser, more humble men as with 'the
great', and, in their attempts to evaluate the quality and
the overall pattern of social and economic life, they com-
pile statistics, preserve artefacts, and discuss theories of
social organisation and progress as well as studying the
careers and influence of individual men and women.
Even so, History remains the study of man—his actions,
thoughts, ambitions, achievements, and failures—so that
historians must always place a high value on such documents as diaries, letters and autobiographies.

The most readily available form of life-story is the
biography. But biography, like all historical writing,
brings its subject to the reader at second-hand. The
biographer is the necessary intermediary. He usually
examines piles of papers concerning his chosen subject,
and then, in the light of his knowledge of the subject's
generation and circumstances, gives us his personal interpretation of the subject's character, intentions, thoughts,
and career. A good biography is a well-written, neatly-
contrived, attractive story, but by its very nature it is
bound to be partial. It frequently ignores what appears
to the biographer to be trivial, and lays undue stress
upon those events which seem to him to lead to major
developments in his subject's career. Important years are
expanded, unimportant years telescoped, and the sole
judge of *importance* is the biographer. Above all, the
degree of the biographer's admiration for and sympathy
with his subject colours the whole of his work. James
Gairdner and P. M. Kendall have given us as different
pictures of Richard III as Robert Graves, David Garnett,
and Richard Aldington have of Lawrence of Arabia.
Since Richard and Lawrence had but one life each, the
differences in their portraits must enamate from their
biographers' judgments.

Because the subject speaks for himself, the autobiography would seem to stand a better chance than the
biography of portraying a true picture. Towards the end
of his life, the author looks back and tells us what he
has seen, felt, and done. The historical value of his work
depends both on the aids to memory that he has been
able to use, and on his purpose in writing. Samuel
Bamford claimed that he based his autobiography on
daily entries. William Stout certainly used notes which he
had compiled over many years, and the detail of Adam
Martindale's life-story points to his use of a similar
memory-prompter. Even so, it is not easy to determine
how near Bamford, Stout, and Martindale got to the truth.
The passage of time and subsequent developments probably clouded their memory and trimmed their recollection
of events. Bamford and Martindale especially tell lively,
fascinating stories, but their very skill as story-tellers and
their natural desire to hold the reader's attention could
have lured them away from a more prosaic but more
truthful narrative. Bamford's account of Peterloo, for
example, is as tense and gripping as a good thriller. It is
a highly personal report as all genuine autobiography
must necessarily be, but how much it owes to the author's
innate romanticism and his intention to justify and exalt
the Lancashire reformers of Regency days, it is impossible
to say.

John Rushton's narrative is less contrived than Bamford's, but even so it has been shaped to some extent by
his wish to demonstrate to his grandson's generation that
working conditions in the coal mines and the artisan's
standard of living had both considerably improved during
the second half of the 19th century. His intent in sitting
down to write actuates the story he has to tell. The
graphic details that have chanced to stick in his memory
give welcome colour to his manuscript, but each reader
has to judge for himself if Rushton's motives and selective
memory in any way affect the truth of his story.

Historical truth is a most elusive quarry. Few records
tell bare-faced falsehoods, but no personal record is free
from traces of self-delusion and from at least one of the

many forms of exaggeration. Consciously or unconsciously,
writers of autobiography cannot escape some degree of
self-justification, of overstating, or occasionally under-
stating, the part they played in events, of explaining away
faults and mistakes, and of recording arguments and
rejoinders that they wished they had made rather than
those they actually made. The reader is left to decide
how much trust he can put in an autobiographer's
narrative. Yet no two readers' assessments will necessarily
agree, for each reader is just as fallible a human being as
the author himself.

Collections of letters or daily entries in a diary are
the personal records most likely to bring the reader near
the truth. In so much as they express one person's
viewpoint, they are prejudiced, one-sided witnesses, but
they do have the merit of being contemporary with the
events they describe. They record immediate impressions
and reactions; unlike autobiographies, they are not emotion
recollected in the tranquillity of much later days. In her
letters and journal, Ellen Weeton expressed herself decisively, often with rancour and bitterness. To be able to
judge more impartially the righteousness of her cause, it
would be necessary also to read the views of her brother
and her husband. But at least Ellen's writings have not
been revised. What she wrote in her joy or anger at the
time has remained, unedited by hindsight, with no
pruning of trivialities or injudicious remarks, and without
the addition of later opinions or impressions. Sir Henry
Hoghton's letters are just as frank and impulsive: free of
the restraint of discretion or second thoughts, both
writers poured out the immediate anxiety, vexation, glee,
and opinion, which different events and circumstances
provoked. Each letter had a single, instant purpose.
Neither author had any thought of future publication.
Such letter-writers as Horace Walpole or Charles Lamb
might always have been careful to safeguard their literary
reputation. But not so Hoghton or Weeton: very probably
they never blotted a single line.

Diaries have similar merits. Assheton, Newcome, Tyldesley, Blundell, Kay, O'Neil, and Fisher form an odd,

miscellaneous collection of men. They have only one thing in common—that, each for his own separate reasons, they all kept a diary. At the end of every day, or at less regular intervals, they wrote down what they considered to be the most important events of the previous few hours or days. All of them had different interests in life, so all naturally differed about what was worth recording. For Blundell, family and estate affairs always had a high priority. Newcome the parson, and Kay the doctor, were constantly watching for the hand of God directing their personal activities. O'Neil filled his pages with political events, Fisher with local disasters, and for Assheton and Tyldesley, the two diarists who are most alike, nothing was more worthy of diary space than a good hunt or horse-race. But none of them attempted to review or amend what they had once written. Unlike George Fox, they have not left us an edited journal, with petty and worthless incidents removed, and, as Fox admitted, 'adding here and there such little reflections as occurred to my mind'. Instead they have left us the raw material itself, and it is up to each one of us to interpret it as we think best.

The Middle Ages had chroniclers in plenty, and such 15th-century writers as Philippe de Commines or the author of *Gregory's Chronicle* might loosely be classed as diarists. But personal diaries such as those chosen for this book are rarely found earlier than the days of Shakespeare. In the 17th century keeping a diary became a fairly popular hobby, and ever since, each generation has had its quota of men and women who have patiently recorded the passing scene. This year's diary is of minimal interest to this year's reader: it is necessary to allow time to enrich a diary's attractiveness. Years after the diarist is dead, his work might well be published and become a best seller.

Of all the diaries mentioned in this book—and, for this purpose, as in the title of this book, *diaries* includes auto-biographies and collections of letters—all but three have been published, at least in part. Until recently, however, all were out of print, and had to be consulted in the reference libraries or hunted in second-hand bookshops. During the last few years new editions of Stout, Blundell, Kay, Weeton, and Bamford have made welcome appearances, and quite possibly the next few years will see the reprinting of some of the other texts. In record offices and libraries throughout the county as well as in personal possession, there are dozens of manuscript diaries, autobiographies, and collections of letters that hopefully await future editing and publishing. Many are too scrappy and others are too massive ever to stand much chance of seeing the light of print, but no one knows the extent of historical treasure yet to be revealed. It is more than likely that many chance finds, such as those that gave us the letters of Ellen Weeton and the diary of John O'Neil, have yet to be made. As they become available, the new manuscripts will give pleasure to many readers, and add their contribution to the ever-growing body of knowledge concerning life in Lancashire during the last three centuries.

J. J. B.

University of Liverpool.
April 1974.

THE JOURNAL OF NICHOLAS ASSHETON OF DOWNHAM, 1617-19

[The original MS no longer exists. T. D. Whitaker published the text in his History of Whalley *in 1818, and F. R. Raines edited it, with much inappropriate sanctimonious comment, for the Chetham Society, Old Series, Volume 14, in 1848. The spelling of the* Journal *has been modernised.]*

The Asshetons are still an important Lancashire family. In 1971 the Crown appointed Lord Clitheroe, present head of the family, Lord Lieutenant of the county. Lord Clitheroe was born Ralph Assheton, and his home is Downham Hall, the house in which Nicholas Assheton lived and wrote his diary in the reign of James I. Could he return, the diarist would find that his old home had been substantially rebuilt in the 1830s, and that the church, although still on the same site, was unfamiliar in design. But he would be quite at home in the countryside round about. Downham has not changed much in the 350 years since Nicholas's death. It is just as much a country village as it was in Stuart times. Some of the houses Nicholas knew still adorn the village street, and, of course, Pendle, which dominates the whole area, changes little. On bright sunny mornings it is a siren tempting the young and able-bodied to spend the day on its broad slopes, but in rain or mist its lowering and forbidding looks turns most people's steps indoors.

The Asshetons did not originate in Downham. As their name suggests, the earliest Asshetons or Ashtons—both spellings are pronounced *Ashton*—are found possessing the manor of Ashton-under-Lyne. This main branch died out early in the 16th century when Sir Thomas Ashton's estates were divided between his three daughters. The Asshetons of Middleton then assumed the leadership of the family. Sir Ralph, vice-constable of England in Richard III's

reign, had increased their fortune, and, his son, Sir Richard,
successfully protected it against any revenge Henry VII
might have attempted to take. In 1563, another Richard,
a child of five years, succeeded to the Middleton estates.
Once he was old enough to look after his own affairs, this
Richard prospered well. In 1597 and again in 1606, he
served as sheriff of Lancashire. He married twice, both
times with profit, and was knighted on the accession of
James I. It was the death of this Sir Richard, which upset
Nicholas's Christmas plans in 1617.

Dec. 26   Word came that Sir Richard Assheton was very dangerously sick.

Dec. 27   I with my Coz. Assheton [Ralph Assheton of Whalley]
to Middleton. Sir Richard had left his speech and did not know a
man. Had not spoken since morning. His extremities began two or
three days since. He departed very calmly about eight at night. No
extraordinary sorrow, because his death was so apparent in his sick-
ness. Presently upon his death there was inquiring after his will,
which was showed by Mr. John Greenhalgh of Brandlesome
[Brandlesholme Hall, near Bury] and Sir Richard's second son Ralph
Assheton, who with my lady [Mary, Sir Richard's second wife] were
executors, and Coz. Assheton of Whalley, supervisor. My now Coz.
Assheton of Middleton, Richard, began to demand the keys of the
gate and of the study for the evidence, and to call for the plate, upon
cause his brother John had some part in them. There were some
likeness of present falling out of him and the executors, which
certainly had been, had not my Coz. Assheton of Whalley so [con-
trived] as was little or no discord. The reason was former unkindness
between Sir Richard and his son, to which Sir Richard was moved
by my lady and those that were of her faction.

Dec. 28   (Sunday) To Church. Parson of Middleton [Edward
Assheton of Clegg, near Rochdale] preached. Text 1 Thess. I, 9. To
Chadderton to dinner with my aunt Assheton [Ann, widow of James
Assheton of Chadderton].

Dec. 29   Executors, heir and my Coz. Assheton in the study all
day, and there well all things set straight.

This short extract illustrates how the several branches of
the Asshetons kept closely in touch with one another.
Ralph of Whalley, who was to be created a baronet in
1620, had recently succeeded his father. He was in his late
thirties, and quite wealthy, for in addition to the site and
buildings of Whalley Abbey, he had inherited extensive
acres and many properties in Great Lever near Bolton,

Manchester, Salford, Worsley, Billington near Blackburn,
and Mallam in Yorkshire. He and Nicholas the diarist were
first cousins, and their inheritances were curiously inter-
twined. In the middle of the 16th century, Richard, a
younger son of Assheton of Great Lever, had purchased
both Whalley and Downham out of the fortune he had
acquired partly from his profession as an attorney, partly
from his wife's inheritance, and partly from the patronage
of William Cecil, Lord Burleigh. When he died in 1579, he
left his estates to his nephew, Ralph of Great Lever, with
instructions that at Ralph's death they should be divided
between Ralph's two sons. Whalley went to the elder,
Downham to the younger. The Ralph of Whalley mentioned in the Diary and Nicholas the diarist were respectively the son and heir of the elder and the younger of
these two brothers. To complicate the inheritance even
further, when Nicholas's second heir died childless in 1657,
he willed his Downham estates to his kinsman, Sir Ralph,
second baronet, of Whalley. And then, when this Sir
Ralph died in 1680, he bequeathed Downham to another
branch of the family, the Asshetons of Cuerdale. Since
then, however, the descent has proceeded regularly.

Nicholas never succeeded to the Downham estates, for
he died in his mid-thirties in 1626, when his father was still
living. But Nicholas had a family of his own. He married
a neighbour, Frances, the daughter of Richard Greenacres,
squire of Worston. They had five children. Two died in
infancy. Ralph, who succeeded his grandfather, and
Richard, his younger brother, were both bachelors, and
their one surviving sister, Margaret, although she married
and had two daughters, had no child to succeed her when
she died in 1652. The most long-lived of Nicholas's family,
surprisingly, was his wife, Frances. Her long widowhood
did not end until 1659, eighteen months after the death of
her last surviving child, Richard. She died mistress of her
childhood home, Worston Hall, which to-day is a farmhouse.
Built into the porch are three stone heraldic shields believed to have been rescued from the demolition of Sawley
Abbey. They serve as a reminder of the days when the
Hall was a social centre of the area.

Assheton's Journal is therefore a diary kept by a young married man, who was heir to considerable property. He belonged to the middle rank of the Lancashire squirearchy. His name alone was a sure passport into any gathering of gentlemen, and he spent his happiest hours in the company of his peers. The pages of the *Journal* that have survived— for surely this fragment cannot be everything he wrote— begin on 2 May 1617 and end on 13 March 1619. Nicholas, then in his late twenties, was bursting with physical energy. It is not surprising that he wrote his *Journal* spasmodically and hastily: the wonder is that he ever bothered to keep one at all, for his heart was obviously far more in hunting, riding, dining, and drinking than in writing. The very first entry reads:

> Hunting the otter: killed one: taken another quick at Salley [Sawley]. Spent Vld.

And the second, ten days later, records a family drinking party:

> Father Greenacres [Richard Greenacres of Worston], mother, aunt Besse [Elizabeth Greenacres?], John [Nicholas's brother-in-law], wife, self, at ale. Spent 1Vd.

What prompted Nicholas to keep a journal is a bit of a mystery. It was hardly necessary as a memory aid. It was certainly not a means of clearing his thoughts or recording his opinions, and it had no pretensions to literary merit. No doubt he would be amazed to know that it survived him, and that later generations have found that it has given them a partial, but clear, picture of country life in the early years of the 17th century.

Hunting was Nicholas's chief sport. Whitaker, his first editor, counted 16 fox hunts, 2 buck hunts, and 2 otter and hare hunts in the *Journal*. Unfortunately, there are no long, detailed descriptions. Nicholas neither effuses about the chase nor gloats over his successes. He is terse and matter-of-fact.

June 11 [1617]. Tried for a fox, found none; rain: wet through. Home again. [Pickwick's Mr. Jingle could hardly have summed up this depressing day more concisely.]

June 30. Self, father, parson, John Assheton [of the Middleton branch], *cum aliis,* a fox-hunting to Harden [Trough of Bowland], up to Scouts Stones; set the greyhounds; found fox . . . lost him in the holds [holes?].

Aug. 23. Downham. Hunting fox on Worsoe [Worsaw End, a hill leading to Pendle]: killed one. Another to Pendle. Killed another fox, and earthed another, afterwards killed in the hole.

Oct. 27. A hunting. Found no fox: killed a hare.

Feb. 20 [1618]. Snow: traced a fox from Harthill [Hart Hill, Trawden] to the warren, and so from want of dogs came home.

One hunting entry, however, is more than usually informative. On 15 November, Nicholas was caught shooting the King's deer in Bowland Chase.

On hill above Walloper Well, shot two young hinds; presently comes the keeper and broke [dispersed] the other deer, had [accepted] the skin and a shoulder and five shillings, and said he would take no notice.

Nicholas found fishing, shooting, and hawking acceptable alternatives to fox and deer hunting, but he did not indulge in these sports as frequently as in hunting.

June 27 [1617]. Coz. J. Assheton, self, father, brother Sherborne [Richard Shireburne of Dunnow, near Slaidburn, husband of Nicholas's sister, Dorothy] fished with two wades [sieves] up to the bridge; sent some fish to the parsonage. Dined at parsonage. Spent VId.

July 10. Home. Parson etc. fished with great nets: got some 47 fishes and laid away.

July 11. Two little drafts, with scamel [small net] only, above Newton [*i.e.* in the River Hodder]. Got about 65 fish, and no salmon; so home.

Dec. 23. To Rowe Moor [Bowland Chase], and killed there 3 heath cocks.

Nov. 4. Down to the water: Dick killed a mallard and a duck at one shoot; Sherborne killed a water ousle, 2 pigeons and a thrush.

And if there was nothing suitable to pursue and kill, Nicholas and his friends would find pleasure in competitive shooting or riding.

Nov. 29 Clitheroe. Ad. Wh. [initials of competitor, or *ad*—towards—
Whalley?] shot W. Walbank at X score [200 (10 x 20) yards], in the
long bow for XXs. Should have shot with steel bows, but Walbank
had broke his string.

They had an insatiable appetite for physical exercise and
open-air sport, and often appear to have had the limitless
energy of schoolboys.

June 24 [1617]. To Worston Wood. Tried for a fox; found nothing.
Towler lay at a rabbit, and we stayed and wrought and took her.
Home to Downham. A foot race.

And for the next fortnight and more, Nicholas was constantly out-of-doors, enjoying the long midsummer days
fox-hunting in Bowland Chase and fishing in the Hodder.
These were the weeks of the year when gentlemen made
longer journeys than usual in order to meet socially, drink,
gamble and hunt together, and ride in competition. On
14 July 1617 Nicholas went to Dunkenhalgh, the home of
Sir Thomas Walmesley, to join the Molyneux family of
Croxeth, the Gerards of Bryn, and the Bradshaighs of
Haigh, near Wigan. This was a gathering of Roman Catholic
families, but that did not deter the Protestant Nicholas
from meeting them, or his cousin, Ralph, from inviting
them to join his house party at Whalley.

July 16.   Sir Richard [Molyneux] with the rest of the gentlemen
to Whalley Abbey; there we had a banquet. Sir Richard Molyneux
junior, Coz. Assheton, self, *cum aliis*, to John Lawe's [the inn];
back to the abbey. All but two old knights to Salbury [Salbury
House in Bowland Chase]; there had one course [coursing hares]
and missed. East Bradford [near Clitheroe]. There Mr. Townley,
Carr [Hall, Pendle], *cum aliis* from London; made merry.

July 18.   Sir Richard and Mr. Assheton made a match, dun gelding
against a dun nag of Sir Richard at Liverpool, for 20 pieces a side;
Sir Richard and my Coz. to ride light as they can, so as Sir Richard
be ten stone.

The following midsummer Nicholas spent in similar fashion.
On 2 June 'we all' went to Prescot to a cockfight, and then
rode to Lever near Bolton. Sir Richard Assheton, Sir John
Talbot of Bashall and John Braddyll of Portfield near Whalley were among the company. 'Very pleasant', comments

Nicholas; 'tabled all night'. Early in July, Nicholas stayed at Gawthorpe near Burnley, and on 19 July, a Sunday,

> Sherborne [Richard], Starkie [Thomas of Twiston Hall east of Downham] etc. to Clithcroe; stayed drinking some wine: so to a summer game: Sherborne's mare ran and lost the bell: made merry; stayed until, etc. 2 o'clock at Downham.

And yet because the gentry took full advantage of the summer months, it must not be assumed that they did not venture away from home during the winter. Nicholas rode to London and back twice during the weeks immediately before and immediately after Christmas 1618, and late the previous January he had been over in the south-west of Lancashire hawking and dicing with William, Earl of Derby, Sir John Talbot, young Thomas Charnock of Charnock Richard, and other gentlemen.

The one aspect of Nicholas Assheton's diary that puzzled and shocked his two 19th-century editors was that he combined a keen interest in church attendance with what they considered to be nothing less than riotous living. Because Nicholas speaks of attending Exercises—religious lectures—Whitaker considered him a Puritan, but Raines rightly pointed out that, in pre-Laudian days, attending *the Exercise* was not limited to Puritans. Nor was the appreciation of a good sermon: no one liked a well-preached sermon more than Henry, fourth Earl of Derby, and yet his love of plays, masques, and songs prevented him from being classed as a Puritan. The characteristic of Lancashire Puritanism was its strong Sabbitarianism: measured by this rule, Nicholas was no Puritan.

May 18 [1617]. (Sunday), to church. Parson preached. Text, 1 Psalm 3. Also in the afternoon preached 1 Psalms 5, 6. Sp[ent] Wine, all alone, xiid. so home. First time I wore my ash-coloured clothes.

[*No date, but July-Aug.*] Sunday. Parson preached; after dinner. Mr. Leigh. To Worston. Spent X11d. there merry.

Sept. 28 (Sunday). Word came to me that a stag was at the spring: Walbank took his piece, and Miller his, but he was not to be found. Miller shot with Walbank at a mark, and won.

Nov. 25.   St. Katharine's Day. To Downham. There an exercise.

To Worston. Tom Starkie etc. very merry, and well all. All at supper.
We were all temperately pleasant, as in the nature of a festival day.

The 17th-century Puritan, however, would not have
been as outraged by Nicholas's drinking as were Whitaker
and Raines. They were astonished that he should go
straight from church to ale-house, and that he should con-
fess to being 'merry' at least a dozen times, 'sick with
drink' once, and on other occasions 'foolish' with drink.
Even more, they failed to understand why he never even
hinted that he regretted these excesses, and never resolved
to exercise greater restraint in future.

Nicholas was none too conscientious a diarist. Now and
again, he made consecutive daily entries in his *Journal,* but
many a time, three or four days, a week, or even a fortnight passed without his putting pen to paper. It could
well be that he deemed these missing days 'ordinary'—days
that were not worth recording because they were wholly
taken up with work on the estate. Occasionally, he allows
us a glimpse of himself at work:

Aug. 22.   A fair day: all to hay; got all we had in.

Aug. 27.   Began to lead first of our corn-wheat.

Feb. 14.   Downham. Grafted some stone fruit which came from
Holker [the home of George Preston, Cartmel].

Mar. 4   Set some apple trees.

Mar. 5.   In the orchard most of the day.

May 24.   Grafted some grafts from Whalley.

All these recorded work days, however, are semi-special;
he might well have wished to recall any one of these dates
on some future occasion. It is a pity there is no record of
routine work, for, from the historian's point of view,
Nicholas would have doubled the value of his diary had he
related the dull and commonplace as well as the pleasur-
able and the unusual.

Two very unusual events occurred during the twenty-
two months covered by this diary. One was Nicholas's
need to make his double journey to London. He does not
explain this business clearly, but he says sufficient to show

that he, acting for his father, was fighting a case in the Court of Wards against 'Midleton'. In August 1615 an inquisition post mortem held at Preston had established that the late James Middleton, yeoman, had held land in Downham by knight's fee. This probably gave the Asshetons the right of wardship if a minor succeeded to these lands, and apparently some member of the Middleton family was contesting this right. The case should have been heard on 20 November, but was 'deferred by the attorney's favour and Sherfield's [Assheton's counsel's] slowness'. Consequently everyone had to return to Lancashire—six days of hard riding—and then journey to London a second time the following term. At length, on 11 February 1619, the court heard the case and gave judgment for Richard Assheton. Three days later at Downham, while Nicholas was still in London, Frances Assheton gave birth to their daughter Margaret. The baby was christened four days later, nearly a month before her father got back home on 13 March.

The other unusual event recorded by Nicholas was the celebrated visit of James I to Lancashire in August 1617. The King was to stay three or four days at Hoghton Tower, and Sir Richard Hoghton determined to make it a memorable occasion both for his family and for the Lancashire gentry. First, he recruited a number of young gentlemen, dressed them in Hoghton livery, and bade them ride with him to meet King James as he travelled from Hornby Castle to stay with the Tyldesleys at Myerscough Lodge, near Garstang.

Aug. 11. My brother Sherborne his tailor brought him a suit of apparel, and us two others, and a livery cloak from Sir Richard Hoghton, that we should attend him at the King's coming, rather for his grace and reputation showing his neighbour's love, than any exacting of mean service.

Aug. 12. To Myerscough, Sir Richard gone to meet the King: we after him to [   ] There the King slipped into the forest another way, and we after and overtook him, and went past to the Yate [gate]; then Sir Richard light; and when the king came in his coach, Sir Richard stepped to his side, and told him there his Majesty's forest began: and went some ten roods to the left, and then to the lodge. The King hunted, and killed a buck.

During his stay at Myerscough, James killed five more bucks. He also found time to receive a petition protesting against the attempt of some Puritan magistrates in Lancashire to enforce a strict observance of the Sabbath. James declared that he approved of 'piping [pipe playing] and honest recreation' on Sundays, and within days, this statement, too freely interpreted, led to some noisy and ugly scenes in different Lancashire parishes. Nicholas probably welcomed the royal decision, but for the moment he was fully occupied 'riding up and down'. On 14 August, he rode to Preston to help make preparation for the king's arrival: 'we were desired to be merry, and at night were so . . . All Preston full'.

James entered Preston on the morning of 15 August. The recorder, Henry Breares, welcomed him with a formal speech, and the corporation entertained him to a banquet in the town hall. In the afternoon the royal party, which included George Villiers, newly created Earl of Buckingham, moved to Hoghton Tower, accompanied by a host of Lancashire gentry, including Nicholas and his cousin, Ralph of Whalley. That busy day ended with deer hunting followed by another meal: 'we attend on the Lords' table'. The next two days were spent hunting, feasting, and merry-making.

Aug. 16.   Houghton. The King hunting: a great company: killed afore dinner [mid-day] a brace of stags. Very hot: so he went in to dinner. We attend the lords' table; and about 4 o'clock the King went down to the Alum mines [at Alum Scar, Pleasington] and was there an hour, and viewed them precisely, and then went and shot at a stag, and missed. Then my Lord Compton had lodged two brace. The King shot again, and broke the thigh bone. A dog long in coming, and my Lord Compton shot again and killed him. Late in to supper.

Aug. 17.   Houghton. We served the lords with biscuit, wine, and jelly. The Bishop of Chester, Dr, Morton, preached before the King. To dinner. About 4 o'clock, there was a rushbearing and piping afore them, afore the King in the middle court: then to supper. Then, about ten or eleven o'clock, a masque of noblemen, knights, gentlemen, and courtiers afore the King, in the middle round, in the garden. Some speeches: of the rest, dancing the Huckler, Tom Bedlo, and the Cowp Justice of Peace [traditional dances].

By noon the next day King James and his company left
Hoghton to stay with the Earl of Derby at Lathom House.
Sir Richard and his more humble guests—Nicholas among
them—relaxed and celebrated the great occasion with a
drinking bout.

> We back with Sir Richard. He to cellar and drunk with us,
> and used us kindly in all manner of friendly speech. Preston :
> as merry as Robin Hood and all his fellows.

The drinking continued for most of the following day—
'all this morning we played the bacchanalians'—but Nicholas seemed capable of a quick recovery. On 21 August he
rode first to Bolton and then home. The next day he
spent hay-making, and by 23 August all was normal again,
for he was out fox-hunting on the slopes of his beloved
Pendle.

THE DIARY AND AUTOBIOGRAPHY OF HENRY NEWCOME, 1627-1695

[In the 1840s the Rev. Thomas Newcome, a descendant of Henry, lent both manuscripts to the Chetham Society. The Society published the Diary *as Vol. 18 of its Old Series (1849) and the* Autobiography *as Vols. 26 and 27 (1852). Thomas Heywood edited the* Diary *which only covers two years, September 1661 to September 1663, and Richard Parkinson the two volumes of the* Autobiography. *The Lancashire Record Office holds the will and inventory of Henry Newcome.]*

Seventeenth-century English records are rich in diaries and autobiographical writings. Pepys and Evelyn are the century's most celebrated diarists, but they do not stand alone. Sir William Dugdale, herald and distinguished antiquarian, kept a journal for nearly half a century. The diaries of Robert Bowyer and Simonds D'Ewes are concerned chiefly with parliamentary matters; Henry Oxinden's letters and Lady Anne Clifford's diary with social affairs. Particularly during the disturbed years of the Civil Wars and the Interregnum, many gentlemen on both sides wrote accounts of their adventures or misfortunes. Some of these writings became the basis for autobiographies or contemporary biographies such as the well-known *Memoirs of Edmund Ludlow, Memoirs of the Verney Family,* and *Memoirs of the Life of Colonel Hutchinson.* But probably the clergy—especially the Puritans—wrote and preserved most autobiographical records in various forms and in different degrees of detail.

Lancashire has more than her fair share of extant clerical writings of this kind. One is tempted to cheat a little and begin with the *Diary* of Dr. John Dee, the notorious chemist, mathematician, astrologer, and magician of

Elizabeth's reign. During his long life he lived in most parts of Europe from Paris to Cracow and from Louvain to Venice. His reputation travelled further afield still, but in 1595 he settled in Manchester as Warden of the Collegiate Church. The manuscript of his *Diary* is in the Bodleian Library, Oxford. The Camden Society published a version of it in 1842, but the pages covering the Manchester years 1595-1601 were extensively edited by J. E. Bailey and in 1880 published in *Local Gleanings relating to Lancashire and Cheshire*. Dee's *Diary* is more intriguing than historically helpful. The irregularly made entries vary from straight-forward notes of dreams remembered, actions taken, people met, or money borrowed to obscure references to burning 'reports of sight and hering spirituall' or cryptic entries which had meaning only for Dee. But occasionally a single line quickens the reader's historical imagination, and makes him wish that he could have overheard the conversation:

9 October 1595. I dyned with Syr Walter Rowleigh at Durham House.

21 June 1596. Mr. Christopher Saxton came to me.

10 July. Manchester town described and measured by Mr. Christopher Saxton.

14 July. Mr. Saxton rode away.

Unfortunately the plan of Manchester which Saxton made on this visit has never been found.

Two generations later than Dee, the Puritan clergymen who regarded Manchester as the centre of their world were prolific scribblers. They have left us extensive diaries, autobiographies, and letters to study. John Angier was probably the most central figure, partly because he won the universal respect of his fellow divines, and partly because, although firmly committed to Presbyterianism, he appreciated the sincerity and arguments of the Independents or Congregationalists. He began his ministry in Lancashire at Ringley near Prestwich, but two years later, in 1632, he moved to Denton, south-east of Manchester, and stayed there until his death in 1677. From its inception

in 1647 to its dismissal in 1660, he served as a member of
the Manchester Classis, the Presbyterian committee charged
with the organisation of the church in South-east Lancashire. Yet, by keeping out of the way at critical times
and by allowing visiting clergy occasionally to read the
Prayer Book services, Angier managed to avoid expulsion
from Denton after the Cavalier Parliament had passed the
Act of Uniformity in 1662. He continued to lead and
minister to his faithful congregation to the end of his life.
Angier kept a diary, but it is no longer extant. Judged by
the few extracts that have survived—some quoted by his
son-in-law, Oliver Heywood, and, some, two hundred
years later, extracted by Canon Raines, who borrowed the
1662-76 volume from its then owner—it was evidently a
full account of Angier's thoughts and pastoral and private
activities couched in the language common to 17th-
century Puritan clergy. Fortunately, Heywood wrote *A
Narrative of the Holy Life and Happy Death of That
Reverend, Faithful and Zealous man of God, and Minister
of the Gospel of Jesus Christ, Mr. John Angier,* which, as
its title suggests, is a pious work of admiration and
appreciation rather than a conventional biography. Heywood published his book in London in 1685, but happily
the Chetham Society reprinted it as Volume 97 of its New
Series in 1937, and the editor, Ernest Axon, furnished it
with introduction, notes, and some of Heywood's and
Raines's extracts from the lost diary.

Oliver Heywood himself was a diarist, and his diaries,
which with gaps cover the years 1666-1702, were edited
by J. H. Turner, and published in 1882-85 under the title
Oliver Heywood's Diaries. Heywood was born at Little
Lever, Bolton, in 1629, and, although he ministered at
Coley chapel, Northowram, near Halifax, from 1650 until
he was ejected in 1662 and again from 1687 to his death
in 1702, he was a prominent member of this group of
Manchester-based dissenting clergy. So were Adam Martindale and Thomas Jolly, despite the fact that the one was
incumbent of Rostherne in Cheshire and the other pastor
first at Altham, west of Burnley, and then, after 1662
further away from Manchester, at Wymondhouses at the

foot of Pendle. Martindale's *Autobiography* is discussed in the next chapter, and *Jolly's Note-Book 1671-93,* which is an edited re-writing of a hurriedly-kept diary, has been published by the Chetham Society as Volume 33 of its New Series. These Puritans formed a closely-knit society and their various memoirs interlock at many points. It was not just that the writers knew each other and referred to one another in their writings. They were all earnest fanatics, who took their responsibilities seriously in the years of authority, and comforted and supported each other during the years of exclusion and harassment after 1662. They all knew, and were well-known by, the faithful congregations in such Puritan strongholds as Gorton, Denton, and Ellenbrook near Worsley, and inevitably from time to time some of them worked closely together. In the late 1660s, John Jolly, Thomas's brother, assisted Angier at Denton, and when John died in 1682, Oliver Heywood preached his funeral sermon. When Thomas Jolly first went to Altham in 1649, he replaced Giles Clayton who moved to Coley Chapel, soon afterwards to be the centre of Heywood's preaching, and in 1648 when the inexperienced Martindale found himself caught in a fierce Presbyterian-Independent conflict at Gorton, he turned to Angier for advice and solace.

In theological and politico-theological disputes the Manchester Puritans formed a formidable group. During the pre-Civil-War years they spoke out boldly against the 'misdeeds' of Laud and the Anglican hierarchy. During the Interregnum, when Anglicanism had been temporarily routed, they debated their own doctrinal differences at great length and with righteous fervour. To use Martindale's expressive phrase, Presbyterians and Independents resembled 'Jacob and Esau struggling in the womb'; but like most quarrelling brothers, they would stand back to back against a common enemy. One of the many orthodox Anglican clergymen who came up against this redoubtable Dissenter opposition was William Langley, the curate at Edenfield. He has left us a fragment of autobiography[1]

---

[1]Published in Chetham Society Publications, Vol. 103, Old Series.

most of which he wasted bemoaning what he imagined was a mis-spent youth. He was angry with himself that he could not match the garrulous arguments of the Manchester Puritans. 'I had to comfort myself', he wrote, 'with St. Augustin, *tu ratiocinare, ego mirer; disputa tu, ego credam'* –'you go on arguing, I stand in wonder; you may dispute, I shall believe'.

Right in the centre of this Puritan brotherhood, in that his most influential years were spent in Manchester itself, stood Henry Newcome. He kept a diary most of his life. He began to write it at Cambridge in 1646, because he heard that a Dr. Ward, an academic whom he respected, had left a diary. He used it 'to set down my sins every day', and although he acknowledged that he did not always enter the most significant events, yet what he did record 'was some restrain unto me sometimes'. He admitted that he left frequent gaps in the *Diary,* but 'I could not be quiet till I had taken it up again', and however 'sapless and empty' he considered most of the entries were, the thought that always kept him going was that 'I knew not but that in time I might have something remarkable to set down'. Soon after his ejection from his pulpit in August 1662, Newcome 'began to review my old diary, and to collect some memorials of the Lord's dealings more historically for the use of my children when I am gone'. This he continued to do until 1693. The result was his *Autobiography,* which has survived and which recounts the chief events of his life. Most of the original *Diary* is no longer extant.

Throughout the whole of his life, Henry Newcome lived in an ecclesiastical world. His father, Stephen, was the Rector of Caldecote in Hertfordshire, and his mother, Rose, was the daughter of Henry Williamson, vicar of Conington, Cambridgeshire, and the niece and granddaughter of parsons. Stephen and Rose had seven sons who grew to maturity, and of these, four, including Henry, eventually took holy orders.

Henry was born in 1627. His father taught him Latin, but in May 1641, on the eve of the Civil Wars, he sent him to Congleton Grammar School, Cheshire, where his elder brother Robert had recently been appointed schoolmaster. Unfortunately, this arrangement did not last long. In the following February, both Stephen and Rose Newcome died within three days of each other. Robert and Henry immediately left Congleton for Caldecote, and after two more years of instruction, Robert arranged for Henry to go up to Cambridge.

> I was admitted, in the very heat of the wars, on May 10th, 1644 [as Prince Rupert was about to invade Cheshire and Lancashire] of St. John's College in Cambridge, pupil to that ingenuous, learned, and pious man Mr. Zachary Cawdrey, Fellow of that College. There was but nine admitted of that great College that year. . . . By reason of the troubles, I discontinued till the 10th May after, 1645, and then I went up to continue. It pleased God to give me good success in my studies . . . and especially to preserve me wonderfully from the infection of ill company.

Newcome eventually graduated in February 1648, but in the previous September he had already followed in Robert's footsteps and had been appointed to the mastership at Congleton Grammar School. Like other schoolmasters who were aspiring Dissenter parsons, he began to accept invitations to preach in neighbouring churches, and in August 1648, almost accidentally, was ordained in Sandbach.

> I did not think of it, but casually asking Mr. Ley whether there would be an ordination or no, he told me there would, and asked me whether I would be ordained. I thought of it, and so entered upon examination. God gave me favour in their eyes, and, though young, they passed me, and I was solemnly set apart that day.

The examiners were of course Presbyterians. They valued ordination as a mark of spiritual authority, but, like all contemporary Dissenters they did not oppose unordained aspirants preaching. Since Newcome was still a few months short of twenty-one, they might well have asked him to wait another year or two before being ordained.

Three or four weeks before his ordination, Newcome had married Elizabeth, the daughter of Peter Mainwaring of Smallwood, near Congleton. It proved to be a happy

marriage, and from a social point of view a most useful
match, in that it gave Newcome connections with the
Cheshire gentry. But in his *Autobiography*, written nearly
half a century later, he expressed strange misgivings that
he had married so early in life:

> I was rash and inconsiderate in this change of condition,
> and sinned in that I took not that advice I should have took
> of my friends in it; and God might have made it sad to me
> and done me no wrong; but he very mercifully turned it into
> good for me. And for the matters of greatest concernment, I
> found a ready compliance in her to further me therein all
> that she could . . .

The Mainwaring influence helped him to be appointed
first, incumbent to the little chapel of St. Luke at Goos-
trey, and then, in April 1650, rector of the important
church of St. James at Gawsworth. He stayed at Gawsworth for seven years, during which he became well
known throughout Eastern Cheshire and even in South-
east Lancashire as a powerful preacher.

In September 1651 Newcome visited Manchester for the
first time. It was partly a sentimental journey, for, since
his maternal grandfather had been born in Salford, he
hoped to discover relatives whom he had not yet met.
But he could hardly have chosen a worse time for a first
visit. The Scots had recently marched through Lancashire
on their way to disaster at Worcester. Charles II had temporarily accepted the Covenant, and therefore the strong
body of Lancashire Presbyterians had been momentarily
torn between supporting the Presbyterian Royalists and
sticking to the Parliamentary cause. Most of them hardly
hesitated before deciding to remain loyal to Parliament,
but that did not prevent the Parliamentarians from
taking precautions and imprisoning a number of leading
Presbyterian ministers:

> . . . at that time were Mr. Heyrick [Warden of Manchester
> Collegiate Church] in prison at London, and Mr. Hollinworth
> [assistant at Manchester] Mr. Angier, Mr. Harrison [incum-
> bent of St. Michael's, Ashton-under-Lyne], Mr. Meeke [in-
> cumbent of Sacred Trinity, Salford] etc. in prison at Liverpool
> upon suspicion of some correspondence with the king in his

going through the country; and they were just in cleansing
Manchester church from the nastiness the poor imprisoned
Scots had left it in.

It was a bad introduction to the place in which he was
destined to do his most important work. Four years later,
in May 1655, he got a much better impression when he
preached at the Collegiate Church. After a lot of debate
with himself, he chose as his text, 'O wretched man that I
am! who shall deliver me from the body of this death?',
because he thought that among 'that great people' there
might be 'hundreds . . . in a carnal condition', whom it
might touch deeply. He seemed satisfied with his efforts:
'a great congregation it was, and the Lord helped me graci-
ously'. And in turn the clergy and congregation seemed
satisfied with him, for he, with Angier, preached there
again in August, and after Hollinworth's sudden death in
November 1656, the parish invited Newcome to fill the
vacancy.

Newcome took up residence in Manchester in April
1657. He was 'sadly affected and broken all to pieces' to
be leaving Gawsworth, but he had five important and
exacting years ahead at the Collegiate Church. Life was
never placid in Manchester. The debates between Presbyterians and Independents reached a climax within the
next two years; there were always sermons to preach and
'exercises' to attend. And pastoral work demanded more
time and energy than it had done in Cheshire: 'I was taken
off my studies by persons coming to me, many of them
about the state of their souls'. The political background
to those five years was equally full of action and change.
Cromwell's death in 1658 eventually led, after an increasingly chaotic period, to the Restoration of the crown
in 1660. Newcome, like most of the Presbyterians,
welcomed the return of Charles II. He heartily disliked
the lack of authority and the 'indiscriminate' religious
tolerance of the last months of the Interregnum, and
believed that nothing less than the restored monarchy
could bring back the necessary discipline. It fell to Newcome to prepare the Manchester congregation for the
peaceful acceptance of the Restoration. At the service on

Sunday, 6 May, he prayed for the king 'by periphrasis';
on the following Saturday he 'went up into the pulpit,
and prayed about half an hour' before formally proclaim-
ing Charles II, and on 24 May, the public day of thanksgiving, he was appointed to preach the sermon. As usual,
the Old Testament gave him just the text he was looking
for—*David bowed the heart of all the men of Judah . . . so
that they sent this word to the king, 'Return thou, and all
thy servants'*. It was a special sermon for a historic service,
so that, as Newcome modestly phrased it, he was 'afterwards persuaded to publish it'.

To Newcome the Restoration was a solemn occasion. It
called for earnest prayer that God would guide the king
and his people to more worthy lives. Yet, in June 1660,
as he rode through the heart of England on his way to visit
his relatives in Cambridgeshire, he found to his disgust
that villagers were openly rejoicing and reviving traditional
pleasures that the Puritans had banned.

> We found May-poles in abundance as we came, and at
> Oakham I saw a morris-dance, which I had not seen of twenty
> years before. It is a sad sign the hearts of the people are poorly
> employed when they can make a business of playing the fool
> as they do. This I found, that in most places they either have
> had bad ministers to rejoice in, or else good ones whom
> they hate.

As the months went by, Newcome and his fellow Presbyterians became further disillusioned. Once the temper of
the Cavalier Parliament had revealed itself, they realised
that the clause in the Declaration of Breda which spoke
of 'liberty to tender consciences' and stated that 'no man
shall be disquieted . . . for differences of opinion in matters of religion, which do not disturb the peace of the
kingdom' would give them no security. They had either
to accept the Prayer Book or be 'ejected'. Newcome
preferred to be ejected. He preached his last sermon from
the Collegiate Church pulpit in August 1662, but, despite
the loss of office, he continued to attend services, avoiding
Holy Communion, and doing his best to be charitable
about the new parsons and their sermons. 'Mr. Browne

preached in the afternoone on Rom. XI, 30, on God's providence, very well. The confidence that the sermon was by him stolen, should make it never the les[s] to me'.

Richard Heyricke continued to hold the wardenship of the Collegiate Church even though he never conformed. Consequently, the ejected clergy and leading Dissenter laymen continued to meet and encourage each other in their old haunts for months after the Act of Uniformity had deprived most of the ministers of their office. But in 1665 the Five Mile Act temporarily dispersed the brotherhood. Newcome officially moved to Worsley, but he spent much of the next five years travelling. He kept in touch with the sympathetic and influential Booth family at Dunham Massey, took every opportunity to meet fellow Presbyterians, to discuss mutual interests, and even occasionally to preach to illegal conventicles. The law was patchily enforced, and at the end of 1670 Newcome decided to risk returning to Manchester. It was still precarious to be there. John Tilsley, ex-vicar of Deane church, was due to appear before the assizes, and Thomas Jolly had already spent a year in gaol for breach of the Five Mile Act. As Newcome wrote, 'Any rascal may fall upon me for being in town'. But, despite a tempting offer of a living in Dublin, he decided to stay in Lancashire and hope that things would improve.

In March 1672, Charles II issued the Declaration of Indulgence which suspended the penal laws against Protestant Dissenters and Roman Catholics alike. Newcome applied for a licence to preach, and by 21 April was legally empowered to hold services in his own house so long as he did so openly and not behind barred doors. The house was too small for the congregation he hoped to attract, so in May he took over a barn and had that licensed as a chapel. He encountered considerable opposition and unpleasantness, for, despite the strength of Presbyterianism in the area, the majority of people in South-east Lancashire dreaded a return of the rule of 'the saints'. In March 1673 they greeted the withdrawal of the Declaration 'with great joy in the town, with bells and bonfires' and 'they expressed much joy and scorn over us'. Newcome did not yield easily. He looked upon the abuse and discomfort as part of the necessary cost of remaining true to Christ: 'the Lord help me to take courage and to do good, and I care not'. After a short interruption he continued to preach in the barn until October 1673, and in his own home until the following April. 'And then I was sent for to Strangeways to three justices, and they took course to stop my further work . . . in my own house'.

Charles II never again felt ready to defy his Parliament and renew the Declaration. He gave his consent to the Test Act in 1673, and for the rest of his reign the Dissenting clergy were banished from their pulpits. Newcome spent his long exile moving from one sympathetic household to another, preaching in private houses in Lancashire, Cheshire, Cambridgeshire, and London, visiting the sick, wrestling as best he could with unaccustomed poverty and the problems of his children's education and welfare, and meditating all the time on the Lord's reason for so reversing the fortunes of himself and his fellow Presbyterians. Considering how firm the law was against him, Newcome was fortunate to have the opportunity to preach to private groups as often as he did. But, as was well nigh inevitable, he eventually ran into trouble. In August 1684, after the disclosure of the Rye House Plot had made the authorities particularly sensitive, officers broke up a religious gathering in Newcome's house. They took the names of eleven people in addition to those family members who were present.

> I kept silence, and said only, It is well it is no worse, and that it is for no worse. If we had been better prepared, it is possible we had not been disturbed. I was advised to go out of the way, lest I should be ensnared.

He went into the Fylde, and on the way took the opportunity of calling on the friendly Hoghtons at Hoghton Tower and Walton-le-Dale. They probably helped him to pay the fine of £40—'The fine was paid after a time, and God found me friends to discharge it'.

These years of oppression and vexation brought
Newcome the joy of grandchildren, but also carried away
several friends and old colleagues for whom he cherished
the highest regard. In September 1677 he returned home
from a prolonged visit to Worcestershire and Hereford-
shire to learn that his 'reverend and dear friend Mr. Angier'
had died, 'which did sadden me no little'. In June 1682
he 'preached a sermon on the account of the death of
that honest, laborious, and useful man, Mr. John Jolly,
at his house in Gorton', and just before Christmas 1684,
attended the funeral of 'my dear friend' John Tilsley at
Deane. At the end of 1683 his son Daniel died—'a sad
(though first) breach that the Lord hath made upon us'.
Daniel had long been a worry to his father—'things are
discomposed and difficult about Daniel'—but Newcome
took comfort from the fact that 'the Lord hath taken off
some of the edge of the affliction' by giving hope that
on his death-bed Daniel had repented of his sins and misdeeds. For compensation there was always his eldest son,
another Rev. Henry Newcome: 'The Lord giveth me much
comfort in my eldest son. His humour good, and his parts
and discretion competent. So that I begin to think that it
is good that he lives at a distance, and that I see him but
sometimes, lest I should over enjoy him'.

The gloomy days of Dissenter exclusion came to an end
soon after James II came to the throne. James had every
intention of destroying the autocracy of the Anglican
Church, and, chiefly as a means of relieving his fellow
Roman Catholics, he issued a second Declaration of
Indulgence in April 1687. The Dissenters did not pause to
examine the king's motives. They heartily welcomed their
new freedom, and none rejoiced more than Newcome. 'I
began to preach in Mr. Barlow's house that is empty, to
our great satisfaction and rejoicing. I continued to preach
on Wednesdays, and after evening sermon on the Lord's
day, a good while'. In June, Newcome and his congregation moved to 'Thomas Stockton's barn': 'I began to
preach there to a great congregation, with much freedom
and ease to myself'. The Dissenters met difficulties, but
now that they were sure that the Lord had ceased to

chasten those whom He loved, they wrestled with their
problems as with 'an unseen spirit'. 'After much struggling
and several sentences of death on the thing', they managed to get the barn enlarged, and with patient resignation
they faced the inevitable hostility from those outsiders
who resented their restored freedom to meet and worship
freely. 'I was troubled to see the malignity that is in men
towards us . . . It may be when they have us under foot
again, they will be kinder to us. That day they are confident to see'.

It turned out, however, that the Declaration of Indulgence was only the beginning of the Dissenters' happy
change of fortune. Political opposition to James was
followed by armed rebellion, so that at length the king
was forced to take refuge in France. Parliament deemed
him to have abdicated, and offered the crown jointly to
his daughter and son-in-law. Newcome welcomed the
coming of William and Mary—'an astonishing providence'
—but the passing of the Toleration Act, which gave
Protestant Dissenters who accepted the Trinity freedom
to worship publicly, pleased him even more:

May 28 [1689]. The news came of our liberty settled by law, a
great mercy, a precious instance of God's goodness; so much
opposed and maligned, and yet effected. I know not that it hath
been abused by any, but not improved by us I well know.

From this basis of legal recognition, the Manchester
Presbyterians moved confidently into the future. The
barn congregation increased in numbers, and inevitably
some of the members began agitating for a more permanent and worthy place of worship. By April 1683 they
were seriously discussing the building of Cross Street
chapel. Some 'were hot about it': others opposed the
scheme. Newcome maintained a nervous neutrality: 'I did
not well understand the likelyhood of the thing. The
matter seemed to fall, and not at all upon my dissatisfac-
tion'. Nothing positive was done until July, and even then
the opposition was so strong that the foundations were
laid in 'many curses and reproaches'. Yet the building
proved a great success, and, on 24 June 1694, Henry

Newcome preached the first sermon in this chapel that
for almost three centuries has been a centre of noncon-
formity in Manchester. He chose as his text, 'An altar of
earth thou shalt make unto me . . . in all places where I
record my name I will come unto thee, and I will bless
thee'. Newcome bade those members of the congregation
who had been foremost in promoting the building of the
chapel not to be boastful about the part they had played.
The Lord alone had made this good work to prosper: they
had only been the Lord's agents.

The opening of Cross Street Chapel was the last big
occasion in Newcome's life. During the next twelve
months he preached an occasional sermon, but in the
summer of 1695 he became too weak to carry out his
duties. He died quietly in September. He kept his *Diary*
until the last fortnight of his life, and his son Henry
rounded off the *Autobiography* with a few last entries, a
copy of his will, and a number of extracts from the funeral
orations. Many people in the Manchester area mourned
for Henry Newcome. He had charmed them with his kindness and concern, won their respect with the way he had
stuck to his principles, and often inspired them with his
fervent sermons. William Bagshaw, the 'Apostle of the
Peak' and a fellow ejected divine, spoke for them all when
he said at the funeral service,

> Blessed Henry, as thy stature and face were comely, thy
> parts, gifts and graces excelled the ordinary portion and pro-
> portion of eminent ministers. There was one in that county
> who, when he heard this our Henry, said, 'If I had this man's
> tongue, I could not scape being proud of it. That he had the
> voice of the learned, and that the Lord spake by him, Lan-
> cashire, Cheshire, Staffordshire, Shropshire etc. have many
> witnesses.

Neither the restoration of his liberty nor his eminence
among local Dissenters had given Newcome worldly
wealth. The inventory of his possessions taken after his
death shows that he was still living very modestly indeed.
His most valuable asset was his library which was
'appraised' at £50. His clothes were worth £5, his bed

and bedroom furniture £35, his linen and plate no more
than £10 each. And yet out of these modest possessions
he had been loaning substantial sums to people in worse
circumstances than himself. In his total estate of
£174 15s. 8d., debts owing to him amounted to £40.

Newcome's own title for his *Autobiography* was *The
Abstract*. It was a truer description, because the work
consisted of abstracts taken from the *Diary* and commented upon in the light of later happenings. Strung
together in chronological order, these abstracts constitute
the raw material for an autobiography, but Newcome
would have had to rewrite the whole work if he had
wished to produce so polished and carefully-constructed
a work as Martindale's *Autobiography*. The original *Diary*
is far more useful to the historian. It has considerably
more detail, and the merit of carrying immediate, rather
than edited, comment upon the events it describes. It
brings the reader nearer to the ordinary life of the period
as well as to the character of the author. The pity is
that so small a section of the whole work has survived.
It begins with the Newcome family moving to a house in
Deansgate on 30 September 1661—'I was ill put to it
amongst the noise and clatter in the house at such a time,
and had a sermon to studdy for tomorrow'—and ends
exactly two years later with Newcome reading his daily
chapter from the Bible and attending church to hear
Francis Mosley, an old colleague who had conformed,
preach against anger. Fortunately, that short span covers
the crisis year of 1662 and we can follow the hopes, fears,
and final disappointment of the weeks leading up to
Newcome's ejection from his fellowship and pulpit.

In his *Diary* Newcome is not so completely absorbed
with spiritual matters that he has no time to comment
upon the secular world around him. However much he
might have resented it, he had frequently to abandon his
reading and contemplation to attend to family and business matters, to the bodily needs of his friends and
parishioners, and to the petty but insistent demands of
ordinary living. Now and again, therefore, secular affairs
intrude, and dominate the daily entry. It might be some-

thing major, as when, in January 1662, 'the Lord poured
raine downe on us all day and the flood was wonderfull':

> Mr. Hartley escaped narrowly, the mill bridge goeinge
> downe within a quarter of an houre after he came over it.
> And just as I was goeinge up into the pulpit the congregation
> was breakeinge up because of fire, but it pleased God it was
> quenched and wee setled again.

Next to a visitation of the plague, flood and fire were
the biggest natural hazards of urban life, but there were a
number of minor ones that could temporarily cause fear
and distress. In November 1661, the Newcome family cow
'was out of the way'—probably slipped its tether – but
fortunately someone caught it and put it in the pinfold.
'Wee were glad to heare of her. It would have beene a
crosse to have misst her one night, but more to have
lost her, and therefore wee should thanke God that gave
us this trouble'. And naturally there were days when
Newcome himself was unwell—'I was troubled with the
collicks this day' or 'I had an ill night with my cough'—
and many more days when he was deeply concerned about
his wife's health or his children's welfare. Family life in
the 17th century had much the same joys and worries
as family life in other centuries. All husbands will
understand Newcome's frustration when he spent time
fruitlessly searching for a particular paper after his wife
had unexpectedly cleaned and tidied his study, and all
fathers will share his anxiety when one of his children met
with an accident or suddenly developed a fever. Once a
family crisis had passed, it was sometimes possible to
smile at it or at least to turn it into such a family legend
as the story of young Daniel's hat. Newcome never
approved of the popular school-boy sport of cock shooting, when boys took it in turns to shoot arrows at a cock
tied to a stump or board. Apparently he did not object
to the cruelty of the sport, only to the danger of boys
getting hurt. And his fears were justified. The entry in
his *Autobiography* for 31 January 1665 reads:

> The children shot at school for their cocks this day; and I
> was moved much with fear about them. I understood I had
> cause, for Daniel's hat on his head was shot through with an
> arrow.

One of the most obvious things in the *Diary* is Newcome's constant need to be away from home, riding to
preaching engagements in neighbouring towns, or keeping
in touch with relations, colleagues, and acquaintances in
Lancashire, Cheshire, and further afield. On the last Sunday in October 1661, he was due to preach at Rochdale.
On the previous Friday he had been, as usual, at Stockport
attending the weekly 'exercise' at which he preached. The
next morning he visited two of his parishioners, and about
3 p.m. set out for Rochdale: 'The Lord made our way
very easy, and wee were brought to Rochdale [11 miles
distant] safe about 6. Blessed be God'. He was worried
about the health of his four-year-old son, Peter. This
natural concern and his physical weariness made it difficult
for him to concentrate upon his preparation for next day's
duties: 'I was huge sleepy . . . The spirit indeed is willing
but the flesh is weake'. But he got through the Sabbath
pretty well. He did not think much of his morning
sermon, but 'in the afternoone the congregation beinge
very great I was helped in prayer and preachinge'. The
day's duties tired him out. After a good night's rest he
spent Monday morning in the town visiting the fair and
talking to his friend, John Hartley of Strangeways, who
happened to be on business in Rochdale. Then, after
dinner, he rode back to Manchester—'got home about 6
or before and found the children well'.

Preaching engagements such as this were routine.
Occasionally, they were at a greater distance from Manchester. In June 1662, at a time when most clergy were
discussing uniformity and the threat to Dissenters, Newcome set out one Friday for Chester. He left Manchester
at 10 a.m., arrived at Northwich about 2 p.m. and reached
Chester 'by sunset'; on most of his journeys he seems to
have ridden at an average speed of about three and a
half miles an hour. On the Saturday morning he 'was soon
engaged to preach to-morrow', and, once that was settled,
he called on his brother and cousin, visited 'the great
church', spent 'a while at the booke sellers', and 'studdied
something on my sermon for tomorrow'. At morning
service at Holy Trinity he was quite satisfied with his

sermon—'The Lord asisted mee very gratiously': in the
afternoon at St. Peter's he 'was somewhat long, but the
Lord did much helpe mee'. Monday, Tuesday, and
Wednesday Newcome spent on social and business matters
in the city. They included some gay hours as well as
'sober discourse'. On the Monday afternoon he and his
friends saw 'the show—the great nothinge', and on Tuesday evening he was in the Sun tavern, 'where wee met
abundance of our Manchester folke to the number of
above 40. Wee were merry together'. On Thursday he rode
back to Manchester: 'Got out of Chester about 9. Dined
at Buckley hill. Got home cheerfully and well through the
good hand of God upon us about 7, and found all well at
home'. The next morning he was off early to his weekly
meeting at Stockport.

In the first week of April 1663, Newcome made an
unusual journey. He set out for Preston to visit James
Hyett, the ex-rector of Croston, who was highly regarded
by fellow Presbyterians, and who was reported to be
seriously ill. Three hours' riding brought Newcome to
Chorley. There he learned that Hyett had died, so he
changed his plans and made for Croston. The next day
he called on the new rector, James Pilkington, and met
Hyett's widow, who asked him to advise her about the
books she should keep from her husband's library. But
the immediate problem was how to bury Hyett without
having the Prayer Book burial service read. Pilkington was
all for observing the new Act of Uniformity, but Newcome
and his fellow Presbyterians considered it essential that
Hyett, who had refused to conform should be buried by a
Presbyterian minister:

> Wee had much adoe about his buryal, but Mr, Pilkington
> at last went his way, and so he was buryed without ceremony
> or booke and Mr. Welsh [Henry Welsh, ex-curate of Chorley]
> his old friend and neighbour preached his funeral on 2 Kings
> ii, 12. A very good sermon he made.

Newcome returned home through the rain the next day.
He was so impressed with Welsh's sermon, which compared
Hyett with Elijah swept up to heaven by a whirlwind

leaving the mourners, like Elisha, sorrowing behind, that
he repeated it to his family at prayers that night. A
subdued feeling of triumph over the law partly assuaged
the grief that Newcome felt at the death of so stalwart a
Dissenter as Hyett.

Newcome fought an unrelenting war against sin as much
in himself as in his parishioners. He was ever repenting
that idleness and indulgence had prevented him from
making full use of an opportunity to preach more con-
vincingly or to study more deeply. Most of his self-
criticism is, by ordinary standards, unjustified: the lapses
he regretted were usually due to bodily weariness or
unavoidable distractions rather than to deliberate neglect
of duty or pursuit of pleasure. But the reader of his
Diary can draw comfort from the fact that even Newcome
had human frailties that neither repeated self-censure nor
repentance in prayer completely removed. In Newcome's
eyes, it was always sinful 'to waste' time and energy on
purposeless recreations and idle amusements. He always
questioned the wisdom of joining the crowd that stood
watching 'the dancers on the rope' or 'the mountebanke
on the stage'—'time might be better bestowed, and
besides wee see sin acted'. For his own comfort he was
too fond of billiards, bowls, and shovel-board. He
enjoyed these games, but, like most sincere Puritans, he
was suspicious of all laughter and enjoyment, and sought
to discipline himself. In his *Autobiography* in January
1658 he explained how he tried to satisfy both conscience
and desire:

> I was about this time much used to go to Zachary Taylor's
> [a fellow divine] at an evening, to play at shuffle-board. I was
> oft checked for this, but I was too much concerned in it; as
> after, about going to Mr. Minshull's [a rich apothecary in
> Manchester] in an evening. And I thought this a rational
> resolution in the case — Not to go forth for this recreation
> unless I had been close at serious business all day; not to go
> forth to this too, if I had been diverted from business other
> ways. And for mirth, which I was afraid of taking too great a
> latitude in—I thought it was my duty to let some [spiritually]
> savoury thing fall, where I had spoken merrily; or to count
> myself truly in debt, for as much serious discourse, for every
> jest I had told.

Even more disturbing and more difficult to control was Newcome's addiction to tobacco. Every few pages he acknowledges that 'tobacco doth too much fill my thoughts' and prays that 'the Lord will helpe me about it'. Yet he went on smoking. If he tried to resist the temptation, he found he could not keep his mind on his prayers, yet if he gave way and smoked a pipe, his prayers and meditations were inevitably postponed. So far as we know, he never achieved the degree of 'selfe denial about such a stinkeinge' that enabled him to break the habit entirely:

> I felt myself lorded over by tobacco and surely I must not give way to it, when it is thus minded by mee as it is . . . I doe see my slavery with this tobacco. When it can hasten a duty to be at it, and when I know it doth not benefit mee, but allmost allways makes mee sicke, it is high time to dismisse it.

Newcome could always wrestle bravely with the Devil when he appeared in the form of injustice or 'heretical' opinion, but he found it much more difficult to resist when the Devil tempted him with what most men regarded as innocent pleasures.

THE AUTOBIOGRAPHY OF ADAM MARTINDALE, 1623-1686

[The text, edited by Richard Parkinson, was published by the Chetham Society, Vol. 4 of the Old Series, in 1845. The manuscript is in the British Museum. The Chetham Library, Manchester, acquired a copy. Parkinson used a transcript of this copy, but had his text checked with the original before going to press.]

Adam Martindale wrote his *Autobiography* in 1685, the last full year of his life. The old man was full of hindsight-wisdom as he looked back over the years, but the display of detail in his narrative points either to an extraordinary memory or to some kind of diary or journal as the basis of his story. What he has to relate is particularly interesting because he lived through such disquieting times. The outbreak of the Civil Wars ruined his plans for going up to Oxford; the 1662 Act of Uniformity spoiled his promising career as a Nonconformist minister, and Monmouth's Rebellion made his last months difficult and uncomfortable. Yet there is little doubt that Martindale enjoyed his life. He certainly enjoyed telling his life-story. And in the telling he revealed so much of himself, ingenuously illustrated the thoughts and feelings of his generation, and made pertinent comments upon many of his contemporaries.

Adam was born at Moss Bank, a village that, since the Second World War, St. Helens has absorbed into a large housing development. His father, Henry, was a yeoman, who struggled to bring up his family partly by what the Scots would call croft farming, and partly by building and repairing cottages and farm buildings. He never had much money, but what he had he was ready to spend on his many children. For example, Adam's elder sister, Jane, insisted on leaving home and seeking her fortune as a lady's maid in London. Henry and his wife did not approve of her going, but they gave her sufficient 'moneyes to carrie her up and to subsist on awhile, till she got a place'. And Adam, the clever one of the family, they were ready to educate for a profession.

Martindale gives us a detailed and, at times almost libellous, account of his education. Until he was nearly six, he sheepishly confessed he was 'all for childish play, and never thought of learning'. Then his godmother gave him an ABC book, and with the help of his elder brothers and sisters and 'a young man that came to court my sister' he learned to read. Once he could read, he wanted nothing else: 'I thinke I could almost have read a day together without play or meat, if breath and strength would have held out'. At seven and a half he began to attend the grammar school at St. Helens. He suffered from a rapid succession of teachers—first, 'a young ingenious sparke', who nearly ruined the school by bad adminis-tration; secondly, 'an old humdrum curate' who, 'simple-ton and tipler', tried to teach Latin grammar without a book; thirdly, a woman 'that had some smattering of Latine'—'with her I did something better than quite loose my time, but not much'; and fourthly, a Winwick-trained scholar—title of some eminence in Stuart Lancashire!— who spoiled good teaching by constantly making new school rules, and by favouring those who 'could fee him well'. Adam at length complained to his father that this schoolmaster denied him his rightful place at the top of the class, because he dared not offend the well-off parents of 'two arrant dunces', and Henry sympathetically trans-ferred his son to a school at Rainford, about three miles west of Moss Bank. There Adam came under another Winwick-trained schoolmaster, who taught him well. Yet he too was far from perfect. He lost his temper easily and often, and after he had moved to St. Helens, with young Adam in tow, he began to drink heavily. 'Then as for his humours and passions . . . they were now growne intollerably high and frequent'.

Henry Martindale's relatives and friends considered he

was foolish to allow Adam to remain so long at school,
'alledging too many instances of such as made no advantage of their learning, though they had been brought up
so long to it as to be fit for nothing else'. Henry heeded
their advice, and put Adam to a trade. A few weeks later,
however, guessing 'which way my mind still went', he
gave his son the chance of continuing his studies. With a
glad heart, Adam eagerly went back to school, first to St.
Helens, then to Rainford, and back to St. Helens again.
He refined his skill as a Latinist and considerably enlarged
his knowledge of Greek, for he was fortunate to meet as
his sixth teacher 'an eminently able and diligent master':

> . . . He taught us also to make Greeke exercises in
> prose and verse; and both in these, and what we made in
> Latine, he expected not onely congruity but elegancie. He
> spake very good Latine to us in a constant way; put us to
> take out our lessons ourselves, and, in examining them, he
> stood not so much upon parsing (as they called it), or
> scanning of verses and proving them, to which he found us
> well enured, as upon rhetorical tropes and figures . . .

By the summer of 1639, this skilful schoolmaster considered Adam ready for Oxford, but, as Martindale wrote
nearly half a century later, 'the worst was, the University
was not so readie for me'.

By 1639 it was clear enough, especially to a Puritan
family such as Martindale's, that serious trouble was brew-
ing in England. The ecclesiastical policy of Archbishop
Laud, the Crown's successive demands for ship money,
and the call-up of unwilling men to march against the
Scottish Covenanters in the Bishops' War were all provok-
ing bitterness and unrest. To so devoted a father as
Henry Martindale, it did not seem the right time for his
son to go far from home. Plans for Oxford were postponed, and Adam joined the household of Francis
Sherington—Adam calls him Shevington—at Booth Hall,
Worsley. Adam thought his duties were to teach Sherington's children and to read family prayers. That would
have been exacting enough for neither Sherington nor his
sons showed him any kindness, but he found himself expected to keep household accounts and act as secretary

as well as teacher. He was not sorry when the beginning of hostilities in Lancashire caused Sherington to shut down Booth Hall and dismiss him. He returned home to find that the war was creating serious financial difficulties for his father and his brothers, and, to avoid being an extra burden on the family, he took a post as schoolmaster, first at Up Holland, a Royalist community that regarded him with suspicion, and later at his old school, Rainford.

Probably in 1643—the autobiography's dates are sometimes a little at variance with the events they accompany —Colonel John Moore, M.P. for Liverpool, recruited Adam as his personal secretary. Adam seems to have liked the colonel, but he had not a single good word for his family. To him they were 'such an hell upon earth', such 'arrant thieves' and 'bitter scoffers at pietie' that he was glad to accept a lesser job to get out of their way. He became clerk to the quarter-master of Moore's regiment, and in that capacity took part in the defence of Liverpool against Prince Rupert in June 1644.

In the Spring of 1644 Charles I ordered Rupert to march from his winter quarters in the Welsh Marches to the relief of the Royalist army besieged in York. The prince chose to go via Lancashire, both to relieve the siege of Lathom House and to recruit more men for his Yorkshire campaign. The Earl of Derby joined forces with him in Cheshire, and the two crossed the Mersey at Stockport on 25-26 May. Their first objective was the Parliamentary stronghold at Bolton. They then marched westward to take Liverpool, which John Moore held firmly for Parliament despite Royalist sympathy that abounded in the countryside round about. Little Liverpool, 'this mere crow's nest' as Rupert contemptuously called it, compelled the Royalists to mount a regular siege, and for a full fortnight Moore held them at bay. Eventually, the besiegers broke through the defences, killing, capturing, and scattering the Parliamentarians. Adam was fortunate enough to be granted quarter. He went to 'a tedious imprisonment' until Rupert's defeat at Marston Moor in July eventually allowed the Parliamentarians to recover

their ascendancy in Lancashire and release the prisoners.
But victory on the battlefield could not repair the damage
the campaign had caused. Adam's brother, Thomas, lost
most of his household goods, and had not 'a great papist
in the neighbourhood' secured his cattle for him by driv-
ing them into his own fields, his loss would have been
much more severe. Adam's father, however, had no such
benefactor :

> . . . [Rupert's troops] tooke the old man prisoner, and
> used him barbarously, forcing him to march in his stockings,
> without shoes, and snapping his ears with their firelocke-
> pistolls. His house they plundered of everything they thought
> worth carrying away, in cartes which they brought to his
> doore to that purpose, and were sore troubled (Good men!)
> that the walls being stone, and the roof well shot over within,
> they could fasten no fire upon the house, though they several
> times essayed so to doe. His stock of cattell they wholly
> drove away, and he never had an hoofe again . . .

Adam was ever a reluctant soldier, and after his release
from prison he thankfully escaped further campaigning
by accepting the offer of a school at Over Whitley in
Cheshire. 'The income was not very great but well paid . . .
and my accidentall gettings (having a full schoole, and
prettie store of rich men's sons in it, and opportunities
for earning moneys by making writings for neighbours)
were a good addition to my salary'. But the biggest bonus
the job offered was time and opportunity to begin studying again. Adam re-opened his Greek texts, and at the
earnest bidding of an unnamed 'minister of Lancashire of
my familiar acquaintance' began to study Hebrew and
Logic with the intention of preparing for the ministry. In
those years of Parliamentary triumph, 1645 and 1646,
Adam's academic hopes began to soar again. He arranged
for his name to be put down as an under-commoner at
University College, Oxford, but the exceptional demand
for more preachers in South Lancashire relentlessly man-
oeurved him into accepting a post straightaway without
reading for a degree. The unnamed Lancashire parson
inveigled him into supply preaching. A good sermon at
St. Helens led directly to an invitation to preach at Gorton.

The Gorton sermon then led to the offer, and, after some hesitation, the acceptance of a permanent appointment. In the early summer of 1646, Adam moved from Cheshire to Gorton, east of Manchester, and, much to his consternation, found himself in the midst of a fierce sectarian dispute.

Once the Parliamentary forces had gained the upper hand in the county and episcopacy had been denounced, the Lancashire Presbyterians began to introduce a Calvinist form of church government. They grouped all the Lancashire churches into nine classes, claimed the right to authorize all ordinations, and insisted upon the obedience of the clergy. Their revolutionary policy, though approved by Parliament in October 1646, could not help but rouse criticism and hostility. Moderate Puritans, to say nothing of Anglicans, considered that they had gone too far; many thorough-going Dissenters wanted them to reorganise more severely. But the most persistent critics were the Independents, who saw no virtue in exchanging episcopacy for the equally rigid discipline of the Presbyterian church, and upheld the right of each 'gathered congregation' to choose its own minister and council, and to worship God as it pleased. In the Manchester area, Samuel Eaton and Timothy Taylor, both of Duckinfield, were eloquent and influential Independents; John Harrison of Ashton-under-Lyne and Richard Hollinworth of the Collegiate Church in Manchester were enthusiastic Presbyterians; and such respected, learned divines as Richard Heyricke, warden of the Collegiate Church, and John Angier, a moderate Presbyterian of Denton, endeavoured to soften the conflict by preaching moderation and tolerance. When Adam Martindale went to Gorton, he soon found that his congregation contained rigid Presbyterians and uncompromising Independents. Each group wanted to claim him as an ally, but bewildered Adam could not convince himself that either side was right. He had an honest respect 'for good and learned men' whether they were Presbyterians or Independents. But to his discomfiture he found that 'to be familiar with them of one partie was to render me suspected to the other'. Neither group in the chapelry would accept his

professed desire 'onely to preach the Gospell to them'.
They raised the awkward question of his ordination, and
pressed him openly to declare his position in the controversy. Adam wisely consulted Heyricke and Angier, and
with their advice and support managed to steer an erratic
but mainly middle course without too much damage.
Eventually, in 1648, 'a brisk calle to preach' at Rostherne,
south of Warrington, 'removed him out of this hote
climate [of Gorton] into a cooler', and introduced him to
a congregation which he was to serve for many years.

Adam went to Rostherne a married man. On the last
day of 1646, in Manchester Collegiate Church, Warden
Heyricke had married him to Elizabeth Hall of Droyles-
den. A year and a day later, Elizabeth gave birth to a
daughter. Greater personal responsibility increased Adam's
natural parsimony, and it often happened that private
financial matters dwarfed his sincere concern about church
affairs and the spiritual health of his congregation. Even
though he was writing so long after the events, he gave
more space and attention to the petty details of the
financial arrangements made for taking over the living at
Rostherne than he did to describing both his excitement
at entering a new parish and the opportunities it offered
for evangelism. Nearly forty years had not reduced the
pride he took in his self-acclaimed generosity in settling
matters with his predecessor's widow, and it still irked
him to remember that she had not moved out of the
vicarage until May 1650, and that he had had to pay her
'for all the wainscote in the house, flags on the floore,
glass in the windows, with all the inner doores, and even the
great double doore full of nailes leading to the hall, or else
she would take all these away, and I must either lose them
or sue for them, which I tooke to be disgraceful'.

Nothing better illustrates Adam's mixture of idealism
and worldliness than his account of his father's funeral
at Prescot. He had a deep love for his father, and after
comforting him in his last hours—'I am not without hopes
that he finished his course with joy'—he determined to
observe the convention of the times and 'bring him home
handsomely'. He kept open house at the funeral—'all that

came to the house to fetch his corpse thence (beggars not excepted) were entertained with good meat, piping hote, and strong ale in great plentie'. The funeral sermon was 'excellent', and afterwards the relatives sat down to 'a rich dinner', a large roomful of other mourners enjoyed 'plentie of wine and strong drinke', and the hangers-on, 'the rest tag and rag' as Adam called them, were given 'sufficient store of such provisions as are usual at ordinary burials'. Yet Adam's chief satisfaction was not that he had honoured his father with a worthy funeral, but that by careful management he had done it cheaply—'I am verily persuaded that some funeralls have cost twice so much, that have not beene so creditable to the cost-makers'.

On 25 July 1649 Adam Martindale was ordained at St. Andrew Undershaft Church in London. He had first applied to the Manchester classis in the previous October. The classis examined him and approved. But in November a small group of parishioners laid objections before the classis. When pressed for reasons, they would neither be specific nor withdraw their charges. Delay followed delay until, in exasperation, Adam decided to go to London and apply there. He arrived on the Monday, the classis examined him on the Tuesday afternoon, and ordained him the day after. He stayed in London a few days longer, partly to obtain from the Committee for Plundered Ministers the necessary order to recover his arrears of stipend, and partly to arrange for the publication of his first book, *Divinity Knots unbound*. The title page declared that Adam, 'one of the meanest Labourers in the Lord's Harvest' intended the treatise specially 'for the Instruction of young Christians in Rothstorne Parish', and its publication, coming on the heels of his ordination, seems to have quietened the opposition he had previously encountered in the parish. 'Now that mine arguments and answers were in their hands to show to whom they pleased, and none of their admired teachers in the neighbourhood, nor any others from abroad, made any returne to them, that pretence [that he could only hold his own in discussion with ill-informed people] vanished into nothing'.

The decade of the 1650s was a turbulent period both

politically and theologically. Conscientious men had difficulty in determining what should be their attitude towards
the Commonwealth and Protectorate governments, and
the emergence of new sects and splinter groups among
the Dissenters could not help but profoundly disturb the
consciences not only of dispossessed Anglicans but also of
disciplined, order-loving Presbyterians. Liberty of conscience could be defended, but the Presbyterians upheld
that usurpation of authority and licence to worship God
as one fancied were impossible to reconcile with the
Scriptures. Adam could not avoid being dragged into endless controversy. His office made it impossible for him to
take refuge in public silence and private thought, and his
temperament made it difficult for him to compromise or
do anything against his conscience. He worried endlessly
about the right and wrongs of the Engagement, which
required men to swear loyalty to the Commonwealth. To
him it was abundantly clear that the Commonwealth was
a usurping government. He searched the Old Testament
for parallel cases, so that he could follow the precedents
set by 'the men of God' involved, but he could find no
satisfactory answer. He attended at Warrington a meeting
of ministers specially called to discuss the Engagement.
He listened to the arguments of several men he admired,
spoke at length himself, but came away as bewildered as
ever. When the magistrates formally required him to take
the oath, he did so along with a number of colleagues in
the neighbourhood, but that did not end his concern. He
made himself ill with worry, and after he had recovered
sufficiently to preach again, he satisfied his conscience a
little by confessing from the pulpit that 'had I known so
much as I now did, I believed I should never have meddled
with it'.

Many parishioners objected to the strict observance of
the Sabbath, which the government was enforcing through
local men nominated by the justices and charged with the
responsibility of seeing the law obeyed. Adam found
himself one of the unfortunate nominees. Every time he
closed his eye to a breach of the law, he ran the risk of
paying a fine of £5 0s. 0d., and every time he reported a

breach to the magistrates, he ran a greater risk of making an enemy for life. Understandably, he did not relish this duty. He felt happier and more confident arguing against Samuel Eaton's Independents in Duckinfield or against the Quakers, who suddenly appeared in North Cheshire in the middle of the decade. He wrote and spoke against both, and was ever ready to take part in public debate against their spokesmen. The debates were deadly serious, but, however curtly he dismissed trivial speakers, Adam always had a kind word for worthy opponents. He held Eaton in constant respect, and described Richard Hubberthorne, a Quaker antagonist, as 'the most rationall calmespirited man of his judgement that I was ever publickly engaged against'.

The 1650s were also important years in Adam's family life. He and his wife suffered the loss of three of their children—John, 'so ripe a child for wit, memory, and forwardness in learning and religion', who died of smallpox in 1659 when he was eight years old; Mary who survived four years, and Nathan who did not live four months. Young Elizabeth still flourished, and so did Thomas, who was born in December 1649, and Martha, Adam's third daughter, who was born at Rostherne in 1656, but the early death of his brother, Henry, and the loss of his father in 1658 threw more dark shadows across Adam's path. One matter, however, gave him satisfaction at the time and greater satisfaction in his old age. In 1655 he bought a house in High Legh in the parish of Rostherne. He had to pay for it in instalments—'paid off yearely in the way of mart'—but it proved a most welcome refuge in time of future troubles.

The political chaos which followed the death of Oliver Cromwell in September 1658 made life very difficult for Adam Martindale. He had never liked Oliver's government: to him it had usurped its power, and had aggravated its offence by encouraging the Independents. Ever since the execution of Charles I, he had held the view that nothing but 'a King and Free Parliament' could ever constitute the rightful government of England. Yet he gave no support to his neighbour, Sir George Booth, whose rebellion

against the Rump in August 1659 had this solution as its
main aim. In his *Autobiography* Adam justified his inaction at great length. He felt certain the rebellion would
fail: 'God seemed to frowne upon them' because the
weather was 'so very foule'; he mistrusted the intentions
of some of the leaders, especially those who promised
universal toleration, which, as a good Presbyterian, Adam
'utterly abhorred'; and he considered that he might do
more good outside the revolt than in it. The venture failed
miserably, but by not taking part and then by trying to
mediate on the part of the rebels, Adam offended both
the friends and foes of Sir George. As long as the Rump's
authority lasted, the authorities regarded him, along with
most of the ministers in North Cheshire, as 'having an
hand in this designe of our gentlemen [the Cheshire sup-
porters of Sir George]'. And after the Restoration of
Charles II, 'wherein no man did more truely rejoyce than
I', he fell foul of an influential, but unnamed, local justice
and deputy lieutenant by refusing to read from the pulpit
a 'precept' forbidding people to assemble 'upon pretence
of preaching, teaching, praying, or hearing of the same
in any place whatsoever but in publick parish churches
and chapells appointed for the same'. Adam answered
the charge against him with reasoned argument, but
neither his competent defence nor two or three adjourn-
ments of the preliminary hearing prevented the justice
from committing him to Chester gaol to await trial. The
case was never heard, however. A Lancashire minister
reported Adam's dilemma to Richard Baxter; Baxter
'shewed it to the Lord Chancellor', Clarendon; Clarendon
'expostulated with the Earl of Derby', the lord lieutenant;
and Derby saw to it that Adam was discharged. Even so,
the hostile justice had fulfilled his promise 'to make me
smart', for his arrest had distressed and harassed Adam
and his family, and, because prisoners had to pay for
their food and lodgings, his imprisonment had cost him
dear. It was consoling to find on his return home that his
youngest son, born in January 1661, was making progress,
and that the bulk of his parishioners had signed a resolution of confidence in his loyalty to the Crown.

But Presbyterian ministers everywhere were finding their work increasingly difficult. The restoration of the Crown meant the restoration of the bishops. The Anglican Prayer Book reappeared, and the Cavalier Parliament was hastening to pass an Act of Uniformity enforcing its use in every church in the land. As early as the Autumn of 1661, Adam was indicted before a grand jury in Chester for not using the Book of Common Prayer. He managed to escape an early consideration of his case, but the following year the requirements of the Act of Uniformity left him no option but to conform or to forfeit his living. He decided to resign. On Sunday 17 August 1662, he preached his farewell sermon on the text, 'And now, brethren, I commend you to God and the word of his grace'. He did not go into details about the particulars he 'boggled at' in the Prayer Book, 'onely saying, in generall, that such things were required as I could not satisfie myselfe to comply with'. He surrendered the vicarage at Michaelmas. The Rev. Benjamin Crosse moved in, and the ejected Rev. Adam Martindale took his family 'to a little house at Camp-greene, about a quarter of a mile off', where he lived for the next three and a half years.

At this point in his life story, Adam gives details of how his ejection affected him financially. The Rostherne living was worth £60 a year. Gifts of about £50 from sympathising friends, together with arrears of stipend and the sale of surplus household goods, more than cleared his debts, and for the next few years he made his living partly from letting his house in High Legh and farming a small-holding he had leased in 1659 at Tatton, and partly by the 'schooling and tabling of young gentlemen' and, after two years, by teaching mathematics. His family did not live quite so well as they had done at the vicarage, but they were far from being destitute. And for a time at least, Adam continued to have spiritual influence in his old parish. He attended church each Sunday, heard his successor's sermon, and then, in the evening at home, preached on the same text 'to an housefull of parishioners of the devoutest sort'. Although he admitted that Benjamin Crosse was a poor preacher despite 'the great assis-

tance he had from the sermon-notes of his dead brother,
who was an excellent scholar', Adam purred with satisfaction when his followers told him that they liked
Crosse's sermons, 'better in the repetition than in the
preaching'.

Adam was well aware that the authorities would not
long allow ejected ministers so to threaten the authority
of new incumbents. He realised he would have to find a
new way of earning a living. At first, he thought of
'physicke', but rejected that idea chiefly because 'the
lives of men were not to be jested with'. Instead, with
the help and encouragement of Sir George Booth, lately
created Lord Delamere, he undertook the study of
mathematics. Thanks to such pioneers as John Napier,
the inventor of logarithms, John Wallis, and Henry
Briggs, mathematics had made great strides during the
first half of the 17th century. By the time Adam
began to study, knowledge of decimals, logarithms, and
indices was becoming available to the ordinary student.
The older generation considered these advancements new-
fangled, but Adam rejoiced in them. By the time the
Conventicle Act of 1663 had reduced his liberty to preach,
he was beginning to acquire quite a reputation as a mathematics teacher. He had short spells teaching at Warrington
and Preston. Then he became tutor to the young Hoghtons
at Hoghton Tower. Sir Richard offered him a full-time job,
but he stayed alternate weeks at Hoghton and Camp-
Green in order 'still to be able to bestow my paines
among mine old people'. After Hoghton he went for a
few weeks to act as tutor at South Tunley, the recently
built home of the Wilson family of Wrightington, and
for a further period to Winstanley Hall, the home of
William Bankes, near Wigan.

The Five Mile Act, which in 1665 forbade dissenting
ministers to live within five miles of a corporate town
or of their old parish, compelled Adam to move from
Camp-Green. He settled down teaching mathematics in
Manchester, which, though it was the biggest town in
Lancashire escaped the restrictions of the Act because
it was not incorporated. John Wickens, the high master

of the grammar school, befriended him by sending him 'a good number of his most ingenious boys'. Adam taught them the new mathematics. Inevitably, he encountered hostility, but he routed his critics in a very practical way:

> . . . But one that was a teacher in the towne, and some others that thought themselves fit for such worke, that knew nothing of decimalls, logarithmes, or the new species way, contemned and assaulted me, sending me questions: which I quickly returned answered, and propounded another to every one that had sent any to me, and then I had done with them . . .

Thomas, Adam's son, was one of Wickens's pupils, and in 1667 Wickens advised Adam to send him to the university. But the religious tests stood in the way: '. . . I was not free to have him engaged in such oaths, subscriptions, or practices as I could not downe with myselfe; not that I would tie him to be of mine opinion when he was once a man of competent yeares and abilities to choose for himselfe'. Adam got over the difficulty by putting Thomas under private tutors first in Cambridge, then in Oxford, and finally in Worcestershire. Then, three years later, Thomas submitted himself for examination at Glasgow University and was admitted to the master's degree.

In the meantime, the magistrates in South-east Lancashire were winking so consistently at the law, that Adam found himself free enough to begin public preaching again. He regularly held services at Gorton and Birch, both today parts of Manchester, and occasionally preached at Cockey Moor chapel in Middleton parish, and to Dissenting congregations at Walmesley, north of Bolton, Darwen, and other places in those Pennine valleys. Dr. John Wilkins, Bishop of Chester from 1668 to his death in 1672, played with the idea of licensing some moderate Presbyterian ministers to preach in his parish churches, and by the royal Declaration of Indulgence in March 1672, Nonconformists were able to apply to have their chapels licensed for regular worship. Adam welcomed this far more relaxed situation. In September 1671 he had thankfully accepted the post of Lord Delamere's chaplain at Dunham Massey, and, after the Declaration, was able to combine

his duties as chaplain with regular preaching to a nearby
congregation. But the Declaration did not please him
entirely. Freedom for Presbyterians was one thing, but
a general freedom for all kinds of Dissenters was quite
another:

> I did so little like an universal toleration, that I have oft
> said . . . that if the King had offered me my libertie, upon
> consideration that I would consent that Papists, Quakers, and
> all other wicked sects should have theirs also, I think I should
> never have agreed to it.

Unfortunately for all Dissenters, the Declaration of
Indulgence was short-lived. In 1673 Parliament clamped
down again with the Test Act, and from the beginning of
1675 withdrew all licences to preach. Adam had to take
great care what he said and what he did. His life assumed
a quiet annual routine. The summer and early autumn he
spent at Dunham Massey attending to his duties as chaplain. Then, when Delamere and his family went up to
London in October or November, Adam went visiting his
'noble and religious friends, and neare relations in Cheshire,
Lancashire, Staffordshire, Warwickshire, Worcestershire,
etc. and sometimes at London'. From January to May he
was usually teaching mathematics to young men who came
to board at his house. Adam admitted that it looked as if
he was comfortably situated. Other Dissenting ministers
might envy him such security. But he explained that
though he was glad to serve Delamere, the chaplaincy
carried no retaining fee. He was paid at the rate of £40 a
year but only for the weeks Delamere was in residence at
Dunham. And because he had this post, the useful gifts
of money and goods from sympathetic friends ceased to
arrive: 'and I could not well undeceive them, for feare of
reflexion upon that noble family'.

Inability to continue his work as a preacher meant more
time available for writing, and during the last dozen years
of his life, Adam busied himself writing on both mathematics and theology. He contributed several articles to
books on agriculture edited and published by John
Houghton, a fellow of the Royal Society. He wrote on
such diverse subjects as marling and navigating sailing

boats and, for a different publication, on the significance of the recent discovery of rock salt in Cheshire. His chief mathematical work, published in London in 1682, was *The Countrey-Survey-Book: or Land-Meters' Vade-Mecum*, a guide to methods of land measuring. More important to his mind, was the writing he did on theological matters. In 1683, or thereabouts, he published *Truth and Peace Promoted* to guide those 'raw youths', who 'had never studied the controversies concerning Calvinisme and Arminianisme' and who were making such a 'clutter' in the pulpits. In manuscript he circulated among his friends and colleagues both his critical review of a new book, *Julian the Apostate,* which, obviously anticipating trouble when James succeeded to the throne, was a rejection of passive obedience, and a much longer consideration of the lawfulness of 'receiving the Lord's supper' kneeling.

This time-consuming writing, together with his evangelical work which continued quietly whenever opportunity offered, was a refuge from troublesome and often distressing family concerns. Adam's daughter Elizabeth, aged twenty-five, died in 1673. Four or five years later a younger daughter, Hannah, was struck down with what appears to have been poliomyelitis: '. . . for anything that belongs to head or hand, she is as active and diligent as any one needs to be; but for her lower parts . . . she hath ever since beene so lame that she cannot stand upright, much less goe soe, nor not with crutches'. And to these sad blows must be added the disasters that befell Thomas, his scholarly son. He was appointed second master at Merchant Taylors' School, London, but by attempting to keep pace with richer friends, he ran into heavy debt. In October 1677 he and his newly-wedded wife turned up in Cheshire destitute:

> . . . I admitted him and his wife to come to our house, dieted them as well as ourselves, clad them warme, and bestowed a deale of money on them in physick; got him a small place for the present to preach at one Lord's-day in a fortnight, till a better would be had; paying a deale of money for him that he ought [owed], and lending him more to pay others himselfe . . .

With Adam's help and advice, Thomas gradually recovered his self-respect. He learned to preach and teach more effectively, and in September 1679 took over the mastership of Witton School at Northwich. It looked as if a satisfactory if modest career was opening for him, when, in the following Summer, he developed a fever and died. Adam felt his loss very sharply indeed. The respect that many local gentlemen showed to his son by attending the funeral gratified him as much as the compliments paid by the Rev. James Livesey, who preached the funeral sermon, but, as he wrote, 'all that could not call him againe'.

Adam's last years were clouded with further misfortunes. In 1684 his patron and employer, Lord Delamere, died, and his son-in-law, Andrew Barton, a tallow chandler, suffered a disastrous fire. Both these adversities caused Adam distress, but a few months later he found himself in worse trouble for he was in danger of being charged with treason. The Duke of Monmouth had revolted, and, as a precaution, James II ordered the lords-lieutenant to arrest Dissenting ministers. Adam had been careful not to allow himself to be entangled in political conspiracy. He had his defence ready and his witnesses waiting, 'but of these things the soldiers that fetched me away were no judges, their warrant being indisputable'. Ill though he was Adam had to ride under escort to Chester at once. But things turned out better than they originally threatened to do. Within three weeks the authorities offered to release him on bail. He found the necessary security, and on his return home discovered that his friends had rallied round with 'visits, presents, and gratuities, that upon the whole matter, I think I rather gained than lost by that imprisonment. A mercie (I'll assure the reader) not usuall with me'.

Hardly had Adam returned home than he was summoned to appear at Lancaster assizes, but this time as a witness in a civil action. The journey taxed his strength, but by limiting his riding to twelve miles a day, he managed to get there, give his evidence about the two fulling mills near Rochdale that were the cause of the dispute, and return home again without disaster. He had to recognise, however, that his strength was failing. So many of his contemporaries were dying too: such leading Dissenters as William Bell of Huyton, James Bradshaw of Darcy Lever, John Tilsley of Deane, John Wright of Billinge, and John Mallinson of Melling had all recently 'left their earthly habitations in Lancashire for a better in heaven'. As Adam observed in the last sentence of his *Autobiography*, 'When God is housing his sheep (or rather sheep-herds) so fast, it is a dangerous prognosticke of a storme ere long to come'. He died in September 1686, well within twelve months of finishing his life story.

THE JOURNALS OF TWO QUAKERS, GEORGE FOX, THE FOUNDER OF THE MOVEMENT, 1624-1691, and WILLIAM STOUT OF LANCASTER, 1665-1752

[The Short Journal of George Fox, *ed. Norman Penney, was published by Cambridge University Press in 1925. The two-volume* Journal of George Fox, *also edited by Penney, was published by the same publishers in 1911. Both MSS. are preserved at Friends House, London.*

Manchester Public Library is the guardian of the Stout MS. In 1851 John Harland published an edition in modern spelling. The Autobiography of William Stout of Lancaster, 1665-1752, *ed. J. D. Marshall, is a transcription of the MS. enriched by introduction, notes and appendixes contributed by half a dozen experts. It was published in 1967 as Volume 14 (3rd series) of the Publications of the Chetham Society.]*

George Fox was neither a Lancashire man nor a diarist. A good number of his letters and pastoral epistles have survived, but the chief justification for including him among a group of Lancashire diarists and letter-writers is his so-called *Short Journal,* which he began to write, or possibly dictate, in Lancaster gaol in 1664. This is not a true journal, rather a chronological collection of reminiscences, but it does relate to a number of incidents in Lancashire and, from its own peculiar angle, portrays several interesting Lancashire men and women. Ten years after writing the *Short Journal,* Fox dictated an autobiography to Thomas Lower, the Cornish husband of Mary Fell of Swarthmoor Hall, Ulverston. This manuscript, compiled at Swarthmoor, is known now as the Spence MS. and has been published under the title *The Journal of George Fox.* It retraces the ground covered by the *Short Journal,* and brings the author's life story up to date. To get the fullest possible account of Fox's activities in Lancashire, therefore, it is necessary to use both *Journals,* and supplement them with relevant letters, the writings of Margaret Fell, her daughters and other early Friends, as well as the official papers referring to Fox's trials at Lancaster.

Fox paid a brief visit to the Manchester area in 1647, the first year of his ministry. Early in 1652 he looked westward from the top of Pendle and 'saw Lancashire sea', but he did not begin his ministry in the county until midsummer that same year. The weeks immediately following his ascent of Pendle he spent in Wensleydale and Westmorland, so that he next came to Lancashire from the north. His first encounter with a 'hireling priest' in a Lancashire 'steeple-house' was with the Rev. Gabriel Camelford, the zealous Puritan minister of Staveley chapel near Newby Bridge. Camelford had a reputation as a serious, God-fearing man, but, to George Fox, he appeared both misguided and inadequate:

> . . . on the first day [Sunday, 20 June 1652] I went to one preist Camelford's chappell and after hee had donne I began to speake the worde of life to them and Camelforde was in such a rage and such a frett and soe peevish that hee had noe patiens to heare but stirred uppe the rude multitude and they rudely haled mee out and strucke mee and punched mee and tooke mee and threw mee headelonge over the stone wall of the graveyard . . .

An unshakeable conviction that he was right hardened Fox against violent reactions to his preaching. Rough handling merely strengthened his resolution. That same afternoon to the congregation at Lindal chapel he spoke 'what the Lord commanded me', and a day or two later he began, what was destined to be a momentous and long struggle with William Lampitt, the Presbyterian incumbent of the parish church of Ulverston.

Fox first met Lampitt at Swarthmoor Hall, the home of Judge Thomas Fell and an unofficial open house for Dissenters. Both men were convinced that God had revealed truth to them personally, so that it was inevitable that each would regard the other as a false prophet. They harangued one another at their first meeting. Next day they continued their wordy battle, and Fox claimed an early success in that Judge Fell's wife, Margaret, 'soone

then discerned the priest cleerely and a convincement came
upon her and her family of the Lords truth'. But when
Fox carried the fight into Ulverston church he met strong
resistance. Margaret managed to persuade the congregation
to give him a hearing, yet, despite his fervent oratory, the
people grew hostile and 'the Constable putt mee out'.
During the next few weeks, Fox used Swarthmoor Hall as
his base while he evangelised the scattered small townships
of Lower Furness. Some congregations, especially those at
Rampside and at Gleaston, received him well, but opponents in North Lancashire were steadily gathering their
forces. Had not Fox had the powerful protection of Judge
Fell, influential men like Justice John Sawrey of Plumpton
—'I told him his heart was rotten and he was full of hypo-
crisy to the brim'—and Captain Adam Sandys of Colton—'I
told him his god was his belly'—would have driven him and
his biting tongue out of Furness and probably had him
imprisoned in Lancaster Castle.

As it was, Fox had two or three most unpleasant experiences. He was 'haled out' of Lancaster Church and 'stoned
along the streets', all because, as he protests in his innocent
way, he had 'declared the Truth to both priest and people
and showed them the deceits they lived in'. Later that
year, his intervention at Ulverston turned a 'lecture day'
into a brawl: 'The Lord opened my mouth to speak' as
Lampitt was 'blustering on in his preaching'. John Sawrey
checked him, the congregation turned against him, and
within minutes the constables were frogmarching him out
of town, 'some takeinge holde of my collar and some by
the armes and shoulders and shooke and dragged mee'.
On the common, the constables struck him across his
'backe with there willowe rodds, and soe thrust mee among
the rude multitude', who beat him with sticks until he lay
almost senseless on the wet grass. And yet that amazing
man walked back to Swarthmoor through the middle of
Ulverston market with his head as high as he could hold it,
'and there was none of them had power to touch me'. A
fortnight later the people of Walney Island treated him just
as cruelly. James Nayler's wife was convinced that Fox had
bewitched her husband, so she organised her neighbours to

prevent him from landing on the island. Fox resisted the hostile demonstrators' efforts to compel him to return to the mainland, and, consequently, once again was 'mazed' with sticks and stones. Somehow or another he managed to stagger three miles to sympathisers at Rampside. Next day Margaret Fell sent a cart to bring the dishevelled and bruised evangelist back to Swarthmoor.

During the winter of 1652-3 Fox was never far away from Swarthmoor. He preached, among other places, at Lancaster, Kellet, and Cartmel, and renewed contact with individual converts in Furness and the Cartmel peninsula. But in the spring of 1653 he headed northwards again. Cumberland, Northumberland, the Midlands, London, the Home Counties, the West Country, East Anglia, and Wales, all heard his compelling voice before he re-entered Lancashire in 1657. Manchester's 'rude people' welcomed him back by breaking up his meeting. But fortunately the justices intervened and next day Fox and his small company left the town quietly. They travelled north, managed to hold general, or area, meetings at Garstang and at Sandside, and then took 'a little respite from travel' at Swarthmoor before carrying 'the Truth' to the Scots. While in Lancaster, Fox re-encountered Colonel William West, a local justice, who confided to Judge Fell that, since he had last seen him, Fox 'had mightily grown in the Truth'. Fox rejected this opinion outright: he had not changed a whit. It was West who had 'come nearer to see the Truth', and therefore 'could better discern it'.

Judge Fell died in October 1658, so that when Fox next visited Lancashire in the spring of 1660 he had no influential friend to protect him. He was arrested in Swarthmoor Hall itself, taken across the Sands under escort, and committed to Lancaster gaol. But, thanks chiefly to Margaret Fell's personal intervention with the recently restored Charles II, he was set free just before Michaelmas to make his own way to London and plead his cause before the court of King's Bench. Over three years later he returned to Swarthmoor and to another period of imprisonment. Thomas Preston of Holker Hall and Sir George Middleton of Leighton Hall were among his foremost accusers.

Robert Rawlinson of Cark Hall was chairman of the quarter
sessions bench that sent him to gaol. The magistrates considered Fox's replies and statements to be arrogant, insul-
ting, and occasionally blasphemous, and the accused made
his case worse by not taking off his hat in court—and by
refusing to swear the oath. In the *Short Journal* Fox relates
the sequence of events in his usual homely vivid style of
writing:

> So when I came to Swarthmoore againe Collonel Kirbey
> [Richard Kirkby of Kirkby Ireleth] had sent for to seek mee
> by Soldiors, and the Constables came to seek for mee. I went
> upp to Collonel Kirkbey if hee had any thing to say to mee
> I was comed to visite him and when I came to him he told
> mee hee had nothing against mee, and told mee If I would
> stay at Swarthmoore, and not keep great meettings and not
> many strangers, none should meddle with mee. I told him our
> meettings were peaceable and we had the word of the king
> for our meetings . . . and so I passed from him and left him
> seeming loving, and so came to Swarthmoore and so after a
> little while the Deputy Leiutenant of the County [Thomas
> Preston] sent for me to Hoolker Hall and Examined mee . . .
> And they asked me If I could understand languages I said
> sufficient for my selfe . . . And so they asked mee if I had
> heard of the Plott [the Fifth Monarchy Plot popularly
> attributed to Quakers as well]; I told them I had heard the
> noyce of such a thing of one which had heard it from the
> Sheriffe of yorkshire, but I know no friend that was in any
> such thing but only I heard of such a thing, I had written
> against all such plotters and all such thinges, and I had sent
> them papers against such thinges and so they were in a rage,
> and cryed make a Mittimus [a warrant directing him to be held
> in custody] . . . and when I came there [to the Quarter Sessions
> court at Lancaster] they called mee to the Barre. And I said
> peace be amongst them twice. And the Clerk of the peace
> cryed peace to all the Court, in pain of Imprisonment, and so
> the Chayre man asked mee If I knew where I was and I told
> him yes, and said It may bee it was the not putting of my hatt
> that troubled him and that was not the honour that came
> down from God, that was a low thing I hope hee looked not
> for that. And hee said hee looked for that too, and bid them
> take off my hatt which they did.
>
> And so a pretty space wee looked att one another, till the
> power of the Lord God arose over all. And then one of them
> asked mee if I heard of the plott, I told him in the same
> manner as I did to the Deputy Leiutenants before . . . And
> they asked mee if I did not know of a law against Quakers

meettings. I said there was a law that took hold of such that were a terror to the kings subjects . . . It was truth that wee held, and were Enemies to no man but loved all men . . .

They asked mee if I would take the Oath of Allegiance. I told them I never took Oath in my life. I could not swear this was my coat; if a man took it, I could not sweare that hee was the man. They asked mee if I did [owned] my self to bee a Quaker. I told them Quakeing and trembling at the word of God I owned according to the Scriptures but for the word quakeing it was a Nickname given to us by Justice Bennett, that cast mee into a Dungeon because I would not take up armes against the king . . . It was Christs Command that wee should not swear . . . our Allegiance did not lie in Oaths but in truth and faithfullness . . . And so they cryed take him away Gaoler. And so I bid them take Notice it was in obedience to Christs Commands that I suffered.

And so I was sent to prison where now I am with 8 more.

Fox remained in Lancaster Gaol until 1665, when, along with Margaret Fell and a number of other leading Lancashire Quakers, he was brought before the assize judges at Lancaster for refusing to take the Oath of Allegiance to the King. He protested faithfulness to Charles II, but refused, as did the other prisoners, to swear an oath. Once again the court committed him to prison, but the local justices, led by Richard Kirkby, one of the members of parliament for Lancaster, were so anxious to be rid of his disruptive presence, that they arranged to have him removed from Lancaster to Scarborough Castle. Margaret Fell and the other prisoners served their sentences in Lancaster.

Two years later, Fox was free again. He resumed his evangelism as if nothing had interrupted it. In 1667 and 1669 he paid brief visits to Quakers in Warrington and Liverpool, but it was not until 1675, after he had preached his way through the West Indies and the American colonies and had suffered further imprisonment, this time in Worcester, that once again physically exhausted, he returned to Swarthmoor. In 1669 he had married Margaret Fell in Bristol, and from 1675 to 1677 they spent their longest period together in comparatively undisturbed peace at Margaret's home. The Spence MS., which was written during these months, ends almost idyllically with a few sentences describing the 'precious meetings' the Swarthmoor Friends were having, and the lack of interference from the authorities.

In March 1677, Fox went travelling again. He returned in September 1678 to enjoy another prolonged stay at Swarthmoor, but when he next left home in March 1680, it was to be for the last time. He continued preaching and travelling until his death in London in January 1691, and Swarthmoor Hall remained the acknowledged centre for the faith he taught until the death of his wife in 1702.

As other powerful evangelists have done before and since —indeed, as Christ himself did—Fox provoked strong reactions wherever he went. Some men loathed him and considered his influence pernicious; others, convinced that he spoke the Truth, undertook, whatever the consequences, to live by the precepts he taught. The hostile laws of 1661 and 1670 caused much Quaker suffering, but the consequent fines, imprisonments, and abuse, did not discourage the growth of the movement. Instead they ensured that Quakerism thrust its roots deep enough to withstand the severest gales of official disapproval. Fox just managed to live to witness the passing of the Toleration Act which eased the legal position of his followers, and by that time there were scattered through Lancashire, not least in the north, a number of small, resolute groups of Friends. Already a second generation was beginning to share responsibilities at the various Meetings, and Lancaster had become the centre of a Monthly Meeting attended by Friends from neighbouring Yealand, Wray, and Wyresdale, and of a Quarterly Meeting which brought representatives from Meetings still further afield. The Toleration Act allowed Dissenters to worship freely, and in 1696 a further statute permitted Quakers to affirm instead of taking the Oath in court, but, even so, Friends and the law were still constantly at odds chiefly over the payment of tithes. The Quakers refused to pay 'the Steeple house rate' because it maintained two things which they rejected—an established church and a professional clergy. Therefore the authorities had to distrain to recover the tithes and the legal costs of suing in the courts. They frequently took goods to a value considerably in excess of the debt.

Minority groups under pressure tend to develop strong bonds of loyalty and mutual help. The early Quakers formed a close-knit body of men and women, held together not only by their faith but also by a protective exclusiveness that was both a help and a hindrance. One Friend trusted the word of another Friend implicitly. He could confidently appeal to other Friends for help, but if he fell in any way from the strict standards demanded by the Meeting, he could find himself repudiated and excluded. Many Friends were disowned for not observing the strict business ethics and principles set by their Society; others found themselves expelled for marrying outside their faith.

Partly to minimise the demand for tithes, many young Quakers moved into the towns to earn a living in trade or industry. Most of them found that the discipline and mutual aid of the Meeting helped them to prosper. Fox had never despised the material rewards of hard work and fair dealing. On the contrary, he had encouraged his followers to demonstrate to their fellow men that Quaker practices and ethics ensured success in business. The four unmarried daughters of Margaret Fell, for example, coupled an iron-smelting business in High Furness with coastal trade between Morecambe Bay and such ports as Liverpool and Bristol. Fox himself invested money in their forge—Force Forge in the Rusland Valley—and other local Quakers bought their iron and used their ships. By the turn of the century, several Quaker families were prominent in the developing industry and trade of North Lancashire. Names such as Satterthwaite of Hawkshead, Rawlinson of Rusland, Dilworth of Wyresdale, Lawson, Casson, and Townson, all of Lancaster, stood for probity and reliability among businessmen. Fortunately, one of these second-generation Quakers, William Stout of Lancaster, took the trouble to put down on paper an account of his life. Through his eyes we are privileged to examine his activities, problems, hopes and fears. We can compare his almost placid life with that of the Quakers of the previous generation, meet many of his contemporaries, and assess the progress which industry and commerce were making in Lancaster and area during his lifetime.

William Stout, like Adam Martindale, wrote his *Autobiography* in a comparatively short space of time in the evening of his life. He did not leave the work, as Martindale did, to his last year, for although he was about seventy-seven before he sat down to his task—probably early in 1742—he lived almost another decade after he had finished it. There is little or no doubt that Stout had other aids besides his memory. On the table as he wrote probably perched a collection of personal notes kept over many years, and for further details he could always refer to legal, business, and Quaker records in his possession. The editor of the 1967 edition and his scholarly collaborators were able to test Stout's accuracy at many points. They did not find him faultless—he is inaccurate, for example, in a number of family dates—but they were all impressed by the care he had taken to tell the truth as he saw it. Stout's neatness of mind was matched by his neatness of execution, for into two, three, or four *complete* pages of tiny, tidy writing he compressed what he had to say about each year. Acting like a newspaper sub-editor, he trimmed his matter to fit arbitrarily allotted spaces.

Stout was not born of Quaker parents. He did not join the Society of Friends until he was twenty-one, and, apart from his well-beloved sister, Ellen, none of his family followed his example. But Stout never wavered in his loyalty to the Meeting or to his interpretation of Quaker ideals. He lived a simple life, and carried the directness and honesty of his religion into his business. To succeed in what one set out to do was to him a sign of spiritual as well as of mental and physical health. Therefore, he aimed to make a reasonable profit from his business, and he regarded those who failed to do so with pity or with scorn. He was very sorry for his old master, Henry Coward, whose debts in 1698 'drew him into despair and broke his hart, so that he kept to his house some time and dyed for greif or shame'. He owed so much to Coward, who had known what it was to suffer for the 'Truth', and who had been a customer of the Misses Fell. It was he who had taught him the trade of an ironmonger and his admirable example that had converted him to Quakerism. He prized the respect and trust which Coward inspired not only in 'people of his own religious proffesion' but also in 'alothers of all professions and circumstances, as well gentry as the most substantiall yeomanry'. But in the end Coward failed, and the dogmatic Stout laid the blame partly on the way he allowed sporting gentlemen, 'loose' business acquaintances, and 'persons of declining circumstances' to distract him 'from his nessesary business', and partly on the conduct of his wife, 'a very indolant woman', who 'drew money privetly from him', and 'took noe notice of trade or of anything but indulging her children'.

Stout was more severe on his Quaker neighbour, William Godsalve, 'who for some years had followed his trade of a draper and grocer repuitably', but who, in 1708, became bankrupt, and, 'sottish and unsencible of his own interest', refused to co-operate with his creditors. This time 'some decayed Popish gentry' were the culprits: they had 'drawn Godsalve into costly treats, which much reduced his creddit, and which caused him to be otherways very expensive and negligent, and his crediters urgent upon him'. Before long Stout lost all patience with Godsalve, especially when he 'continued obstinat and idle, and very abusive to his wife', the daughter of Henry Coward.

Stout had an unusually high regard for 'our neighbour and my particular friend', Robert Lawson, a Quaker merchant, ship-owner, and sugar refiner, but he had to report in 1720 that Robert had misjudged the soundness of the South Sea Company and had become a victim of the infamous 'Bubble'. Lawson had bought his £800 worth of shares in good faith 'as a well wisher to the government'. When the stock began to appreciate, he decided to spend £4,000 on an estate 'fully expecting that his advance in the stock would pay it'. Stout urged him to sell when the South Sea shares continued to rise in value, but 'he was so far infatuated that it [the price] would still advance till the payment for the estate was due', that the stock was still in his possession when the 'Bubble' burst. Fortunately the loss did not ruin Lawson: he had sufficient reserve to

recover quite easily. But eight years later, his namesake
and nephew, Robert Lawson of Sunderland Point, had no
such resources to cushion him against financial loss. He had
enjoyed 'good success in trade', but, like many of his contemporaries, struck a bad patch and in 1728 had to ack-
nowledge bankruptcy. Stout's diagnosis was that he had
'imployed the proffit in superfluety of buying land at great
prices, and building chargeable and unessary houses, barns,
gardins, and other fancies, and costly furniture'. Had he
been content to live humbly, he could, according to
Stout, 'have been worth 3 or 4 thousand pounds'.

In his own opinion at least, Stout avoided most of the
pitfalls which for him made man's journey through life
so hazardous. He found his humble beginning an advantage
in that he had not been reared with a taste for luxury and
extravagant living. His father had bred sheep on the marsh-
lands of Bolton-le-Sands, and, from about the age of ten,
William had been expected to help with ploughing, hay-
making, and shearing, as well as to satisfy the demands of
the master at Bolton Grammar School. He completed his
schooling at a small school in Heversham, and at fifteen
years of age, a month or two after his father's death,
became Coward's apprentice at Lancaster. Coward was an
exacting master, and young William a hard-working, serious
apprentice.

> . . . I attended the shop in winter with the windows open,
> without sash or screen till nine in the evening, and with the
> windows shut and the dore open till ten o'clock without
> coming into the house except to our victuals or to the fire,
> having our bed in the shop; and had my health well all the
> time . . . when out of nessesary business, I passed my time
> in reading; or improving my selfe in arethmatick, survighing
> or other mathamatikall sciences, which I was most naturally
> inclined to . . .

This account is probably coloured by the old man's ideal-
ized remembrance of his industrious youth, but after Stout
had set up shop for himself in Lancaster in 1688, he continued to work hard and made an outstanding success of
the business.

Nine years later, Stout sold his ironmonger's shop to
his old apprentice, John Troughton of Overton. He had

begun with £120 capital, and in 1697 he reckoned that
his 'clear estate was eleven hundred pounds or upwards . . .
so that my improvement in nine years was above one
hundred pounds a year, one year with another . . .'. He
had achieved this success by living frugally, giving his
mind to the business, and dealing straightforwardly as a
Friend should;

> And I tooke of the shop [which he rented for £5 0s. 0d. a
> year] a smal room, for a bed, table and a smal light, where
> I lodged. And upon the 28th day of the 3rd month, 1688, I
> went to bord with Alderman Thomas Baynes at the price of
> five pounds a year, victuals and washing. But lodged in the
> shop, so was seldom in the house, which was adjoyning to my
> shop, but at victuals summer or winter; for in my apprintiship,
> and some time after, we were frequently caled up at altimes
> of the night to serve customers, [which] obliged us to have a
> bed in the shop.
>
> At Midsummer Fair I had good encouragement, without
> inviting any of my master's or neighbour's customers, which
> was a practice much then used, but by me always detested as
> being contrary to the golden rule to do to others as I would
> they should do to me . . . And I always detested that [which]
> is common, to aske more for goods than the market price, or
> what they may be aforded for; but usualy set the price at one
> word, which seemed ofensive to many who think they never
> buy cheape exept they get abatement of the first price set
> upon them—and it's common for the buyer to aske the lowest
> price. Which, if answered, the wilful insist of abatement; to
> whom I answered they should not tempt any to breake their
> word . . .

Stout had no thought of retiring at the age of 32. He combined his responsibilities and work for the Friends with
helping to equip and load the *Imployment,* a ship which
he part-owned and which he hoped would make money
for him across the Atlantic.

During the previous thirty years, a growing number of
enterprising men had been successfully 'venturing' in com-
mercial voyages between Lancashire ports and the West
Indies. Latterly, a few had made extra profits by sailing
first to West Africa, exchanging their export goods for
slaves, and then heading for the Indies as fast as sail could
take them. Usually on the outward voyage, their ships
carried linen or linen-and-wool cloth together with food-

stuffs and a miscellany of household goods. They returned laden with sugar, tobacco, ginger, barrels of rum
or molasses, or bales of cotton wool. The 'venturers' who
financed each voyage ran a high risk of losing their stake,
for there was always the likelihood of shipwreck, piracy,
and, in time of war, capture by the French. But the profits
from a successful voyage were compensatingly attractive.
Stout was particularly unfortunate in his ventures. On its
first voyage, the *Imployment,* built near Warton of all un-
likely places, had an incompetent trader for a captain. She
returned no more than half full of tobacco, and Stout,
who had taken a sixth share in the voyage, suffered a loss
of £40. He broke even on the *Imployment's* second
voyage, but in the same year, 1699-1700, lost 'at least
£70' when another ship, the *Britannia,* made a disastrous
crossing to Philadelphia. 'Infectious distemper' did the
damage this time. It carried off half the men on board
including George Godsalve, a fellow Quaker from Lancaster, to whom Stout had entrusted his business. But the
climax of Stout's ill-fortune occurred in 1702. The French
captured the *Imployment* as she was bringing to the Lune
her cargo of sugar, ginger, cotton, and molasses. The
captain bargained with the enemy; he surrendered himself
as a surety for a ransom of £1,100 in return for the French
allowing the mate to sail the vessel home. Even that did
not end the *Imployment's* bad luck. The mate reached the
Isle of Man with difficulty, but on the last leg of his
journey, mistook

> . . . Rossall Mill for Walney Mill, and run in that mistake till he
> was imbayed under the Red Banks behind Rossall, so as he
> could not get off. . . . She struck off her rudder, and at the
> high water they sliped her cables and run her on shore in a
> very foule stoney place, where she beat till she was full of
> water. . . . We got the sugar in to Esquier Fleetwood's barn at
> Rossall Poynt, and the cotton wooll into Bispham Chappell. . . .'

Stout reckoned that this voyage lost the owners £2,450. It
cured him of wanting to continue in transatlantic trade.
With some eagerness he returned to the more prosaic
retail business, in which, untroubled by the hazards of the

deep, Quaker honesty and hard work could determine success.

In April 1701 Stout's friend and neighbour, Augustine Greenwood, died. His widow thankfully and trustfully left William Stout to settle the estate: '. . . she brought the keys of the warehouse to me, and desired me to make use of them as I thought nessesary for the safty of the goods and disposing of them . . .'. Alice Greenwood felt herself incapable of running the family grocery business, and so, on her behalf, Stout accepted Richard Leconby's offer to buy it. But when Leconby failed to raise the purchase money, Stout himself bought the business for £279, 'the same [price] that Leconby should have had to pay'. Three years later, he bought at auction most of the bankrupt stock of his old apprentice, John Troughton, and for the next few years combined wholesale grocery with retail ironmongery. It was quite a profitable combination. For the year 1709, for example, Stout recorded a net profit of over £132. Tobacco constituted about one third of his total trade, and if he could buy it direct from the shippers, he could retail it 'spun up' in rolls at a good profit. He handled considerable quantities of sugar, and journeyed to Leeds to buy Swedish iron for nailmaking. Not until 1717, when war in the Baltic forced up the price of Swedish iron, did the iron-smelters of Cartmel and Furness 'build furnasses to run iron, which makes it as good as Swede iron, and brings a great benifit to the north part of this county, where mine and coals are plentyful and labour cheap'.

Stout never married. At the age of thirty-eight, when, as he puts it, he could reasonably have expected 'that reason and prudence might have overbalanced affection and passion', he became infatuated with Bethia Greene, a sprightly young woman in her mid-twenties and elder daughter of 'my antient friend and neighbour, Thomas Greene'. Stout confesses that at one time he resolved that 'if ever I marryed, it must be to her', but, needless to say, though Bethia 'was aprehensive of my respect for her . . . she was very averse to it in respect of my age and plaine appearance and retired way of living'. Bethia obviously had no intention of marrying William or of becoming a Quaker. She accepted an Irishman 'of a facetious and agreable disposition . . . but of no substance', and William 'contented himself' with living with his sister Ellen. In succeeding years Stout could never resist recording news of Bethia, but Ellen and he supported each other with affection as they quietly jogged through the years towards old age and infirmity.

In 1706, when Stout was safely back in the retail trade and his sister Ellen was caring for him at home, he 'had a parish apprentice put upon me'. The law charged parish overseers of the poor to ensure that the children of paupers did not grow up to become paupers themselves. It gave them authority compulsorily to apprentice to a trade any pauper child over seven years of age. This right was often abused, and many masters simply used parish apprentices as cheap labour. But Stout was too honourable a man to take such an advantage. His apprentice, John Robinson, aged ten, he sent to school for four years, then bound him apprentice to a weaver. Once out of his time, Robinson set up his own business, 'but was not so industrious or carefull as he ought, fell to drinking and broke'. He went to London, married, and then, leaving his wife behind, sailed for America. Stout was left to ponder whether he could have spent his money more wisely.

Stout began his entry for 1719 with the statement that his principal motive for continuing to trade was 'the preferment of my brother Leonard Stout's children'. Five girls and three boys grew to maturity, and in time of trouble or need every one of them looked to Uncle William for help. In Stout's opinion, his nephews and nieces fell short of the standards he expected them to achieve. He accused them of flighty behaviour, of choosing unworthy friends, and of wantonly rejecting the good advice he poured on them. But probably the fundamental 'fault' was that they were young men and women who, welcoming opportunities for fun and lively company, found solemn and staid Uncle William difficult to stomach. Yet, however much Stout censured their conduct, he always helped in the end.

Leonard's second surviving son, William, became his uncle's apprentice, and in 1728, when Uncle William was 63 years old, young William took over the business. The old man was generous to a fault.

> . . . I made an inventory of what goods I had in the shop, sellers and warehouse for sale, which amounted to three hundred and seventy pounds. And I gave him in money therty two pounds, which he went to Sheffield with to buy goods: was in all fower hundred and two pounds, all which I gave, and also the use of weights, scales, chists, boxes and other utensils to the value of twenty pounds, and also the use of the shop, sellers and ware house rent free, and also his bording free, and the offer of my assistance in the shop upon any ocation; all which was great satisfaction to his parents . . .

The one thing Stout did not give his nephew was freedom: 'I assisted him as diligently as if I had been his servant' conjures up a picture of him constantly in the shop, proffering comment and advice at every turn. Naturally, the young man resented this perpetual scrutiny, and in defiance deliberately did the opposite of what his uncle wisely but too tenaciously advised. His actions saddened and perplexed his uncle:

> I did not find that he had any due regard to my advice; which was a great trouble to me, that, as I had taken soe much pains and charge for his education, and given him such encuragement to begin to trade, and to be so sleighted. And it put me upon a resolution wholly to leave him, which I tould him, but found he was void of a sence of my care for him or what I had done for him, nor expressed any sorrow for his conduct or of my forsaking him, so that I had no hopes of his doeing well in trade . . .

Even so, Stout did not allow his disapproval to build a permanent barrier between his nephew and himself. Three years later he restocked his shop to save him from imminent bankruptcy, but even further financial help in the following years did not prevent him from eventually going bankrupt in 1737. This disaster seems to have driven young William into acute depression, but his uncle competently handled the settlement, paid the creditors 15s. 0d. in the £, and, out of his own pocket, supported William's wife, Jennet, and their two children.

In the meantime Stout had been helping his nephew John, Leonard's youngest son. He thought that John should be a farmer, and offered, 'if he was industrious and frugall', to buy him a farm. But John wanted to be 'a draper or mercer or a gentleman'. His parents encouraged him in his ambition, and bound him apprentice to Edward Holme, a Kendal draper. William thought this most unwise. He prophesied disaster, but nevertheless produced the necessary £40 fee for Holme, and paid for John's new clothes. In 1738, when John had successfully served his apprenticeship, Leonard and his wife, Ellen, again scorned William's advice. He wanted to set up John in business in Kendal, but they insisted that John should begin in Lancaster, notwithstanding the formidable competition which William told them John would have to face. Stout once again fell in with the family wishes. He gave John £300 to go to London and buy stock for his shop. In his will, he left him another £500. But this time the money was well spent. John and his youngest son, another John, carried on a successful business in Lancaster for the next hundred years.

Ellen, Stout's housekeeper-sister, died in November 1724. Janet, Leonard's second daughter, moved to Lancaster to keep house for her uncle. She stayed 'near three years', and then married Matthew Wright, a yeoman from Preston Patrick in Westmorland. Stout contributed £140 to her dowry of £300. Ellen, Janet's younger sister, took over the vacant post of housekeeper. As she marketed 'she came into the aquaintance and company of Thomas Cort, a young man, a chandler by trade, which I was displeased at, and tould her parents of, diswading her and them to discurage their future courtship for some time of consideration'. Cort was bad enough, but when Stout discovered that Ellen was 'keeping company privtly' with one of the dragoons stationed in Lancaster, he walked through 'a frosty and snowy' night to get her mother to take her back home.

Two years later, he had similar 'trouble' with Leonard's fourth daughter, Margaret. She became friendly with Isaac Nicholson, a young grocer, 'but of loose conversation'.

Leonard and his wife 'thought but light' of the news, but William insisted that Margaret must not stay in Lancaster. He felt justified when, 'less than a month after', Nicholson quietly left Lancaster and never returned, 'to the great loss of his creditors'. But Margaret came back to her job as housekeeper in 1734. Yet again her uncle advised her 'to be carefull who she contracted familiarety or freedom with', but 'in three months time, I perceived she kept company with a young man at that time noe way acceptable to me'. This time Margaret ignored her uncle's displeasure. In January 1735 she took advantage of his temporary absence from Lancaster to marry Walter Burnskill. Stout was most upset: the way that Margaret had 'slighted' him disturbed him far more than her choice of husband. But later he befriended them both most generously. He lived to revise his opinion of Burnskill, who, the year after Stout's death, was elected mayor of Lancaster.

Ellen had married Thomas Cort soon after she had been carted back to Bolton-le-Sands, and Uncle William had overcome his disapproval of the bridegroom sufficiently to give them substantial sums of money and his newly-repaired house in Penny Street. Later, in 1736, he rebuilt the Burnskill's house and shop in Market Place, and three years later contributed generously to the cost of enlarging them. Again, when Leonard's eldest daughter, Elizabeth, lost her husband in 1733, William, who from the first had had 'noe hopes they would do well', settled her business affairs and volunteered to pay her a pension of £10 a year. Later, when Elizabeth died, he took responsibility for the maintenance of both her children. Every member of Leonard's family had reason to be thankful to Uncle William however much they had misused him or he had criticised and angered them. Fortunately, the relationship between the youngest daughter, Mary, and her uncle carried no scars, for exacting William actually approved of the man she married. James Dixon had served his apprenticeship as an apothecary and surgeon in Lancaster and had worked a further year in the London hospitals. William found him 'diligent', and not 'frequenting unnessesary company or

devertion'. James and Mary needed no financial rescue,
but William thought it only right 'to contribute to them
equaly what I have done, or intend to do, to all the other
daughters of my said brother Leonard, who were befor
marryed'.

In less than six months after his marriage to Mary,
Dixon had need to attend her Uncle William professionally,
for in April 1743 a runaway horse knocked him down and
trampled him. The accident broke Stout's leg and bruised
his whole body. 'The people that stood by thought I was
slaine and laid me by as such', but, despite his seventy-
eight years, he slowly but steadily recovered. He lived
for another nine years, but he did not continue his
Autobiography once he had recorded his accident and the
beginnings of his recuperation.

The Autobiography of William Stout has many uses as
a primary historical document. As we have seen, it provides
a portrait gallery of many of Stout's contemporaries. The
'painter' made particularly strict judgments, but he possessed a keen eye and delineated sharply. His sights ranged
far wider than the Lancaster area, for he was interested in
party politics and in European affairs. Naturally enough
he favoured the Whigs if only that they supported toleration of Nonconformists, but he did not automatically
swallow Whig propaganda. He suspended judgment, for
example, upon the birth of James II's son in 1688:

> And upon the tenth day of the fourth month this year
> [10 July 1688], it was published that the Queen was delivered
> of a sone, which was published Prince of Wales, and con-
> sequently to be successor to the Crown if living at the King's
> death. But as the Princess of Orange and Princess Anne of
> Denmark were not at the birth . . . it was suggested that he
> was not born of the Queen's body, but was an imposter; and
> many pamphlets published to prove the same, but never
> proved by any authority apoynted therupon.

The Jacobite rebels marched through Lancaster in 1715,
but Stout made no mention of seeing them. After com-
menting on George I's coronation and the enquiry into the
conduct of the Tory government in the last months of
Anne's reign, he merely referred briefly to the Earl of

Mar's rising in Scotland, and to Lord Derwentwater's defeat at Preston. The event of 1715 which earned most of Stout's space was the death of Louis XIV. He recognised this as the end of an epoch, and summarised the events of the reign shrewdly and knowledgeably. He wrote a similar obituary on Peter the Great of Russia in 1725. He commented upon elections both local and national, and in a well-informed way upon the reason why George II discharged Walpole and his colleagues in 1742. Most of these political facts Stout would probably gather from news-sheets which relayed information from pamphlets and broad-sheets printed in London, but his selection of the items to record in his diary and his assessment of events were as personal as the rest of his writings.

Thanks to Stout, economic historians can colour their interpretation of shipping figures, price variations, import and export graphs, and production costs with some account of personalities and personal experiences and fortunes. Details of retail businesses as early as Stout's are too rare not to be precious. The historical geographer and social historian can profitably search Stout's pages for topographical descriptions and for incidental accounts of social customs and ways of living. In 1687, for example, he went on business to the Isle of Man—'mountainous and barren and thinly inhabited exept in Duglas, Peel Town and Castletown'—and his general comment has almost a modern ring about it:

> '. . . one may live plentifuly there at halfe price they may in England, and many goe there to dwell who are reduced to strates here by extravigance here or other misfortunes; who are safe there from any prosecution of the laws in England for any debts contracted here, or other misdemeanures comited in England or Ireland.'

Even the meterologist can cull fact and description from Stout's book, for particularly in his later years, the author frequently commented in detail on unusual weather.

Somewhat surprisingly, Stout devotes comparatively little space to Quaker beliefs or activities. He writes about going to London and to Whitehaven to represent Lancaster at Meetings. He occasionally remarks upon his relations

with fellow Quakers, and describes how in 1708 the Lancaster Meeting entrusted to Robert Lawson and him the
task of doubling the size of their Meeting House in order
to house the General Meeting of the Northern counties.

> We got it built and finished in about six months, with
> flore, seats, galerys and ceiling, to the generall satisfaction
> of our friends in the county and others. The whole charge
> whereof was one hundred and eighty pounds, which was
> thought moderat.

But between the lines of Stout's book there is Quakerism
in plenty. His way of living, his business ethics, his
distrust of the 'superfluity' of material possessions, his
denunciation of 'light and airy company', of indulgent
parents, and of inconsiderate and selfish children, his
constant sobriety and his mild-mannered attitude even
towards those who misused him, all give us a picture not
only of the man but also of the religious sect of which he
became a leading member. Many of his fellow townsmen
must have considered he led a narrow, dull life, unexciting
and laughterless. But, from the evidence of his writing,
Stout enjoyed life in his sedate and sober way. He welcomed the solitude of his room and he sought no company
when he walked through the countryside. He read much,
and he found satisfaction in quiet contemplation. It
cannot be said that the mantle of George Fox had fallen
on his shoulders for he did not have a burning desire to
go out and convert. But Fox would have acknowledged
him as a worthy follower. The two men had compatible
outlooks on life and ethics.

THE DIARIES OF TWO ROMAN CATHOLIC SQUIRES, THOMAS TYLDESLEY of MYERSCOUGH LODGE, near GARSTANG, and NICHOLAS BLUNDELL of LITTLE CROSBY, CONTEMPORARIES IN ANNE'S REIGN

[In 1873 Joseph Gillow and Anthony Hewitson transcribed, edited, and published The Tyldesley Diary *at Preston. The Lancashire and Cheshire Record Society has published* The Great Diurnal of Nicholas Blundell *in three volumes, 1968-1972. Frank Tyrer transcribed and enriched it with numerous quotations from other Blundell papers; J. J. Bagley edited it for publication. The original manuscripts are preserved by the Blundell family.]*

Thomas Tyldesley, the elder of these two well-known Lancashire diarists, lived from 1657 to 1715. His father, Edward, is hardly remembered except for having built the original Foxhall, now a popular Blackpool hotel, but his grandfather, Sir Thomas, was the distinguished Royalist major-general, who fell at the battle of Wigan Lane in 1651 and whose memorial obelisk still stands near the spot where he died. Nicholas Blundell was twelve years younger than Thomas Tyldesley. His father, William, was just as undistinguished as Edward Tyldesley—he was only head of the family for four years—but his grandfather, another William, fought, as did Sir Thomas, under the Earl of Derby's command, and locally earned the sobriquet *Cavalier*. Blundell the Cavalier was more fortunate than Sir Thomas Tyldesley. He survived the Civil Wars albiet with a game leg, and lived until he was seventy-eight. He took a keen interest in his grandson, the diarist; letters which he wrote to Nicholas when he was a pupil at the Jesuit College at St. Omer reveal a close sympathy and understanding between grandfather and grandson.

Both diarists were brought up in the Roman Catholic faith, and both remained loyal to it all their days. This, of course, restricted and shaped their lives in several ways. It closed the professions to them, denied them the chance of holding public office and made it advisable that they should not attract undue attention especially in times of political tension. Nicholas Blundell's father had the ill-luck to be one of the eight gentlemen in the dock at the notorious Lancashire Plot trial of 1694. He should never have been arrested, for the warrant had been issued against William the Cavalier. But when the King's messengers arrived at Crosby Hall, they realised they would never be able to get the old man on a horse. He was far too heavy and too lame to move. So they took the son 'as the likelyest man of the two, tho' hee also is very lame'. As Roman Catholics, the Blundells could not help but be sympathetic to the Jacobite cause, but it is very doubtful indeed if either the Cavalier or his son was a plotter.

There is no such doubt about Thomas Tyldesley. He was an active Jacobite. He accepted a commission from the exiled Old Pretender, and his signature was one of ten which endorsed a declaration of loyalty to James. The document, dated November 1693, was found over sixty years later among hidden papers at Standish Hall. Thomas was a kinsman of the Standishes—his grandmother was Frances Standish—and he frequently visited Standish Hall, which, if plot there ever was, was the most likely place for it to have been hatched. But, when Jacobitism quickened again in 1713-14, especially after the dangerous illness of Queen Anne in December, Thomas was too old and too uncertain in health to be among the most active Lancashire Jacobites. Yet his heart was with them. Had he lived another year, he would almost certainly have been involved in the 'Fifteen Rebellion in some capacity.

Throughout his life, Nicholas Blundell did his best to keep in the political background: he endeavoured to live according to his personal motto *in omnibus requiem quaesivi*, 'I have sought tranquillity in all things'. But in November 1715 suspicion of Jacobite collaborators was so strong that troops searched Crosby Hall on the 13th—'This Hous was twice sirched by some Foot as came from Leverpoole, I think the first party were about twenty six'—

and three days later Nicholas thought it prudent to take refuge in the priest's hiding hole. He feelingly recorded, 'I set in a Streat [straight] place for a fat Man'. A week later he decided to seek anonymity in London, and in March 1716 made his arrest even less likely by sailing from London to Flanders. His wife and daughters joined him there in July, and Nicholas did not return to Crosby before September 1717.

Like Samuel Pepys and John Evelyn, Tyldesley and Blundell were on nodding terms. Tyldesley does not tell us that they were acquainted, but Blundell does:

28 December (1703). I went to Ince after dinner to solemnise Mr. Blundell's Birthday, he being now 40 years of Age. Mr. Ralf, Thomas and John Tildesley were there.

13 January (1704). I dined at Mr. Levins his at the Moor-side with Mr. Thomas Tildesley, Edmund Trustrom etc.

The *Mr. Blundell,* whose birthday was being celebrated, was Nicholas's neighbour, Henry Blundell of Ince Blundell. He was the son of Bridget, Thomas Tyldesley's aunt. *Mr. Ralf* was presumably Bridget's brother, Ralph, but who John Tyldesley was is not clear. Thomas had two brothers, Edward and James, but had no known relative named John. Quite apart from the relationship between the families at Myerscough Lodge and Ince Blundell, it was almost inevitable that these two heads of prominent Roman Catholic families would know each other. The Lancashire gentry as a whole tended to be quite well acquainted: quarter sessions provided regular meeting places and there were enough social occasions to maintain most contacts. Roman Catholic Gentlemen had extra ties. Numerous marriages between Lancashire Catholic families, as well as the common danger of legal penalties, strengthened the natural bonds of rank, and priests moving from household to household helped to keep contacts fresh with up-to-date news. Even gentlemen who had never met knew of each other's activities through mutual friends. The two diarists reveal that Tyldesley and Blundell were in the same company at Ormskirk races in May 1712. Tyldesley records that he crossed the Ribble—probably by the horse

ford from Warton to Hesketh Bank—about eight o'clock
in the morning and rode to Ormskirk where 'were a greatt
company off the best in the County'. Blundell, who
arrived by coach with his wife and daughter, mentions
meeting Lawyer Starkey of Preston, a well-known Jacobite
sympathiser, Parson Letus of Sefton, and Lord and Lady
Petre, who, according to Tyldesley's *Diary,* were frequently
in Tyldesley's company during the next few weeks. It is
almost beyond doubt that Thomas and Nicholas said 'how
do you do' to each other that day.

Although it was natural in those penal days that
Roman Catholics would wish to marry Roman Catholics,
for the landed gentry marriage was as much a financial
contract as it was a personal union. The bridegroom
looked for a tempting dowry as well as for an agreeable
bride. Soon after his father's death in 1702, Nicholas
Blundell began negotiations to marry Frances, daughter
of Lord Langdale of Holme, Yorkshire. The bride was a
Catholic and the dowry a welcome £2,000 which considerably eased Blundell's financial straits, but the *Diary*
makes it clear that this money was not extracted easily.
The marriage itself is dismissed in a single short sentence:

17 June (1703). I was Married to Lord Langdales Daughter by
    Mr. Slaughter a Clergyman.

But the ceremony that initiated Nicholas into a reasonably
happy marriage was the climax of several weeks of bargain-
ing. The earliest mention in the *Diary* is dated 28 February:

    I went to Scaresbrick to discours my Cozen Robert
    Scaresbrick about going to Hathrop

Hatherop in Gloucestershire, the home of Lady Webb,
the bride's grandmother, became the centre of negotiations. Blundell paid his first visit there in April:

17 April. I came from North Leech to Hathrop, found the Family
    all there, and also my Lord Langdale.
19 April. I discoursed Lord Langdale in his Chamber and Lady
    Webb in the Dining Roome. I made my first adress to Mistress
    Frances Langdale.
23 April. Mr. Trynder the Lawyer came to Hathrop for Instrucsions
    to draw Artickleys of Marriage.

24 *April.* Mr. Trinder drew up the Heads of Artickles of Marriage.

25 *April.* Mr. Trinder brought to Hathrop the Heads of Artickles of Marriage fairly transscribed which were agreed to by Lord Langdale, Lady Webb and myself.

That, however, was not the end. The dowry was agreed but not the method of paying it. Blundell wanted the money straightaway: on 30 May he recorded that Langdale was subject to 'much intercession' to pay the dowry in a single draft. Langdale insisted upon paying half then and half later, and made certain that Frances would receive £200 a year if she were widowed. On 12 June the revised marriage deeds were carefully scrutinised by Blundell's lawyers in London. Three days later they were accepted by both sides:

> Lord Langdale, Lady Webb, Sir John Webb Etc. heard the Marriage Deeds read, all we at Hathrop concerned therein subscribed them before Four Witnesses.

Grandmother Webb sweetened the occasion by gratuitously granting the bride an annuity of £100, and next day everyone gaily attended the wedding.

The Tyldesley Diary was written far too late in the author's life to give us an account of either of his two weddings. For his first wife, he married Eleanor, daughter of Thomas Holcroft of Holcroft in the parish of Winwick. The Holcrofts were anything but Roman Catholics, but the marriage served Tyldesley well financially. When Thomas Holcroft died, his estates were divided between his two daughters: Eleanor took the lands in Holcroft itself, and her sister, Margaret, who had married Richard Standish of Duxbury, took nearby Peasfurlong. For his second wife, Tyldesley chose Mary, the sister of Sir Alexander Rigby of Burgh and Layton. This branch of the Rigby family had been strongly Royalist in the Civil Wars —indeed Mary's grandfather had served under Thomas's grandfather and had later erected the Wigan Lane memorial to him. Most members of the Rigby family conformed by attending the parish church, but there was a tradition of Roman Catholic sympathy in the family. Very probably

Tyldesley was more at home with the Rigbys than he had
been with the Holcrofts, but he did not find his second
marriage profitable financially. An unlucky trading venture
put his father-in-law in the Fleet prison for debt in 1713,
and the Rigbys never recovered from the disaster.

These two diaries are very different in size and scope.
Tyldesley's only covers three years, 1712-14; Blundell's
begins in 1702 when he became head of the family,
continues—with only one day missing—to 1728, and is
supplemented with a wealth of family accounts, letters,
and miscellaneous papers which has enabled the editor,
Frank Tyrer, to enlarge and explain most of the cryptic,
obscure entries. Yet, despite these obvious differences, the
diaries have much in common. In a simple, straightforward
style both note the happenings of every day. Neither
diarist attempts to reflect upon events, or even to express
opinions, and both write in homely language couched in
their own onomatopoeic spelling. Such phrases as Tyldesley's 'tucke phissick', 'cock feights', or 'very could
eivening', and Blundell's 'mesured them with the cheane',
'the bargain is since brock', or 'eather last night or yesterday' reflect dialect pronunciations in 18th-century Lancashire. Above all, each diarist gives us a detailed picture
of the annual round of events, his chief interests in life,
and the problems that beset him and his family.

Both Tyldesley's and Blundell's incomes derived from
their estates. Therefore, throughout their lives they were
constantly concerned with farming, with the care of
tenants, and with gardening, which could add variety to
their diet and colour to their homes. Each of them had
ample labour available outside and inside the house, but
on occasions both were ready enough to take off their
coats and lend a hand.

2 *August* (1712). Alday very bussy in my hay; and in the evening
    cleared the Bryory Feild.
29 *June* (1713). Got up beffor 4, and with severall Freinds helpe
    gott a boat load off terfe into my seller beffor 6
12 *August* (1713). Very bussy in my hay. About 2 post prand[ium]
    godson and Mr. Crage went towards Natby; I brought them to
    Aldclife. Remainder of the day bussy in my hay, and Finished
    the getting of it all.

These extracts from Tyldesley's *Diary* can be matched by similar items from Blundell's on almost the same dates:

9 August (1712). I went to my Work-men that were Scouring the Ditch between the Winterheys and Brownbills Lane. I finished Mowing this year and paid some of my Mowers.

4 June (1713). George Abbot being gon to the Morehous Turf-Moss I went after him betimes in the Morning and helped him to sell Turves, it being the first dayes sale there this yeare.

16 August (1713). I was most of the day in the Little-More-hey and Pick with my Leaders [carters] and Turners of Oats and Reapers of Barly.

17 August (1713). I went to my Mowers in Nichols Hey then thorrow the Hightown and so to the same Mowers againe who were then Mowing Beanes in the Nearer Wheathey, I was also with my Shearers of Barley in the Pike and with my Leaders of Oats in the Little-More-Hey.

In the first quarter of the 18th century, some English farmers were beginning to try out new methods to see if they could increase the yield from their fields: Turnip Townshend and Jethro Tull, the two most celebrated of these agricultural reformers, were both born a mere five years later than Blundell. Lancashire was not unduly troubled by enclosure disputes, and Blundell at least was ever ready to experiment and spend money on improving his estates. He tested new fertilisers and different kinds of grass seeds:

5 May (1712). I Sowed 18 Bushells of Cole-Seed-dust [sea-kale remains] in the Slip and 14 Busshells in the little Moss-hey, I also sowed in the Little Moss-hey about 24 Busshells of Malt Dust and about 32 Busshells of Shiling Dust [husk and dust of grain after winnowing], there was two Busshells sowed on one Rood, I find the Dust above to have done some good espetially in the Meddowing in the Little-Moss-hey . . . I sowed four sorts of Grass-Seeds viz.: Clover, Trefoyl, St. Foyn and Rye Grass Seed in the Middle-North-hey but none of them did well, one reason was becaus the Moulds were not fine enough.

He experimented with fruit tree grafting:

23 March (1720). I finished Grafting the Apple Tree in the new Grounds, it has in it 25 Imps or Grafts and I think they are 24 different sorts of Apples.

He tried to minimise the constant nuisance of blown sand by regularly planting broom and marram grass in the sand-hills that bordered his lands. He planted conifers, oaks, and chestnut trees in the park and plantations near the Hall, and windbreaks of willow, holly, wild rose, and hawthorn along the sides of fields.

1 March (1726). I made my Third Seeding of Haws [hawthorn berries] this year in the Vistow Wood . . .

2 March (1726). I Finished my Great Seeding of Haws in the Vistow Wood, I sowed there about 64 Bushells this yeare, the best time to sow them I think is the begining of January. . . . I sowed about three quarters of a Bushell of Heps [rose-hips] in the Vistow Wood . . .

He took a keen interest in his 'knot' or nursery garden, and later developed other seed beds around the house:

28 August (1706). I Planted in the Knot severall Sets of Riculasses [auriculas] which Mr. Cooper gave me.

6 October (1707). I Lead some Run-Sand from the Ford for my Flower Knot, and also some muck and old Chips for the same use . . .

3 April (1708). I helped Banister [a gardener] to remove some Cowslops and Polianthus into a more regular order in the knot.

25 August (1714). . . . This is the first day as I perceived my Indian Wheat to have any thing on lick [like] Ears of Corn, they seem to be two Inshes and a half long and 12 or more upon the top of one Stalk and a great many more appeered soon after, they Looked very lick Ears of our Wheat but they were onely Blossoms or Flowers.

14 February (1722). I Sowed severall Sorts of Salleting in the Kill [Kiln]-Garden and Close-Hedg Garden and one Bed of Carrots in the Stone-Garden. The New-Bed next to the London Appletrees in the New Orchard, I sowed with severall sorts of Peas all for Seed and Beanes, all the Beans and the farthest Peas were George Smiths Hot-Spurs, the Border next to it sowed with Robert Bushells Hot-Spur Beans.

Like many of his generation, Nicholas Blundell was fasci-nated by tulips. He tried dressing bulbs with different coloured inks 'in hopes to change their colour but to no good effect', and he planted bulbs in profusion around the

Hall. Spring 1719 must have been particularly colourful for in the previous September Blundell recorded:

> I made an end of seting my Tulop Roots, I set this year in all of Tulops and their Chives 3123 besides some as I gave away and some as were not worth seting.

Mid-September was Blundell's usual time for preparing for his next Spring display. On 19 and 20 September 1722, for example, he wrote:

> I set my Forren and best Offsets of Tulops on their Propper Bed and set seedling Tulops and sowed Tulop Seeds on their Propper Bed, I put a good deal of Compost into boath Beds. . . . I filled the two Tulop Beds in the Knot with Compost and set them with Tulops, if they had been set three Weeks sooner, it had ben never the wors.

Yet despite the constant attention which they gave to their estates and despite Blundell's inborn curiosity which led him to experiment, neither Tyldesley nor Blundell seem to have initiated any fundamental changes. In general they followed the well-tried methods they had inherited. They arranged tenancies in the traditional way—Blundell relied on the Tenants' Book which his grandfather had left behind—and the annual cycle of duties and work did not change. Rents were paid partly in cash and partly in services known as boons or boon-rents. There is more than an echo of feudalism in such entries as the following, the first from Tyldesley's *Diary* and the rest from Blundell's:

17 February (1713). In the morning Ben Corney left mee after wee had bargened pro Wood End ground, at £4 10s. 0d. per annum, and his tenant or servant is to have a beaste gatte for his care and tending that gate, which said tenentt is to pay me two days work and 2 hens yearly.

6 October (1707). . . . The Jury met in the Townfield about seting out some wayes. I was with them part of the While, we discoursed about the Doostone [boundary marker] thats set in Richard Harrisons But.

11 August (1709). . . . This is the first day this year that I led Turf with Boone Carts, there was 12 Boone Carts and one of my owne.

21 May (1719). I met severall of my Boons at the West Lane Gate when they came from the Cole-pit with Sleck [slack] for my

Brick [making] . . . Some of my Boons as led Sleck for me
today [25 May] came past the Hous to shew me their Loads.

22 December (1719). Thomas Syer and I stated Accounts for what
he had Disbursed for my use and for what he ought [owed]
me for Turves and for my Boon Shearers.

The repetitive cycle of the farming year—ditching,
ploughing, sowing, turf cutting and stacking, hay-making
and harvesting—and the constant calls upon time and
attention made by horses, cattle, pigs, and sheep, were
broken and relieved by occasional days given to sport.
Horse racing attracted most gentlemen because it provided
a good opportunity to meet neighbours and exchange
news and gossip. The races at Layton Hawes, south of
Blackpool, always drew a good crowd. On 28 June 1704
Captain Robert Fazakerley borrowed one of the Blundell's
horses 'to goe to Leaton Rase on', and on the same date
five years later, Nicholas Blundell rode after Henry Blundell
of Ince, 'when he was going towards the Rase at Leyton
Heys and gave his servant Thomas Sweetlove a Note to give
to Mr. Leomand of Preston'. Thomas Tyldesley enjoyed
Layton Hawes being conveniently near to Foxhall. He
has described the company that gathered for the races
on 18 June 1712:

> Alday att Fox Hall, till the eivening, when sister and Mrs.,
> about 4, went to wate on my Lady Peters, and I went to
> Rogers to meet my Lord and company about the messuring
> the horses to run nextt day, viz.: Sir Francis Andrew's gray,
> 14 halfe; younge Lord's gray, 14; Mr. Harper's gray mare, 14
> and an inch; Jem. Singleton's, bate off 14; and old Fenick,
> 14, son's [i.e. the horse, Old Fenwick, belonged to Edward ,
> the diarist's son.] . . .
> Went to Lit'ium to dinner; thence to the raice; won
> 10s. 0d. of Sir. Francis Andrews but Jem. Singleton treated
> all, soe I spent nothing, only gave Dick Osboldeston's man
> one shilling, pro riding old Fenwicke well, who bette 3 off
> them . . .

Lord and Lady Petre—Catherine Walmesley of Dunkenhalgh before marriage—and Sir Francis Andrews of Denton,
all kinsmen of the Cliftons, were members of Thomas
Clifton's house-party at Lytham, but the rest of the
gentry rode from their own homes to be present at this

sporting event. That evening Tyldesley entertained at Foxhall 'younge Mr. Whitingham' of Whittingham Hall, north of Preston, and a close friend, Will Hesketh of Mains Hall, Singleton. Both were Roman Catholic gentlemen who had spent the day at the races. They 'stayed till 12', and then presumably, each with a manservant, rode home through the short night hours.

Blundell usually rode across to Ormskirk for the races, and on one occasion at least, in September 1726, joined a race party at Knowsley Hall, but most of his race-going was on Crosby shore. By tradition going back to the 1620s at least, the Blundells, at the request of Lord Molyneux of Sefton, undertook to mark out the course each summer. The distance round the oval track was over a mile and a half, and the horses ran two laps. There was, however, no regularity in the meetings; anytime that suited Molyneux between April and October seemed to be the rule. In 1718 it happened to be 1 September. On 8 August Blundell went to Crosby Marsh with three neighbours 'to see where was proper to set out Ground for a Hors Race'. A week later Caryll Molyneux, son of the viscount, dined at Crosby Hall, 'and then I went with him to Crosby Marsh and helped to set out the Cours'. On 26 August, 'I went to Crosby Marsh and ordered where the Distant Post should stand and saw them fixing the Chear' which marked the starting line. The horses were measured on 30 August, when the visitors were beginning to arrive for the race. Blundell entertained at least seven guests at Crosby Hall, and Lord Molyneux sent a side of venison to enrich the board.

September 1. I was at the Gallaway Race on Crosby Marsh and was in the Chear with my Lord Darby and my Lord Molineux and four Horses ran and Mr. Bosloms won the Plate.

Race meetings such as this were major social occasions, but hunts were much more informal. A few neighbours merely arranged to spend a particular day hunting foxes, or hares, or deer, or otters. Tyldesley hunted more frequently than Blundell. Although his *Diary* only covers the last three full years of his life, it records many days spent with the hounds.

25 and 26 August (1712). Went in the morning in order to meet the
hound about Sellery [Sellerley, south-west of Galgate]   where
Brother Frostt's gray-houndes killed a sorell [young, male
fallow deer], which wee tucke to the Cockes [inn at Conder
Green], and were very merry over a parte off him; Sir Pears
[Sir Piers Mostyn, father-in-law of John Dalton of Thurnham],
Mr. Dalton, Frost, Dunlop, and others were there; spent
1s. 6d.; soe to Lancaster.

  Went in the morning to Ashton a hunting, where a wager
off a ginny was layed that wee killed noe bucke; but after
3 howrs good sport wee did, and went to eate part off him
at Cockes, where Brother Frost and I keep company with
the yemonmen, who had helped us in our sport . . .

8 June (1713). As soon as day, wee went to meet severall company
a hunting. Wee earthed the bitch Fox; and tucke a cub beffor
the hounds, alive, affter running him 2 miles . . .

25 June (1713). Went about one a Fox hunting towards Cloughall
[Clough Hall, north-east of Lancaster]; called of Mr. Taylor
at Parke Hall [Quernmore Hall]; thence to Jemmy Gibson's
where we parted hounds; I tucke the Finders; Jemmy Gibson
went with Lawrence C[utler] and mee; wee meet Tommy
Hodhshon who went with us; att 2 brigs, wee tuke kine trall
[cow track], which never left the brookes till wee came to
Barkin bridge, butt no oter could wee stire; soe parted and
went home.

28 November (1713). Alday a hunting, in Booke [Bulk?], with
Cos. Go. Carus and Jo. Yeats; we killed two hares; so home.

Nicholas Assheton would have appreciated Tyldesley's
frustration on 25 June, and been just as excited as he was
over the successful deer hunt in the Conder valley. In this
respect at least, these two diarists, although a century
apart, were twin souls: life could hardly offer either of
them anything more satisfactory than a strenuous day with
the hounds followed by a convivial evening spent with
friends.

  Nicholas Blundell did not show the same enthusiasm
for hunting. Apart from occasional forays, chiefly for
social reasons, he left deer and fox hunting to others, but
fairly frequently he would course hares or go fishing.
Coursing was chiefly a winter sport, and on Blundell's
fields there was no lack of game. Throughout his long
Diary, there are many entries that refer to it:

26 December (1709). Walter Thelwall, John Hunt, etc. went a
Coursing with me, we started about 8 Hars in I think less then

two Hours time, but it was so exteamly Windy that several
of them stole off and we had but little Sport.

19 November (1717). I met severall a Coursing in the More-houses,
being we were a great Many we devided into three Companys,
we all killed 7 Hares, I found one set. In my Company was
Captain Thorp, Young Mr. Robert Fazakerley, Captain Burch,
etc. Burch told me that about the 14th of October last he
with some others were a Coursing in the Haws [sandhills]
and started 24 Hares all of them as I think in my Warant
[Warren] . . .

Both Tyldesley and Blundell did most of their fishing in
ponds or pits specially stocked with pike, or carp, or
tench, or eels. Occasionally, Tyldesley would fish in the
Wyre or the Lune, and Blundell off shore in the Mersey,
but fish was so necessary and so desirable an item of diet
that both men took care to keep their pits well stocked
and in good order. Tyldesley, for example, had a busy day
at Myerscough Lodge on 14 May 1714. He emptied the
trout pond, 'stored the wheat Feild pitt with 77 15 inches
carps; putt 19 into the breeding pond, and 2 tench carps'.
It was a full day's work for ten workmen and himself: they
all celebrated with a supper of eels washed down with
'2 dossin of ale'. Six weeks later, on 1 and 2 July, they re-
constructed and restocked the trout pond. The following
March, Blundell cleaned out his Carthouse pit:

> I got most of the Water out of it so as to get the Flat Fish
> and some Eles, we took six Large Carp, and was 2 Ft-4¾ in.
> long. Since we began to fish it this bout, we got 9 Tensh, 7 of
> them were put into the Horspoole; Carps got in all eight
> larg ones of which 4 were put into the Pike New pit and two
> into the Horspoole. Breames got in all besides smalle Fray
> about 557. Brames stored in the Horspoole 20 lb., in the
> Duckcoy about 30. Eles got in all about 30 lb.

In September 1727, cleaning the same pit was just as
rewarding;

> I having drained a great deale of Water out of the Cart-
> hous-Pitt, I drew it with my own Net and took six large
> Pikes, some Hundreds of small Breames and I think about 20
> Large ones. I sent Mr. Blundell [of Ince Blundell] some
> Scoars of Breame Fray to stoar his Pits and some Fish to eat.

Such restorative work was routine at both Myerscough and Little Crosby. Each pit needed regular 'slutching' or cleaning. The men allowed the old water to flow down the dammed water-course or to run over the fields. They took some of the stranded fish for cooking, but the young and the surplus they put into other pits; they then cleared away the weed, mud, and silt, and restocked the pit as soon as it had refilled with fresh water. It was, of course, always possible to fish a pit for sport. Nicholas Blundell and his chaplain, Robert Aldred, apparently enjoyed some night fishing at this same Carthouse pit in August 1707:

> I went the first time with Mr. Aldred to fish for Shoulers [dace], we got some and bated Pickhooks [pike-hooks] with them and layed them in the Carthous Pit, as we were busy at the Pit by Candle-light Ned Hatton called Mr. Aldred . . .
>
> I fished with Mr. Aldred the first time for Eles in the Carthous pit, we layed a line from the Island to the side and had very good Sport. Mr. Aldred and I plated at Night a very long line to tye Ele Hooks to. . . .

Fowling and ferreting for rabbits were two other sports that enriched the larder, but bowling and cockfighting merely provided relaxation, excitement, and opportunities for betting. Cockfighting was a popular sport, and both Tyldesley and Blundell enjoyed it. On Easter Monday 1713, the men of Little Crosby staged 'a great Cocking' at Ann Rothwell's inn in the centre of the village. There had been weeks of preparation. The decision to hold the event was made on Shrove Tuesday after four successful battles had been fought at Rothwell's on the new 'cock-clod', which Blundell had recently helped to construct. On 25 February, William Ainsworth, one of Blundell's most trusted servants, returned from Blackburn fair—'he brought a Cock with him to fight at Mrs. Anns in Easter Week'. Nearly three weeks later he brought another cock from Ditton—'I designe to feed him against the Cocking as is to be at Mrs. Anns on Easter Monday'. Within a few days, Blundell acquired two other new cocks, and put them with four of his old ones on a special diet. As early as 25 March he was taking bets, and matching his 'Ditton Cock Clumsy' against one of John Rose's cocks. On

Easter Monday nothing mattered but 'the cocking': excitement was so strong that Nicholas uncharacteristically neglected his duty as host:

> We had a great Cocking at Mrs. Ann Rothwells they played Battle Victory, I had two Cocks in the Battle and one of them got two Battles, there were nine Battles played this after-noone. Captain Robert Fazakerley and William Atherton etc. Lodged here. Mrs. Blundell and Mr. Turvill made a Viset here, but I came not to them from the Cocking.

The prospect of this cockfight and his preparations for it enlivened the gloomy weeks of Lent for Blundell that year, but it is doubtful if Tyldesley would have thought so much of the occasion. He accepted cock-fighting as an entertainment which was commonly available: when it suited him to do so, he called at the pit for a couple of hours' excitement and pleasant company. In June 1714, he was an interested spectator at fights at Skippool near Poulton. He had called there a week earlier 'to see Sir Edward Stanley's cockes', but on 9 June he rode from Lancaster to attend a two day meeting:

> Left Lancaster about 11; thence to Skipall, where att a cockin I meet with a deall off gentlemen. Gave Ned Malley 1s. 0d. for his expences; spent 1s. 0d. and won 2s. 6d. of Dr. Hesketh's cockes; thence to Polton . . .
> Gave John Malley and Jo. Parkinson 1s. od. to see the cock Feights. Gave Ned Malley 1s. 0d. pro subsistence. Dined in the cockpitt with Mr. Clifton and others. Spent in wine 6d., and pro dinner 1s. 0d. . . . Spent in the pitt betweixt battles 6d.; I won near 30s. . . .

Excitement rather than profit probably prompted Tyldesley and Blundell to take part in smuggling. The people living on the Lancashire coast had an unenviable reputation for both smuggling and exploiting wrecks, and, in a *Whisky Galore* mood, the gentry were ready to share the booty. Despite the obvious wisdom of saying nothing at all, neither diarist could resist recording his daring. In April 1712 Tyldesley entertained a Mr. Madrell, a Manxman, who later that day brought along Evan Williams, 'the skipper of the Frigot of 12 tuns'. That night Williams slept at Tyldesley's Lancaster house. The next day's entry reads,

25 April. Almorning in the house; gave Evan Williams 8 duble botles to Fill with brandy. Gave him apice of beuff to take with him to Iland.

Blundell's biggest involvement appears to have been in 1720 and 1721. On 27 April 1720, the local customs officer searched the priest's house and the outhouses of Crosby Hall 'for Brandy as he heard was conceiled here'. He found nothing, but during the next six or seven weeks *The Great Diurnal* has several entries which suggest that the squire and his chaplain, Robert Aldred, had out-witted him.

5 May. I mixed about eight Gallons of Frensh Brandy with Water and all other Ingredients and set them a runing to make Aqua-Coelestis on. [Blundell made this drink with crab-apples, lemons, sugar, and brandy.]

27 May. Charles Howerd [a neighbour]botled off some Claret. Mr. Aldred had some of it and I had above eleven Gallons of it.

8 June. Thomas Howerd botled off the remainder of his Claret as was in my Seller.

In the following February, Blundell was again busy making aqua coelestis. He must have made a large quantity of this 'heavenly drink' for he used a hundred lemons, and he ended his entry for 3 February with the significant words 'I had a Cargo of 16 Larg ones [casks] brought to Whit Hall'. His groom 'covered the Cargo very well with Straw', and a week later 'Charles Howerd brought me a good provision for Aqua-Coelestis, I shewed him his goods well stowed in Whit-Hall'. Wisely he does not explain where Whitehall—ironic name!—was, but we, like the customs officer, can assume it was not too far away from Crosby Hall.

More legitimate business of various kinds required each of our two diarists to be frequently away from home. Blundell had land and tenants in Ditton; Tyldesley divided much of his time between his three homes, Myerscough Lodge, Foxhall, and his rented house in Lancaster.

Blundell occasionally rode to Liverpool to attend to legal business, to buy for the household or estate, or, in the first years of his *Diary*. to arrange to send cases of goods to his brother Richard, who was an agent in Virginia. He had many friends and acquaintances in the rapidly-growing borough as well as in the whole of South-west Lancashire, and he and his wife were often entertaining or being entertained. But compared with the restless Thomas Tyldesley, Nicholas Blundell was almost a stay-at-home. So long as he was well, Tyldesley liked to be on the move. He never seemed to settle anywhere for long: restlessness soon forced him back into the saddle, and he was on the road again calling on friends, joining different groups of sportsmen, or just moving from place to place. To the end of his days his appetite for change and movement seemed insatiable. The second half of May 1712, for example, illustrates his unsettled pattern of living: on 15 May he left Banister Hall for Preston, and from then until the end of the month visited or stayed at, in order, Foxhall, Thornton Marsh near Poulton, Lancaster, Crook near Glasson, Kirkby Lonsdale, Cockerham, Bolton-le-Sands, Holme in Westmorland, Foxhall again, and Layton Hawes. For most of that fortnight, Tyldesley slept at his Lancaster House, and even on the two or three days he stayed in town, he was out meeting friends at the King's Arms or the Sun, or discussing matters of business. He traversed the roads and horse tracks of Lancashire so often that he must have known every short cut and every particularly bad patch in the county. Certainly, in the years covered by his *Diary,* Tyldesley seems to have spent little time at home with his wife.

Blundell, on the other hand, derived much of his contentment from his home and family. He found his wife tiresome and unco-operative at times, but he delighted in his two daughters, and, in his last years, in his grandson, Christopher Peppard. His one disappointment was that he never had a son. Yet despite the constant attraction that Crosby Hall had for him, Blundell was a more widely travelled man than Tyldesley. He did not ride so constantly, but he undertook journeys, which, as far as we know, had no parallel in Tyldesley's life. He visited such

places as Blackburn and Ashbourne to buy cattle, but
mostly he travelled to call on friends or stay with one or
other of his many cousins. In 1706 Nicholas and his wife
visited Langdale relatives in Yorkshire and Blundell relatives in Durham. The following year they went on pilgrim-
age to the shrine of St. Winifred in Holywell, and in the
1720s spent two or three interesting holidays in York.
Within the space of nine months in 1713-14, Nicholas
made no less than three journeys to Stockeld, the Yorkshire
home of his brother-in-law, Peter Middleton, who had
married Frances Blundell's sister, Elizabeth. In October,
1713 he took his daughter, Mary, to stay with her Aunt
Elizabeth and Uncle Peter 'for change of Aire'. In the
middle of June 1714, his wife, his younger daughter,
Fanny, and he began a three weeks' holiday in Yorkshire.
They brought Mary home with them, but they had been
back at Crosby less than three weeks when Nicholas was
crossing the Pennines again, this time to attend Peter
Middleton's funeral. It was a two- or three-day journey
each way. To be at the funeral in time, Nicholas had to
make a special effort: he set out an hour before midnight,
and riding through Preston and Skipton arrived near
Bolton Abbey for breakfast—a journey of almost seventy
miles in seven hours.

Cross-Pennine journeys, however, paled into insignifi-
cance alongside Blundell's two 'explorations' in the Low
Countries. His boyhood experience of life at St. Omer in
no way diminished his excited anticipation of adventures
ahead as he sailed from the Thames to Ostend in March
1716. From 8 March, when he rode out of London for
Gravesend, to 5 August 1717, when he landed back in
London, each entry in his *Diary* witnesses the satisfaction
and joy which the journey gave him. Through the grille
of the convent, he was able to greet again his three sisters
and his aunt, all of whom had left Lancashire to become
nuns in Flanders. He spent week after week admiring the
countryside and visiting towns from Calais to Aix la
Chapelle and from Antwerp to Cambrai. Everything was
new, and therefore fascinating, to him. Tirelessly he went
on sight-seeing: intelligent curiosity constantly triumphed

over physical weariness. Palaces, churches, windmills, coal-pits, unfamiliar plants, canals, markets, methods of cultiva-tion, all intrigued him, and all earned mention at the end of each day in pocket notebooks which he later trans-formed into his *Great Diurnal.* His wife and two daughters travelled from Crosby to join him, and when at last Frances and he sailed back to England, they left Mary and Fanny as new girls in the Convent School at Ghent. Six years later, Nicholas and his wife visited Flanders again in order to bring the two young ladies back home. This time they were away from Crosby from 26 May to 5 October 1723, but they only spent three weeks in Europe. For most of those four and a half months, they were in London buying fashionable clothes for their two eligible daughters, enter-taining and being entertained by many Roman Catholic and Lancashire visitors, and enjoying the experience of living a few weeks in the busy city. The *Diurnal,* supple-mented by the detailed financial accounts and the *Letter Book,* answers most of the questions anyone would want to ask about both these journeys abroad.

Two of the most obvious characteristics which Tyldes-ley's and Blundell's writings have in common are the detailed accounts of personal spending, and the frequent references to medicines and other treatments for illnesses. In his *Disbursement Book,* Blundell kept a meticulous record of all his expenditure. Nothing seemed too trivial to be ignored, and, of course, these full accounts are now valuable historical records. Wages, such as 'joyners at 12d. per day, at 8d. and 5d., masons at 8d. per day and 10d. per day, plasterers at 6d.'; food prices, such as 'onions at 1d. per pound, honey at 5d. per pound, and butter at about 4½d. per pound'; luxuries, such as 'almonds one pound 1s. 8d., coffy 3 lbs. £1. 0 0, and candles at 5s. 4d. per dozen'; and the cost of furniture, domestic animals, services, clothing, travel, and customary gratuities in this corner of pre-industrial Lancashire all appear in Blundell's 'disbursements'. Tyldesley has nothing as comprehensive as this. He just made notes of what expenditure he could remember at the end of each day.

6 June (1712). Gave Mrs. [his wife] £3, 0s. 0d., viz., £2. 0s. 0d. to

pay Mr. Walbanke, 20s. 0d. to send to London; gave her 1s. 0d.,
and gave a boy 6d. that brought my colt from Thurnham.

1 July (1713). Went in the morning to Cockerham sale; bought a
bull pro £5. 1s. 0d. spent on Mr. Holden, who went with
mee, 4d., and spent with Mr. Charnley and Ned Reeder 6d.,
thence home.

4 February (1714). Paid pro horses 4s. 0d., pro servants' meat
1s. 0d., and 1s. 8d. pro ale; and gave the maide 1s. 0d., and
the boy 6d. Thence to Garstange. Dined with Mr. Beardsworth,
Doctor Batson, Dick Gorney and Jos. Tounson. Gave them a
hare and treated them; spent 2s. 8d.

Neither Blundell nor Tyldesley had money to spare. Both
frequently had difficulty in making ends meet, so that
keeping accounts in some fashion was as much a necessary
discipline as a convenient way of remembering what bills
they had settled and what sums they had paid for particular purchases.

Tyldesley's last years—the years covered by his *Diary*—
caused him several bouts of acute illness and pain. He made
every effort to shake off indisposition with physical activity and to quieten pain with alcohol, but there were times
when he had to admit defeat and take to his bed. In
November 1712, for example, he had a severe attack of
'gout'. He was out hunting most of the first week of the
month, but on 7 November, at White Hill, Goosnargh,
where he was staying with the Heskeths 'he fell lame off
the goutt'. The next day he spent 'taking phisick to prevent
the gout, but very lame'. By easy stages, though with
considerable difficulty, he managed to reach his house at
Lancaster on 14 November, and for the next ten days he
was bedfast. The daily entries in the *Diary* are brief but
explicit: 'Fell lame off my hand'. 'Very lame in both
Feet'; Very lame and the goutt beginning in my right
hand'. On 24 November he went out hunting hares, and,
hardly surprisingly, the next day was 'very sicke' again.
Warm cabbage leaves did something to relieve the anguish
in his left hand, but on 13 December the pain had become
so acute again that he 'was Forsed to take 12 or 14 ounces
off blood from the same arme'. This treatment brought no
relief. The gout continued, and to add to his distress he
suffered an attack of 'the gravel'. Tyldesley blamed his

troubles on 'the snow meltin and the severity of the angry wether'. He endured a painful Christmas, and by the middle of January was just as bad as ever.

9 January. Trobled with a Fowle stomach; tuke 3 vomitts . . .
10 January. Bloodded in my right arme for a could and stitch . . .
11 January. My stitch not removeing, Mrs. tuke from the left arm 12 ounces—as bad as the other.
12 January. In paine all over . . .
15 January. Alday in much paines and helpless.
18 January. My paine increasing seassed most joynts in my body, viz.—both ankles, both knes, both hands, both elbows, both shoulders, and both collar boans; God knows all at once . . .
27 January. In much paine occasioned by the bad wether off angry winde and vast great snow, which fell in great fleakes, licke the largest off goose quills . . .

So the sad story continued off and on for the next three months. A course of manna taken as a laxative seemed to improve his general condition, but Tyldesley had to wait until the warmer weather came before he could get out and about again with any freedom and pleasure.

Blundell's much longer diary, of course, gives him many more occasions to write about illnesses and remedies. Moreover, he was interested in experimenting as much upon himself as on other people. In his Recipe Book he compiled a long list of cures and treatments. He had, for example, more than two dozen 'recipes' for eye-trouble, from which he was a chronic sufferer, but in practice he relied chiefly on eyebright, which he usually boiled, sieved, and drank as 'eye-bright tea', but sometimes dried and mixed with his food, or smoked in his pipe. On 7 August 1722 he commented on his spectacles:

> I began to uese Spectacles but not as a Constansy, onely when the Print is too Small for me or that it is rather too dark to see my Letters plaine without them for now they are of advantage to me, though formerly they were not.

Blundell had occasional spasms of fever or ague. Now and again he complained of gravel or bladder trouble, and at the end of March 1712 he suffered from a short, sharp illness which resulted in 'a continuall Fit of Heckoping

which lasted for about 15 Hours without ever any Long
intermission', and which brought two doctors and four
priests to Crosby Hall. Yet, apart from his eye trouble,
Blundell enjoyed good health for most of his life.

Frances Blundell was not so fortunate especially during
her early married life. For more than a fortnight in July
1708 she stayed as a resident patient at Dr. Worthington's
in Wigan, drinking the spa waters in an unsuccessful
attempt to cure the gravel. A year later Nicholas and she
rode to Whitchurch to consult the well-known Dr. Bostock
about her persistent backache, and she regularly submitted
to 'bludding', sometimes by a visiting doctor, but more
usually by Malthus the innkeeper, Cartwright the butler,
or one of the knowledgeable women whom she called in
from time to time. Blood-letting, purges, and vomits were
standard treatments for most illnesses, but curious, inquiring Nicholas liked to try less obvious methods when he
could. He steeped his feet in hot whey 'to make my Cornes
come out by the Roots', lowered one daughter into the
cellar well and pulled hairs from the other's head to cure
skin disorders, shaved his head and applied blistering
plasters to treat severe headache, and, on the occulists'
advice, put clary seeds in his eyes to improve his sight. In
August 1709 he arranged for his daughters to be immersed
daily in the salt waters of the Lower Mersey to clear their
skin of 'outbreaks', and he was not above suffering cuts
in both ears to judge the effect upon his sight, prescribing
herbs for a tenant's child's convulsions, or recommending
treatment for ague, gravel, and eye ailments, for which he
had something of a local reputation. Nicholas does not give
us sufficient evidence to determine the success of all these
cures, but most of them seem to have been as disappointing as the waters of Chaudfontaine and Spa, in which
Nicholas and Frances solemnly bathed in the summer of
1717 in the vain hope of being granted a son. 'We went
into the Bath in the Morning, it is my Wives 13th. time
and my eleventh.'

Lancashire historians regard the first decades of the
18th century as the period when the early signs of
the approaching industrialisation of the county were

becoming increasingly obvious. Lancastrians everywhere still maintained a keen interest in growing crops or in rearing cattle and sheep, but infant industries were developing, more colliers were digging coal, the need for far better communications was being felt more keenly every day, some of the ship builders working on the banks of most of Lancashire's rivers were constructing the bigger ships which the exporters were demanding, and each year the ports, Liverpool especially, were attracting scores of new burgesses. Neither Tyldesley nor Blundell was directly concerned in industrial matters, but their writings could not help but reflect something of these changing times. Tyldesley speaks of doing business with John Blackburne of Orford, who was very active in developing the rock salt industry. He was well acquainted with the two Quaker brothers, Robert and Joshua Lawson of Lancaster, who were pioneers in establishing trade between the Lune and the West Indies. On 12 July 1714 Tyldesley wrote, 'Went to the ship. Gave them 12 of ale in order to oblidge Joshua Lawson to bee kinde to litle Dick Shutlesworth'—a cryptic entry which, in the light of a later reference to the launching of 'the ship', might well refer to Lawson building a new ship, in which Tyldesley had a financial interest. Six weeks earlier, in the second half of May, Tyldesley had shown a sudden and intense interest in coal mining. Along with William Beardsworth, a Lancaster attorney, he had visited 'the New cole pitt' and three other pits at Ellel, Quernmore, and Crag, to the east of Ellel township. Since he paid three visits to Ellel, took presents for the colliers, and stayed there a full day on one visit, and since during that fortnight he met Beardsworth almost every day, it might fairly be inferred that Tyldesley's visits had more to do with business than sight-seeing.

Coal-mining in and around the Lune valley was a rather desperate and ultimately unsuccessful attempt to develop an industrial hinterland for the port of Lancaster. South west Lancashire was already demonstrating what industrial development could do when plenty of coal could be mined in the neighbourhood of a wide, navigable river. Blundell was able to take coal for granted all his life: every summer,

when the roads were less muddy than at other times, his
carts brought to Crosby Hall his usual annual supply from
comparatively-near Huyton, Prescot, and Whiston, or from
more distant Haigh, near Wigan. He was well aware that
coal, as one of the basic requirements for industrial
advancement, was a profitable possession, and he showed a
keen if amateur interest in the mining of it. The following
three entries, well-spaced in time and place, illustrate this:

3 November (1708). . . . I lodged at Dungenhall [Dunkenhalgh],
going thither I called at Seath Woodcocks [at Wrightington]
and saw Mr. Barlows Water Engin thence I went to Cozen
Thomas Gelibrond [at Chorley] and dined there, I saw his
Cole-Work it being the first time I had seen it . . .

19 June (1717). Mr. Wright went with me [from Liège] to some
Cole Pits, we went most of the way by Bote, they wind up
about one Hogshead and a half of Water at a time with 3 or
4 strong Horses, the Cole Pits are generally very deep and
some of them about 80 Fathom, at one Pit I saw a place like
a well made of Brick with a Bucket of Fier which hung down
in it to prevent the Damp, and over it there was a Chimney
like that of a Glass-hous . . .

5 May (1719). I went to Mr. Case his [at Red Hazels, Prescot], but
he was not at home so I smoaked a Pipe with his Son Henry
and then went to the New Engin [a Newcomen engine] as is
to draw up Water from one of the Cole-pits . . .

Eighteenth-century Liverpool had a growing appetite
for coal. The furnaces of the salt refiners, sugar boilers,
pottery makers, metal and other workers competed with
an ever-increasing number of domestic grates to burn the
precious fuel. The goods which coal helped to manufacture
were wanted on Merseyside itself, elsewhere in Britain, and
more than ever in the holds of ships bound for North
America and the West Indies. From far and near, merchants gathered cargoes of all kinds, from linen cloth to
nails, soap to gunpowder, copper pans to looking glasses.
They loaded them in Liverpool ships, and took them across
the Atlantic either directly, or indirectly by way of the
African coast and the slave trade. In exchange, they purchased load after load of sugar, tobacco, timber, molasses,
and rum, most of which required refining or maturing in
Liverpool before being distributed to British customers or

re-exported to Europe. Such constantly expanding industry and commerce could not survive of course without a constantly expanding labour force.

In Blundell's lifetime, Liverpool grew from a small borough of little more than 2,000 inhabitants to a thriving port about ten times that size. Three years before Nicholas's birth, William the Cavalier had taken shares in the venture of the *Antelope,* the first Liverpool ship known to have made the long voyage to the West Indies and back. He doubled the money he had invested. In the 1690s, Nicholas's father had apprenticed his younger son, Richard, to be an agent in Virginia for a Liverpool merchant, Richard Houghton. This agreement caused Nicholas much anxiety during the first five or six years after becoming the head of the family. Because he could not get Richard to send him satisfactory financial accounts, Houghton expected Nicholas to take responsibility for his brother's dilatoriness. Richard's ill-health and family duties made communications between the brothers more difficult than they should have been, and, until, and indeed after, Richard's early death in November 1704, Nicholas was busy buying and crating goods to send him, standing surety for him, paying his debts, and finding him an indentured apprentice.

During these years of involvement, Nicholas himself seems to have invested £500 in Houghton's business, but nowhere in the accounts he left behind is there mention of profit or of subsequent investments in other trading ventures. Yet throughout his life, Nicholas was an interested spectator of Liverpool's spectacular growth. He knew better than his contemporary Defoe that 'Liverpool was one of the wonders of Britain', for he was frequently in the borough mixing with the men who were most involved in its commerce, industry, and administration. He numbered such key personalities as William Clayton, Thomas Johnson, Richard Norris, Sylvester Morecroft, and George Tyrer among his friends and social acquaintances, and they, along with many less distinguished Liverpool burgesses, continue to live in the pages of his *Great Diurnal.*

THE DIARY OF RICHARD KAY OF BURY, 1737-1750

[The Manchester Central Reference Library possesses a typescript copy of the original diary. A few general extracts were published in A Lancashire Doctor's Diary *(1895), but in 1968 the Chetham Society published a much bigger selection of extracts under the title* The Diary of Richard Kay, 1716-51, of Baldingstone, near Bury. *The editors were W. Brockbank and F. Kenworthy.*

The diary of Elizabeth Byrom is printed in Chetham Society Publications, Old Series, Vol. 44 (1857).]

Kay was, and still is, a commonly-found surname in Bury and district. The frequent use of two or three favourite Christian names led to confusion, and still makes the tracing of Kay family connections doubly difficult. The only way to distinguish one Richard Kay from another in the 18th century was to add to each his place of residence. Our diarist was Richard Kay of Baldingstone, as was his grandfather before him. His uncle and cousin were both Richard Kay of Chesham, and three less close relatives—brother, uncle, and great-uncle of John Kay, the inventor of the Flying Shuttle—were each known as Richard Kay of Sheep Hey, which was an older family house, close to the Irwell and about four miles north of Bury.

Richard Kay of Chesham, uncle of our Richard, was also a diarist. His original manuscript has long been lost, but a copy covering the years 1705-31 still survives in the Raines MSS. in Chetham's Library, Manchester. Uncle Richard, who was very wealthy by Bury standards, was an active Dissenter. Much of his diary is taken up with financial accounts and with the building first, from 1712 to 1714, of his new house, Lower Chesham Hall at Chesham Fold, no more than a mile from the centre of Bury, and secondly, in 1719, of the Dissenter chapel in Silver Street, Bury. The hall, considerably altered and modernised

earlier this century, is still in use, but the chapel, the first
to be built in the township, eventually became too small
for its congregation. In 1837 it was replaced by the
predecessor of the present Bank Street Chapel.

Our diarist's father, Robert, was the local doctor. He
was a younger son, but he had inherited the family home
of Baldingstone, two miles north of the centre of Bury.
Robert's practice was quite extensive: he had patients in
places as far apart as Turton and Middleton, or Pilkington
and Edenfield, so that any day he might be called out to
visit houses five or six miles distant in any direction from
Baldingstone. He prescribed and prepared medicines, and
performed operations in his patients' homes, but, apparently, he had had no more training than he had acquired
from his apprenticeship and his subsequent experience.
Compared with his nephew, Samuel, he was poorly
qualified, for Samuel, trained at the University, could
claim the title *physician,* which gave him much higher
status in his profession. In 1752, the year after our diarist
died, Samuel was to be appointed physician to the new
Public Infirmary in Manchester.

Richard's mother, Elizabeth, was the daughter of
Samuel Taylor, a Dissenting or a Nonconformist minister
of Moston, near Manchester. Elizabeth and Robert brought
up their five surviving children to attend Silver Street
Chapel, and as a young man Richard found difficulty in
choosing between medicine and the dissenting ministry
for his profession. His father early taught him sufficient
doctoring to meet the routine needs of occasional patients,
but he neither expected nor encouraged him to train to
take over the practice. He left his son to make up his own
mind, and, in common with many young men before and
since, Richard found the decision anything but easy. He
spent hour after hour in his room, praying for guidance
and thinking over the problem.

16 Nov. (1737). [Richard, born 20 March 1716, was twenty one.]
This Day I've assisted Father some little in his Business;
we have Coz. Richard Kay's Company of Chesham; vacant
Times I've spent in my Closet; this Evening Father gave me very
free Instructions concerning his Business, chiefly about his
Remedies; I've often wondered within my Self what Calling

of Life I must fix my Self to, since I cannot reconcile my
Self to the Thought of living in the World without an
Employment, tho' Father's Business and calling of Life be
free and open, yet through the Difficulty that many Times
attends it he gives me but little encouragement to fix my
Self to it, but 'tis my Resolution to commit my Self to God
and his kind Providence, and in the meantime to give my Self
very much to Closet Duties and Closet Employments. Lord
bless and provide for me and crown my Desires and Endeavours with Success.

Gradually, Richard became increasingly involved in his
father's work. 'This day I've attended on Father's Business
at Home' came to be a frequent entry in his *Diary,* and
from time to time he recorded riding with his father to
visit patients, witnessing and even assisting with operations,
and attending lectures and demonstrations on mechanics,
mathematics, and various aspects of physics as well as on
anatomy. From 1738 onwards he and his father appear to
have assumed that medicine was to be his career.

By September 1740, twenty-four-year-old Richard was
visiting patients and mixing medicines:

> In giving Father an Account this Evening of the Patients I
> have been concerned for to Day, and of some Doses of Physick
> I made up this Week which I had not given him account of
> before he has blamed me very much for prescribing as he
> fears a few Grains too large a Quantity of Calomel. Sextus
> Sublimatus to a Man at a considerable Distance of a very
> Strumous Habit: It happened thro' Mistake, I am no little
> uneasy about it, but I hope it will be a Means to make me
> very careful for the future, and hope by God's Blessing it
> will succeed well, the Quantity exceeding not 15 Grains.

Soon afterwards he was dressing wounds, and by 1742 he
was obviously feeling confident enough to make important
medical decisions. On 28 April he wrote:

> This Day Father being Abroad [visiting patients] I've been
> attending on Business at Home, could not in the Evening
> well excuse myself visiting a Patient near Heywood under a
> Scrophulous Disorder in his Ancle Bones, I advised him to
> an Amputation or taking off of his Leg which he complyed
> to and never would before, as being the only Method for
> his Cure as also the only Chance he stands for his Life . . .

Dr. Robert certainly provided his son with plenty of practical experience. Sometimes the *Diary* mentions a 'throng of patients' in the house, and occasionally gives us details of cases. For 27 June 1743, we have an unusually specific entry:

> This Day in the Morning with attending on some necessary Concerns I waited on Father in the Shop, we had a Patient with his Glutaeus Medius or the Muscle which extends the Thigh cut from the Patella or Knee pan by a Fall, we had a scrophulous Tumour in the Shoulder with a Caries of the Bone, and Stiffness of the Joint, a strumous Tumour in the Leg infested with Pus from near Ham to Heel, a broken Arm, a Broken Thigh, besides other Patients; in the Afternoon went to Manchester, heard a Lecture concerning Mechannicks, Father ordered me as I went to Manchester to visit a Patient one Martha Peake near Blackfordbridge [near Radcliffe] not much out of my Road having been long confined under a Spina Ventosa in the Tibia of her Leg . . .

We cannot assume that the *Diary* faithfully reflects the distribution of Richard's time and energy. He probably took his apprentice-doctor work largely for granted, and recorded the exceptional rather than the routine. Yet he makes it quite clear that he gave many days wholly to farming, gardening, looking after the horses, visiting friends and relatives, and, above all, attending services, listening to sermons, and studying theology. His activities in the last week of April 1740 are typical of the life he led outside his church and study in his early twenties. On the 21st he rode to Stockport to visit friends, and 'to bring back Sister Alice [seventeen years old] who went thither on Saturday last with Coz. Neddy Kay of Brookbottom'. He stayed the night with his cousin, Joshua Taylor:

> . . . In the Evening betwixt 8 and 9 o'th'Clock Cousin Joshua was troubled with Sickness, occasioned as was supposed by being too long in the cold Evening upon the Bowling Green, and then coming to a hot Fire; tho' he had thought himself not very well by eating an improper Breakfast in the Morning; they called in Mr. Fletch an Apothecary, but we differing in our Opinion, they sent for Doctor Watson who order'd him to be bled, and prescribed for him a Vomit and a Sweat successiviely.

Joshua recovered considerably during the next twelve hours, 'tho' the Doctors wou'd have him blistered', and therefore Richard and Alice felt free to travel to Manchester to stay overnight with another cousin, John Kay. Presumably, on the next day, for which there is no entry, brother and sister returned home, for Richard spent 24 and 25 April moving 'a large Stone Trough' which his grandfather had built 'in a Wall below the House' to a 'new Wall in the Garden I am making above the House'. On the 26th Richard was back at his father's side, 'concerned to Day for several Patients that have had Disorders in and near their Eyes'. This work caused him to worry about his own sight. He was sure his vision was not so steady as it ought to be:

> . . . but I ascribe it to Reading and Writing so much by Candle Light, notwithstanding I always used a thick Candle, and endeavoured to keep a steady Light; I have likewise at present some other prejudicial Effects in my Body of my late close Thought and Study . . .

Once or twice Richard shows an inclination to hypochondria. He suffered real trouble especially with his teeth, but prolonged meditation or harrowing experiences with patients led at times to depression and imagined illness.

Occasionally, but only occasionally, Richard rode off on holiday. In August 1739 he and his favourite cousin, Samuel Taylor of Moston, spent a couple of days in Buxton taking the waters and having 'a Deal of good and profitable Discourse' with the local clergy. This was Richard's second holiday in that exceptional year, for he had spent the last days of April and the first days of May touring the West Riding. Five years later he visited Yorkshire again, but his most adventurous and enjoyable holiday was in June 1742 when he and Samuel Taylor set out for Cumberland. Samuel was on business—he dealt with Whitehaven merchants in linen check—but to Richard it was 'a very unexpected Journey'. They rode through Lancaster, Kendal, Ambleside, Keswick and Cockermouth on the way out—all new country to Richard—and returned through Workington, Carlisle, Penrith, and Shap. They heard sermons, and held discussions with clergy and at least one doctor, Mr. Carlisle, 'Doctor in Physick' at Kendal. At Whitehaven they even listened to a comedy 'where there was a considerable Appearance of Gentlemen and Ladies'. Yet not one word did Richard write about the magnificent country through which he passed. The first sight of Windermere from the Kendal road, the charm of Grasmere, the dominance of the Skiddaw range, and the wildness of Shap apparently did not merit a single word. Yet Richard Kay was not a town dweller: unlike his contemporary Samuel Johnson, he did not think that 'the full tide of human existence was at Charing Cross'. Perhaps the trouble was that Thomas West's *Guide to the Lakes,* which firmly established the appreciation of the Lake District in English hearts, was still almost forty years in the future.

At least three items in the first part of this *Diary* will raise the eyebrows of those who derive their picture of serious Nonconformist behaviour from Victorian and Edwardian days. In May 1738 Richard attended a race meeting on Kersal Moor: on 18 October 1739, he went coursing hares, and, two years later, he bought two tickets in a state lottery. Eighteenth-century Dissenters did not consider these pastimes so outrageous as did their late 19th-century successors, but even so they were a little out-of-character for so serious and devout a young man as Richard Kay. Throughout his *Diary,* Richard ended each entry with a short prayer or invocation. Usually, this last sentence was a general plea for divine help and guidance such as 'Lord give me Patience, and help me to make a wise Improvement of all', or 'Lord sanctify all Providences both in Church and State'. But sometimes the final sentence was an obvious pointer to how the diarist had reacted to the events of the day. A trying spell mixing drugs once provoked 'Lord give me a Genius for the Study of Medicine', and a long struggle to reduce a dislocated hip occasioned 'Lord, Teach me the Knowledge of Anatomy which is not only honourable and pleasant, but profitable and highly useful'. So, probably it is a sign of regret and remorse that Richard ended his entry about the race meeting with

> Lord ever keep me in good and sober Company, and ever
> give Grace and Strength to watch and guard against mad

Frolicks, foolish Sports, unseasonable and dishonourable
Diversions, and wicked and sinful Irregularities.

In August 1743, Richard, then twenty-seven years old,
began a year's training at Guy's Hospital, London. His
father had broached the matter in the previous January,
'but says he knows not how to advise me for the best'.
Cousin Samuel Kay, the Manchester physician, urged the
proposal forward and sent off the necessary fee of twenty-
four guineas. The other requirement, a certificate of good
character, presented no difficulty, and on Monday, 1
August, the great adventure began. From Bury to Manchester a veritable cavalcade of friends accompanied
Richard and his travelling companion, Edward Sparrow, a
young apothecary returning to London after visiting
relatives in Lancashire. Samuel Taylor and Benjamin
Gaskell of Clifton Hall then took them as far as Knutsford.
But from breakfast on Tuesday the two young horsemen
rode alone. They travelled by the well-worn route, known
to the Romans as Watling Street and to motorists as A5,
and by hard riding arrived in London on the Friday
evening.

Richard enjoyed a busy year. He studied under Benjamin
Steade, the only resident medical man in this hospital of
about four hundred beds. Hospital rules restricted Steade,
officially entitled *apothecary,* to no more than three
pupils, so that Richard had intensive instruction. He
attended lectures by physicians and surgeons, was present
at all kinds of operations, watched dissections of corpses,
and took a course in midwifery. He realised how fortunate
he was—'the Operations and weekly Anatomical Lectures
I have here the Opportunity of are very good and edifying'
—but he put little detail into his *Diary.* For the most part
he was content merely to record the occasion—'Mr. Sharp
lectured to us on vision', or 'This Day I've attended the
Hospitals [St. Thomas's as well as Guy's] there hath been
two Legs took off and a Girl cut for a Hare Lip'. On
13 October 1743, the diarist explained his reluctance to
write too much:

This Day I attended the Hospitals; I'm here I think every
Day seeing something very remarkable in one or both of these

Hospitals, but think it best not to mention the Particulars only my Attendance here because it will swell my Diary too much; I send Father a Journal of my Going on, and of what falls out here that is remarkable.

That journal, if it were ever discovered, would be keenly studied by medical historians, for even the little that Kay records about his tuition is unparalleled in the archives of Guy's Hospital.

Richard was very conscious that his stay in London would soon pass and that most probably he would never again visit the city. He determined to use every moment. He fitted in a lot of sight-seeing, including Bedlam, a favourite tourist attraction in the 18th century; the Lord Mayor's Show; St. James's 'to see the Quality go to the Ball, his Majesty's Birthday being celebrated as this Day'; and the public hanging of five men and a woman on Kennington Common. Occasionally, he went to Covent Garden or Drury Lane to see a play. He accepted a few invitations to meals, but his chief delight was attending religious services and listening to sermons. For this year the denomination did not matter: away from home and neighbourly tongue-wagging, this young Presbyterian busily enlarged his experience by worshipping in Anglican, Quaker, other Nonconformist, and even Roman Catholic churches. Only ten days after he had arrived in London, he wrote:

August 15. This Day in the Morning I took a Walk to St. James's Park, went to a Popish Meeting heard Mass afterwards attended the Business of the Hospital . . .

August 16. . . . I heard Mr. Westly [John Wesley] the Field Preacher in Moor Fields this Evening . . .

Whenever hospital duties allowed, he continued to spend Sundays sampling the many London churches. Two or three services a day, all in different places, were not unusual:

October 30. This Day this Sabbath Day in the Morning I heard Mr. Reade near the Hospital Gates preach from John 7. 46, in the Afternoon heard Mr. Spillsbury preach at Salters Hall from Heb. 10. 31, heard the Evening Lecture at the Old Jewry preached by Mr. Foster from John 3. 3 . . .

These varied experiences did nothing to shake Richard's certainty that Presbyterianism was the right sect for him.

He returned to Baldingstone with as strong a belief as
ever in the virtues of Calvinistic theology and chapel life.

No prodigal ever had a more hearty homecoming than
Dr. Richard Kay, newly armed with his certificate signed
by Samuel Sharp, Guy's outstanding surgeon, and proud
owner of a box of 'Chirurgic Instruments' which Steade
had helped him choose. He did not race home: on the
contrary, he wisely used the journey to do some more
sight-seeing. He travelled first along the Thames valley to
Richmond, Hampton Court, and Windsor, then struck
north-westwards to Oxford, Woodstock, Stratford and
Birmingham. At Lichfield he left the usual route in order
to ride to Derby and approach Lancashire through the
Peak District. His 'very agreable Friend', the Reverend
John Jolly, accompanied him as far as Woodstock, but for
the next five days Richard journeyed on his own. Bad
weather delayed him, so that when he arrived in Buxton,
he found that a number of his friends had been waiting
for him 'since the Night before',

> *Sept. 11.* . . . there I met with the Revnd. Mr. Braddock, Brother
> Joseph Baron, Coz. Richd. Kay of Chesham, Coz. Joshua
> Taylor from Stockport, Brother Robert and my Nephew
> Samuel Baron, spent the Evening very agreably with them at
> Buxton in company with the Revnd. Mr. Harrison there . . .

> *Sept. 12.* This Day in the Morning we left Buxton came through
> Stockport to Manchester, I dined with Coz. Kay's in the
> Back Square; Coz. John Kay came with me, and Friends, I met
> with my dear Mother and Sisters at Brother Baron's in Bury,
> we went together on Horseback to Baldingstone, and blessed
> be God, I have a comfortable Meeting with dear Father and
> Friends. Lord, Joyn with Friends, and as it were bid me
> wellcome likewise at Baldingstone . . .

The next day he spent listening to the monthly lecture at
Bury Chapel. A week later, he was busy with the practice:
'the Number of Father's Patients seems to be considerable'.

The last half of this *Diary* is concerned with Richard's
life as a qualified doctor. After his return from London,
he took full responsibility for his work, and steadily
became the more active of the partners. The family practice extended in area. He was soon writing of patients 'a
considerable distance from home', and of a single round

of visits being 'upwards of 20 Miles or near 30'. From Haslingden and Rossendale in the north to Middleton and Blackley in the south, from Bolton in the west to Rochdale in the east stretched his usual area, and for special patients he sometimes rode as far as Padiham, more than a dozen miles to the north, and Manchester, ten miles to the south of Baldingstone. Like all doctors, he could not allow darkness and bad weather to keep him from his patients and during the six years covered by the rest of the *Diary*, he and his horse had some nasty experiences. To be soaked with rain was common enough. Now and again he had to seek shelter for the night, and two or three times his horse threw him. Probably his worst experience occurred on 27 December 1748. After he had had dinner at noon, he set out to see a patient at Crawshaw Booth, north of Rawtenstall. There he was asked to see a new patient further up the valley, so that he did not turn for home until after nightfall. A Mr. Lord of Newchurch in Rossendale led him back over the unfamiliar road. As they were crossing a stone bridge near Crawshaw Booth,

> I said, It is very dark; he [Lord] answered, So dark It is all I can do to see the Bridge; he had no sooner said so but my Horse in the highest Part of the Bridge went over the Battlement, I light flat upon my Hands and Knees in the Water with my Face down the Stream, and my Horse in the Fall turned so much that he lay upon his Feet on my right Side with his Head up the Water, I immediately got up upon my Feet; Mr. Lord called out, How are You, Doctor; I answered All is Well, God be thanked for it; he said, How is your Horse, I felt on the Side of me at his Tail and Buttocks, and said I believe my poor Horse is killed, but feeling towards his Head (I was in great Darkness and Confusion) he began to stir, Upon that I found my right Foot to be still in the Stirrup and the Stirrup Leather to be twisted; when I had quitted my Foot from the Stirrup, I called upon the Horse, and he got up; after bringing him into the Road, I mounted and rode Home neither Man nor Horse having received any visible Harm. A wonderful Preservation . . .

Two days later Richard crossed the same bridge in daylight. He took the trouble to measure the height of the battlement above the water, and calculated he must have fallen 'about eight Yards'. His escape from 'being much bruised

or taken up dead' strengthened his belief 'that a Divine
Providence frequently interposeth both for our Safety and
Comfort'.

Once Richard had returned from London, he began to
pay increasing attention to medical matters in his *Diary*.
The entry for 13 August 1746 explains how Richard and
his father (62 years old, but 'appears to be only at the
Meridian of his Life, and at his best Age for doing
business') carried on their practice. Robert's work lay
chiefly in seeing patients at home. Richard undertook most
of the visiting, and on 13 August he wrote down details of
the eleven patients he had visited that day during a '12 or
14 Miles ride'. Two fever cases he treated by bleeding, and
a threatened 'mortification of bowels' he attempted 'to
divert by blistering'. He dressed a woman's 'sore leg' and
a young woman's 'very sore stinking leg', comforted a
nervous young wife 'near the Time of her Delivery',
visited a brother and sister both suffering from consump-
tion, prescribed for 'An Antient Woman with a bad Pain
in her Hip', and treated a girl with a 'strumous disorder'
under her chin and a man with a similar affliction in his
arm. He considered that to mention such particulars every
day would be 'abundantly too tedious and prolix', but
from time to time he did allow himself space to record
some of his unusual and outstanding cases—the trepan-
ning of a fractured skull; the lancing of an acute quinsy;
his attendance at difficult and often fatal, confinements;
the attempt to control an outbreak of smallpox and an
epidemic of spotted fever; the setting of fractured bones
and the reducing of dislocations; the amputation of
gangrenous limbs and the surgical treatment of cancer.

The case of Mrs. Driver of Crawshaw Booth is a good
illustration of Dr. Richard's skill as a surgeon, and of the
incredible pain that some patients had to suffer in those
pre-anaesthetic days. On 22 December 1748 Richard gave
details of the first operation:

> . . . with the Assistance of my Father I took off Mrs.
> Driver's right Breast that was Cancerous, the Cancer weighed
> near 3 Pound Weight; the Revnd. Mr. Picup of Bacup and the
> Revnd. Mr. Thos Ashworth of Clough-fold were present, Mr.

Pickup went to Prayer before and after the Operation, all
Friends seemed to behave in a Christian Manner, and to be in
a serious good Frame, I lodge at Mr. Driver's for fear of any
Blood-Vessel bleeding . . . Lord, Prevent ruinous and inconsiderate Undertakings, and succeed all our Labours.

Richard and the minister, Thomas Ashworth, stayed with
the patient the whole of the next day and night, and
Richard returned to visit her every alternate day for the
next week or ten days. Mrs. Driver recovered well; she was
'hearty' during the rest of the winter and the spring, but
early in June she turned up at Baldingstone 'to show us a
Knot she had discovered that Morning about an Inch and a
half below the old Wound'. Richard soon discovered 'other
Kernalls closely joined together' round her ribs and abdo-
men. On 7 June, at Mrs. Driver's home, he 'dissected from
her at a moderate Computation five hundred different
distinct Schirrous Knots or young Cancers'. Inevitably,
the patient was 'sick and very poorly'. Richard stayed with
her all night, and next morning left her 'pretty easy'. But,
exactly a month later, he found it necessary to do more
dissecting round her armpit and neck, and after another
five weeks to repeat the operation. By the end of
September, Mrs. Driver was very ill indeed. On the 25th,
Richard 'took from her right Side 3 different Cancers
about the Size each of a Hen's Egg', and within a week
and again on 5 October cut five or six more from the
same wound. This seems to have arrested the progress of
the disease a little, for not until four and a half months
later, 20 February 1750, did Richard record attending Mrs.
Driver's funeral at Goodshaw church.

Despite the long hours which he spent with his patients,
Richard managed to attend Bury Chapel pretty regularly, to
fit in occasional visits to other chapels, to call on relatives,
and to attend an extraordinary number of funerals. His
constant contact with death set him wondering about life
hereafter. Devout Christian though he was, he sometimes
had niggling doubts:

. . . I cannot, nay I dare not, but believe the Immortality
of the Soul; tho' I know not what shall be after death; know
not where I shall be, what I shall be, nor what I shall see
when I come to see unseen Things . . .

And again, four years later, after the death of his namesake, Richard Kay of Chesham:

> . . . I believe the Immortality of the Soul; tho' I can form
> no certain Idea where my deceased Friends are, or what they
> are doing; yet I believe in a future State of Happiness or
> Misery. Lord . . . Let me ask, Is all well, O that I were
> answered, All is well. . . .

The answer, whatever its nature, came to Richard sooner
than he could reasonably have expected. The *Diary* ends
with an unfinished sentence on 19 June 1750, in the
middle of recording an epidemic of spotted fever. The
epidemic had already carried off several friends and his
brother-in-law, Joseph Baron. Before the year was out
his father was to die. Then, in October 1751, death struck
its heaviest blow. Within the month, Richard, his sister
Elizabeth, and his mother, in that order, all perished.
One funeral sermon served all three.

Richard Kay saw something of the Jacobite march
through Lancashire in 1745. So did Elizabeth, the
twenty-three-year-old daughter of John Byrom of Kersal
Cell. Both confided their thoughts, hopes, and fears to the
pages of their diaries, and it is interesting to see how
differently these two Lancashire neighbours reacted to the
same sequence of events. Predictably, Presbyterian Richard
dreaded a Jacobite success. His heart sank when he heard
that the Highlanders had defeated Sir John Cope at
Prestonpans outside Edinburgh. His immediate alarm is
evident in the prayer with which he ended his diary entry
for 24 September, the day the news reached Bury:

> Lord, We hope thou wilt be favourable to these Lands,
> notwithstanding the Sins that are committed among us; we
> hope thou wilt still espouse the Protestant Cause whereby thy
> Name is known and worshipped amongst us; we hope thou
> wilt preserve us from Popish slavery and vain Idolatry; God
> be merciful unto us, we know we are in the Hands of that
> God who governs all Things for the Purposes of his own
> Glory.

strengthened Richard's first impression that God was using
the Jacobites to chastise the loyal subjects of George II
for their sins. He implored God to show mercy, to let
His rod 'be for Correction to us, and not for Destruction',
to 'Suppress the Pride of these Rebells, these rebellious
Wretches, in due Time', and not to 'laugh at our Calamity,
nor mock when our Fear cometh', Elizabeth Byrom was
neither so apprehensive nor so solemn. She tingled with
excitement. She looked forward to seeing the Jacobites
on the march and, with herself committed to neither side,
she watched with amusement the way different groups of
people behaved. As early as 8 October, a month before
Charles Edward crossed the River Esk into England, she
reported:

> . . . everyone in hiding for fear of the rebels; Mr. Hoole,
> Mr. Nichols, Mr. Lewthwaite [all clergymen at Manchester
> Collegiate Church, now the Cathedral] preached against
> rebellion . . . The Presbyterians are sending everything that's
> valuable away, wives, children and all for fear of the rebels.

Richard Kay's relatives and friends did not panic quite
so easily as that, but when, in November, news reached
them that the Jacobites were besieging Carlisle and
threatening to march south, they took reasonable precautions. Baldingstone, nicely removed from the north-south
roads, they considered relatively safe, and consequently
Dr. Robert became host to a crowd of refugees:

Nov. 13. Cousin John Kay from Manchester lodges here tonight,
has this afternoon brought his two daughters, with a servant
to attend them, for fear of the Rebells, who we hear are
marching towards us in England.

Nov. 28. . . . O, How Persons are removing their Families and
Effects out of Manchester. We have here [at Baldingstone]
a numerous family.

Elizabeth was at the other end of this dispersal. On
26 November she wrote:

> . . . everyone is going out of town [Manchester] and
> sending all their effects away, there is hardly any family
> left but ours and our kin; they have . . . shut up shop, and
> all the warehouses in town almost are empty; tonight the

bellman is going about to forbid anyone sending provisions
out of town . . .

She herself showed no signs of alarm. She heard various
estimates of rebel numbers—rumour offered anything from
7,000 to 30,000—but she felt she could rely on the report
that the Highlanders had 'behaved very civilly' in Preston.
She seemed quite indifferent to the news that soldiers
were pulling down bridges at Warrington, Barton, and
Stockport, but she understood and probably approved of
those Mancunians who said they would 'set fire bells off
ringing to raise a mob' if the authorities attempted fo
destroy Salford bridge which spanned the Irwell so close
to the heart of Manchester. Several things tickled her.
She could not help laughing at the local militia, which,
called together far too late to be effective, had only found
time to remove stocks of gunpowder and weapons into
safe places and to disband itself before the Jacobites
appeared: 'Yesterday [26 November] the militia were all
discharged and sent home, but just in time before the
Highlanders came—well contrived!' And, Parson Lewth-
waite's choice of texts set her giggling. On the Sunday
prior to the Jacobite entry into Manchester, he preached
on 'He that hath no sword, let him sell his garment and
buy one'. That was comical enough, but Elizabeth remembered that a fortnight earlier his text had been, 'Is thy
servant a dog that he should do this thing?'

The Jacobite advance guard reached Manchester on
Thursday, 28 November; the main body followed the day
after. Elizabeth described the entry in some detail:

> About 3 o'clock today came into town two men in High-
> land dress, and a woman behind one of them with a drum on
> her knee, and for all the loyal work that our Presbyterians
> have made, they took possession of the town . . . they beat
> up for volunteers . . . 'All gentlemen that have a mind to
> serve H.R.H. with a willing mind, 5 guineas advance', and
> nobody offered to meddle with them . . .

She added that by eight o'clock about eighty men had
volunteered. News of this extraordinary happening must
have spread rapidly, for before he went to bed that night

Richard Kay had written 'a Sergeant with one Drummer belonging to the Pretender's service are come to Manchester today, and have enlisted several into their service'.

Elizabeth found the next three days most thrilling. She was 'at the Cross' in Market Place to see Charles Edward enter Manchester on the Friday: 'the bells they rung, and P. Cotterel made a bonfire, and all the town was illuminated . . . about 4 o'clock the King ['James III'] was proclaimed, the mob shouted very cleverly'. Next day, dressed in her white gown, she went to see the prince ride from his lodgings in Market Street—'a noble sight it is'—and then went with her escort, an unnamed 'officer', to a service at the Collegiate Church. 'Mr. Shrigley read prayers, he prayed for the King and the Prince of Wales and named no names'. Early Sunday morning, Charles Edward rode south from Manchester, over Cheadle ford into Cheshire. Richard Kay saw nothing of this, but he was busy wrestling with the consequences. Saturday, 30 November, was a very trying day:

> . . . All Things are in a Hurry, Business is confused. We have concealed our Valuables mostly, the Press has been so strong for Horses that for fear lest Ours should be seized we have sent them away to Day. Lord, Send us better Times.

And even when immediate danger had passed and he heard that the Jacobites were moving towards London, he found it unnerving to think of a 'Popish Prince upon the Throne of England'. He prayed that George II's crown might 'sit firm upon his Head'. Nor did the Baldingstone refugees hasten home once the Jacobite whirlwind had cleared Manchester. They remained to see what would be the outcome of events.

Richard first heard of the retreat from Derby on Sunday morning, 8 December. On his way to Chapel, he met his cousins, Dr. Samuel and John Kay, who told him the news. They were hoping to recruit 'Country People' to help Manchester to 'make a Stand against' the rebels, and they prevailed upon Richard to ride with them into Rossendale. Next day, about five hundred volunteers 'came our Road towards Manchester . . . but 'tis thought proper

not to oppose the Rebells: They and Thousands were
dismissed'. Most Lancastrians appear to have wanted the
Jacobites to move through their county as quickly as
possible, and it promised well that this time they were
marching north, back to Scotland. Elizabeth recorded that
a few rash people 'had slutched 'em and thrown stones'
in Manchester, and that the Scots had demanded £5,000 to
recompense them for 'the insolence of the mob'. In the end
they settled for half that sum, and kept 'a party of about
1,000' in the town to see it was collected and handed over.
'Having never seen the Rebells or any in a Highland Dress',
curiosity moved Richard to abandon his patients and go
and watch the retreat. On Tuesday, 10 December, he
walked with a party of friends to Four Lane Ends in
Hulton: '. . . the Rebells marched from one o' th' Clock
till betwixt four and five o' th' Clock in the Afternoon
as throng as the Road could well receive them'. Richard
estimated there were 10,000 men, but it is doubtful if
more than half that number were in retreat. Yet everyone
considered that they had seen 'History' made that day.
Richard and his friends were so excited that, after the last
of the kilted Highlanders had gone, they walked home via
Manchester, nothing less than twenty miles, in December
darkness.

Within twenty-four hours, the bells of Manchester were
ringing again, this time to welcome the Duke of Cumberland's soldiers. Richard saw this as a deliverance, Elizabeth
as a lesser excitement. Each diarist quickly settled back
into normal life. Elizabeth looked back wistfully on the
magic moment when she had seen the handsome prince
riding in the streets of Manchester; Richard prayed
earnestly for the firm handling of the Jacobite threat—
'Lord, Let our Forces go forth conquering and to
conquer', and 'Lord fight our Battles for us'. The following
Spring, he knew God had answered his prayers. On 27 April
he attended a Thanksgiving Service for Cumberland's
victory at Culloden: 'May we all praise the Lord, give
thanks unto the Lord, for he is good, for his Mercy
endureth for ever'. Such a *Te Deum* found no echo in the
church at St. Germaine, nor in the hearts of the Mac-

1. Nicholas Blundell.

2. Samuel Bamford.

3. William Stout.

4. George Fox.

5. Extract from the diary of Nicholas Blundell, 1709.

6. Extract from John O'Neil's diary, 1864

7. Downham Village.

8. Middleton, c. 1880: Samuel Bamford is believed to have lived in one of these terraced cottages.

9. Assheton House, entrance (Whalley Abbey).

10. Cross Street Chapel, 1835.

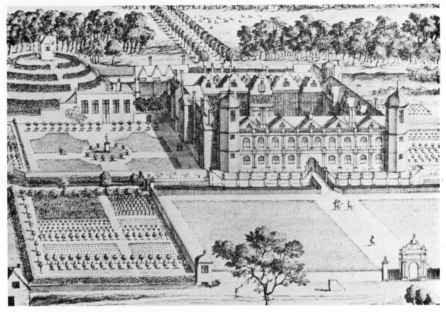

11. Old Dunham Massey Hall, *c.* 1690.

12. Swarthmoor Hall.

13. Little Crosby Hall: Sketch plan, 1738

14. Little Crosby Hall.

15. Hoghton Tower.

16. Swanside packhorse bridge, Downham.

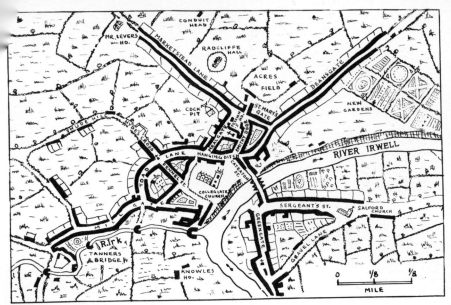

17. Map of Manchester and Salford, *c.* 1660.

18. Manchester heroes at Peterloo Massacre.

donalds, nor yet amongst the families of those men who had accepted the '5 guineas advance' in the streets of Manchester. Almost all were dead or in gaol.

Kay's *Diary* provokes comparison with two other very different records left behind by Lancashire writers. The first is a brief diary kept by Ireland Greene during the years 1748 and 1749, and the second is an autobiography written by R. J. A. Berry, 1866-1963, towards the end of a very long life. Miss Greene's diary is published in *Isaac Greene*, by R. Stewart-Brown (Liverpool 1921), and Professor Berry's autobiography is in typescript in the Lancashire Record Office.

Ireland Greene was the unfortunately named daughter of Isaac Greene, a most successful lawyer and business man, and Mary his wife, who inherited sizable estates both from her father, Edward Aspinwall of Hale, and from a distant relative, Sir Gilbert Ireland of Hale. In the 1720s Greene rebuilt Childwall Hall, near Liverpool, acted as a generous squire of Hale, and steadily began to climb the social ladder in South Lancashire. In February 1748 he and his family rode to London for the season. Ireland was then eighteen years old, her sister, Mary, a year younger. Neither had visited London before, so that both debutantes were excited at the prospect of the journey ahead and of the tea-parties, routs, balls, and theatre visits that would follow. Ireland determined to keep a record, presumably on her return to remind her of the details of the great adventure.

The Greenes travelled by much the same route as Richard Kay had done five years earlier. A broken coach wheel delayed them in North Staffordshire, but they finished a leisurely journey in nine days. Their overnight stops were at Warrington, Talke, Newcastle-under-Lyme, Lichfield, Coventry, Dunchurch, Stony Stratford, and St. Albans. They arrived in London about noon on 20 February. Immediately, they were visited by friends, for many Lancashire ladies and gentlemen had travelled up to London to enjoy the season. Mrs. Fazakerley, the wife of the well-known lawyer-politician, Nicholas Fazakerley of Prescot, and her sister-in-law, Mrs. Lutwyche, sister of Sir Henry Hoghton, were the girls' chief hostesses throughout the season. With their help they enjoyed numerous tea-parties, occasional card parties, shopping expeditions, concerts, including one of the first performances of *Judas Maccabeus*, excursions to Ranelagh Gardens and the wax-works, and theatres, where they saw at least two of the same plays that Kay had done — the farce *The Virgin Unmasked* at Drury Lane, and the *Tragedy of Cato* at Covent Garden.

At the end of March, Ireland and Mary were guests at Mrs. Fazakerley's rout. The diary lists the many Lancashire and Cheshire friends and acquaintances who were present. They included the Grosvenors from Chester, the Cliftons from the Fylde, and Peter Bold, one of their Lancashire neighbours, but, a little surprisingly, not Lady Strange and the two Lady Stanleys of Knowsley Hall, whom the Greenes had met frequently throughout the season. The activities and interests of the two Greene girls were very different from those of the young, earnest Dr. Kay, but they were just as determined as he was to squeeze everything possible out of their stay in London. They failed, however, to get tickets for the highlight of the season, the masquerade at the Haymarket on 28 April. As a compensation, they were privileged in the afternoon to see Mrs. Fazakerley and Mrs. Cooke 'in their masquerade dresses which was Venetian, Mrs. Faz a light dress, blue trim'd with silver and Mrs. Cooke a long dress white trim'd with blue and silver gauze'. It was such a gay and colourful occasion that even the highly-critical Horace Walpole praised it. In a letter to his friend Sir Horace Mann, he wrote:

> We had last night the most magnificent masquerade that ever was seen: it was by subscription at the Haymarket: everybody who subscribed five guineas had four tickets. There were about seven hundred people, all in chosen and very fine dresses. The supper was in two rooms, besides those for the King and Prince, who, with the foreign ministers, had tickets given them.

Isaac Greene and his family rode back to Childwall during the second week of May. In the following February they

left home to enjoy another London season, and once again
Ireland kept a record in her diary. This time the Greenes
rode to Holmes Chapel on horseback, the necessary
luggage piled on pack-horses led by the servants. It was
quite a cavalcade. From Holmes Chapel to London, the
family coach made good time, and by 14 February, exactly
a week after leaving Childwall, Ireland and Mary were once
again engulfed in the swirl of social engagements. The
programme was much the same as during the previous
season, but this time there was a little more theatre-going,
and the circle of friends and acquaintances seems to have
been rather wider and more varied than the year before.
Among the new acquaintances was William Pitt, in 1749
a rising politician holding the office of paymaster-general.

The Peace of Aix-la-Chapelle had already brought to an
unsatisfactory end the War of the Austrian Succession, and
the firework display designed to celebrate the peace was
one of the main events of the 1749 season. Handel wrote
his Firework Music specially for the occasion. On 21 April
Ireland Greene set out for Vauxhall to hear the rehearsal
of this music, but like hundreds of others she never got
there. London Bridge was so choked with carriages that
traffic came to a standstill. She was more fortunate the
following Thursday when the firework display itself was
held in Green Park. Mrs. Fazakerley managed to get her
an invitation to a house in Sackville Street. Like most of
the excited spectators, Ireland was bitterly disappointed
when a burning pavilion brought the show to a premature
end. But she appreciated what she had seen. There is
nothing of Horace Walpole's sour description in her diary
entry for that day. Walpole professed to be most disgusted:
according to his exacting, sophisticated standards the
fireworks

> by no means answered the expense, the length of prepara-
> tion and the expectation that had been raised . . . the immense
> crowds in the Park and on every house, the guards, and the
> machine itself, which was very beautiful, was all that was
> worth seeing. The rockets . . . succeeded mighty well; but the
> wheels . . . were pitifull and ill-conducted . . . The illumination
> was mean and lighted so slowly that scarcely anybody had
> patience to wait the finishing; and then, what contributed to

the awkwardness of the whole was the right pavilion catching
fire and being burnt down in the middle of the show.

No matter what Walpole might think of the show, it is
pretty certain that Ireland Greene told the story of that
evening in several Lancashire drawing rooms after her
return in May, and that she described the crowds, the
music, and the magnificence of the fireworks with
excited enthusiasm.

Professor Berry's autobiography has nothing to do with
visits to London. It matches Kay's *Diary* in that it describes
the training of doctors, not in London in the 1740s but in
Edinburgh in the 1880s. It leaves the reader with the
uncomfortable feeling that he would have been better off
under Dr. Kay's care than at the mercy of many of
Berry's contemporaries.

Berry attended school in Southport from 1877 to 1883.
He spent the next two years training to be a shipbroker in
Liverpool, but he changed his mind, matriculated at
Edinburgh University, and in 1886 began the four-year
course in the faculty of medicine. The course opened with
daily lectures in both anatomy and chemistry, 'the former
unnecessary' because 'every word was to be found in any
standard text-book of the period', and 'the latter quite
unintelligible' because 'the learned man who lectured for
one hundred hours in Chemistry was quite incapable either
of keeping order or imparting his knowledge'. Later in the
course, materia medica, like anatomy, had to be learned
by rote: the students committed to memory 'numbers of
what in those days were known as *elegant prescriptions,*
calculated to cure any of the then known diseases with
which Man was afflicted'. The practical side of the young
doctors' training Berry considered most inadequate:

> I was allotted a lower limb—leg to you—and was directed
> to start on the buttock, or in our more polite medical
> phraseology, the gluteal region. The demonstrator . . . dis-
> sected the buttock for me talking profusely the whole time
> about something else. That was the first and last I ever saw of
> that leg. Yet my certificate says that Mr. Berry has dissected
> the inferior extremity once carefully.

Midwifery was 'appallingly taught', and no student 'was
ever required to attend classes or clinics on fevers, diseases

of children, affections of the skin, diseases of the ear, nose, throat, or eye, and no one bothered overmuch with mental disorders'.

In one paragraph, Berry describes some of the 'brutal surgery' that was current practice:

> I went one morning, as an interloper, to see Mr. Joseph Bell, the prototype of Sherlock Holmes, perform an amputation of the breast in an elderly woman suffering from cancer. . . . One sweep of the knife above the breast, and another below it, blood spurting everywhere, and the deed was almost done.

It sounds as if the patient on Mr. Bell's operating table stood much less chance of recovery than did Mrs. Driver of Crawshaw Booth. And yet, in spite of such training, Berry became a notable doctor. He held the chair of anatomy at the University of Melbourne from 1906 to 1929.

SIR HENRY HOGHTON'S ANTI-JACOBITE LETTERS, 1745-1746

[These letters, which are among the Hoghton papers in the Lancashire Record Office, have never been published. They have been calendared by J. H. Lumby in Volume 88 (pages 276-287) of the publications of the Record Society of Lancashire and Cheshire.]

Henry Hoghton succeeded to the Hoghton baronetcy and estates in 1710. His Tudor ancestor, Thomas, the builder of Hoghton Tower, had exiled himself from England rather than accept separation from Rome, but ever since the death of Sir Gilbert in 1648, the heads of the Hoghton family had been Dissenters in religion and Parliamentarians or Whigs in politics. Sir Richard had represented Lancashire in the parliaments of the Commonwealth and Protectorate, and Sir Charles had served as Whig member for the county from 1679 to 1690. Sir Henry, Charles's son, was as resolute a Whig as his father, and an even more determined Presbyterian.

Five years after Sir Henry inherited the title, the Jacobites attempted to overthrow the Hanovarian succession. In June 1715 crowds of Jacobite sympathisers in Manchester and South Lancashire attacked Presbyterian chapels. In September the Earl of Mar raised the standard of 'James VIII of Scotland and James III of England' at Braemar, and early in November a combined force of English and Scottish Jacobites began marching south into Lancashire. Sir Henry was thoroughly alarmed. He was well aware of the strength of Roman Catholicism in the North-west, and he feared that a single success for the rebels would prompt many Lancashire co-religionists openly to come to their aid. Already such leading Lancashire Jacobites as John Tyldesley of Myerscough Lodge, Richard Towneley, and Ralph Standish had committed themselves to revolt. Sir Henry convinced himself that this trickle of Jacobite support could quickly swell into a torrent. He could not understand how the government could view the situation so calmly as it appeared to be doing. General Wills was belatedly moving troops from Chester to Manchester, and it was reported that General Carpenter was marching from Newcastle. But the authorities were showing no signs of urgency. Obviously, through ignorance of the true loyalties of many Lancastrians, they underestimated the dangers.

Sir Henry decided to take action himself. With the ready co-operation of the Rev. James Woods of Chowbent Chapel, he raised an enthusiastic, volunteer force of Dissenters. These amateur soldiers helped Wills to hold the south end of Walton-le-Dale bridge, while Carpenter marched down the Ribble valley and forced the Jacobites to surrender in the streets of Preston. For Sir Henry the battle of Preston was both a profound relief and a personal triumph. It destroyed all threats of a Lancashire rising, and it gave him considerable satisfaction to look back on those first days of November and imagine what damage the Jacobites could have wrought had not he, Sir Henry, taken the lead and acted promptly and decisively. Without doubt November 1715 was his finest hour—so far.

Fate gives few men the chance to win fame as the saviour of their homeland: it permits hardly any to play this role twice in a lifetime. But exactly thirty years after the suppression of the 'Fifteen Rebellion, Sir Henry found his county and his home threatened with the 'Forty-five. Prince Charles Edward landed on the island of Eriskay on 23 July 1745. Two months later, he had defeated Sir John Cope at Prestonpans and had occupied Edinburgh. George II's government seemed to be just as unconcerned as his father's government had been thirty years earlier, but Sir Henry's ears had pricked at the first rumour of the landing. He felt that his previous experience qualified him more than most other men to assess this new threat to peace and stability in Lancashire—and the rest of Britain. He turned his house at Walton-le-Dale on the main north-south road into an information centre, gathering news from Scotland and relaying it to the lord lieutenant, Edward eleventh Earl of Derby, and to Henry Pelham, first commissioner of the treasury, or, as we should say today, prime minister. Many of the letters which Sir Henry wrote from September 1745 to January 1746 are still available, for the copies which he kept are among the Hoghton papers in the Lancashire Record Office. Together with information gathered from several other sources, they paint for us a graphic picture of the confusion which the 'Forty-five caused in Lancashire.

On 1 September Sir Henry sent Pelham a summary of the reports he had lately received.

> One (who I can depend on) at Wakefield in Yorkshire says that his friend att Edenburgh writes there are 2 Regiments landed in Scottland Cloathed in white turned up with blew supposed to be french, who have Joyned the Rebells near Fort William, they are supposed in all about 4000—make a Camp about a mile square are Commanded by the Person called the Duke of Perth, the Pretenders Standerd is sett up in the front of their Camp, they have a number of small cannon so contrived as to screw sides together to be taken on sunder and carryed on horses over the mountains—that a Company of Sinclairs Regiment are taken prisoners after the loss of 12 men killed. My friend's correspondent was in the Camp and saw the 12 men buried, this he has made affidavitt of before the provost of Edinburgh.
>
> I have another aut[hority] that Fort William is in the hands of the Rebells . . .

Pelham replied from Arlington Street, London, on 7 September. He reassured Hoghton that 'as yet we do not hear of any foreign troops having come with him [the Pretender's son] or followed him', but he admitted that the rebels had 'contrived to escape General Cope' and have 'got to Blair Castle the seat of the Duke of Athol'. He thought it likely that the rebels would next make for Edinburgh or 'your part of England', and, no doubt to Henry's satisfaction, he recalled the events of 1715.

> . . . However, I can't but recommend to you and the Gentlemen in your parts to have a watchfull eye, if they should leave Edinburgh and march your way I don't know

what there is to Stop 'em att present, except the zeal and
courage of the inhabitants, it is thirty years since I had the
honour to meet you att Preston on the like occasion, I can't
forget those times, tho' I am satisfied [that] both the dispositions of the people, and the strength of the Enemy is far
different now from what it was then your Zeal continues the
same, my wishes and endeavors shall not alter, and therefore
if you learn any thing of what passes or is likely to pass
your way, I shall be very glad to hear from you . . .

Sir Henry took this friendly encouragement to heart.
Pelham had recognised his experience and trusted him with
confidential information. It was now up to him, Henry, to
put Lancashire on guard against the threatened invasion.
Within hours of receiving Pelham's letter, he was writing
a long despatch to Lord Derby, passing on Pelham's news
and adding the latest reports that Cope had withdrawn to
Inverness and that some of the rebels were south of the
Forth and near Glasgow. He enjoined the earl to observe
cautious discretion—'I have not [communicated Pelham's
news] to any Gentleman in Preston, for tho' we have
several well affected to the Government, they converse
so much with those of another principle, that I think it
prudent to keep it private as yet . . .'. Above all, he was at
pains to tell Derby what should be done':

. . . I humbly submitt it to your Lordship whether in the
mean time you will not give directions to such Deputy Lieutenants (as you think proper) to have the polls fixed [*i.e.* musters
held] and arms inspected, and new ones provided where
wanted in the hundred of Londsale and Amounderness and
in Derby and Leyland hundreds that we may be in as good
order and readyness as they are in Salford and Blackburn
Hundreds for if the Rebellion comes nearer us, its possible
the disaffected amongst ourselves may rise, and we are
defended less if either that should happen or the Rebells in
Scotland should make us a visitt, especially as Mr. Pelham
writes he dont know what there is to stop them untill the
troops arrive except the Zeal and courage of ourselves . . .

On the same day, 11 September, Sir Henry replied to
Pelham. He thanked him for his information and advice,
gave him the most recent Scottish news, and added,

I can't end this without asking pardon for differing with you
in opinion that the dispositions of the people and the strength

of the Enemy is far different from what it was in the year
1715, as to our Country, our Enemys are as strong as then,
and I know no converts to be depended on.

You are kind in remembering the part I acted then. I am
the same now only 30 years older and am ready still to venture
my life and fortune for my King and Countrey.

Two days later Sir Henry wrote again to Derby urging
immediate action: 'if we wait till they [the Scots] arrive
it will be too late to provide Arms for so many as may
want, I should be glad to know my Captains and Subalterns'. He pressed the earl to appoint 'some proper Deputy
Lieutenant' in Lonsdale hundred, and asserted that the
Militia Act of 1661 gave lord lieutenants power to put the
militia in readiness. Nothing could be done until Derby
gave the command: 'your Order in a very few Words will
be an Authority to us, without it we can't do it nor will
any join therein'.

But mustering the militia was not so easy as Sir Henry
imagined. In 1662 parliament had cleverly amended the
financial clauses of the Militia Act so that neither the
king nor the lord lieutenants could call out the militia
without parliamentary consent. And in September 1745
parliament stood prorogued. Furthermore, George II, the
only person who could summon it to meet again, was in
Hanover. Hoghton might have logic and common sense
on his side, but Derby had to contend with the law. When
he sought legal advice from Lincoln's Inn, he received an
uncompromising reply: 'You'll please to consider you can't
do anything by Law with the Militia'. If he decided that
the situation was too desperate to bother about the
letter of the law, he ran two alternative but equally unpleasant risks. Parliament might leave him personally to
foot the militia bill, especially if the Jacobites avoided
marching through Lancashire. On the other hand, if the
invasion succeeded and the Jacobites took control of the
country, he would not be able to argue that he was merely
obeying orders in raising the militia against them. Patently,
he would have exceeded his legal authority.

Charles Edward entered Edinburgh on 17 September.
The news spread quickly, and five days later, Sir Henry
wrote in some alarm to Pelham:

One Snodgrass a Scotchman who very often comes to buy goods here a very honest man, came to mee Yesterday was at Glasgow the 17th says he heard the Rebels were within 4 Miles of Edinburgh the 16th . . . the Rebels . . . past the Forth about 5 Miles above Stirling the 1st party was judged to be about 4000 of which 2000 good men and 1500 of them well armed, the 2nd party 2000 and about 1200 or 1500 were left behind.

On the 18th Snodgrass came to Mophet 30 Miles South of Edinburgh an Express came there that they had entered Edinburgh that the 2 Regiments of Dragoons were retired to Haddington . . .

This day at Noon one of undoubted Credit sent me an Account from Lancaster that an Express was come to Whitehaven of their having entered Edinburgh the 17th . . .

Sit, I have just now been with an Englishman who we know very well and can credit who says he saw the Pretenders Son in an high land Dress and green velvet Bonnet at Edinburgh upon the 17th and saw the Pretender proclaimed there that his followers were but indifferently armed when they came there but had got about 20 Cannon which were planted upon the Gates and Walls and a great number of small Arms which they took from the City Guard and others in the towne . . .

We are yet quiet in this Country but not knowing how long we may be so we are Securing our Plate Writeings and Effects the best We can for if they are not stopt We have nothing to defend ourselves with, We are arming the Militia but have no power to raise them until an Act passes for that Purpose, and as the Parliament is prorogued to the 16th next Month we shall probably be all in Confusion before that Time . . .

Apparently at Sir Henry's suggestion, Lord Derby agreed to appeal for voluntary subscriptions in an attempt to overcome the legal obstacle to mustering the militia. On 29 September, Sir Henry informed Pelham that 'it dont yet amount to above £6000, but hope it will be much more before it has travelled thro' the County'. So far the subscriptions only consisted of promises, but Sir Henry was already planning how the money should be spent: 'we shall want Armes Cloaths and Officers for the men we raise'. The recent news of Cope's defeat at Prestonpans had confirmed his worst fears. He saw nothing left to prevent the victorious Jacobites from crossing the border, and he fully anticipated that they would be approaching Lancashire within the next few days:

> . . . We hear of Troops marching to Nottingham and other Places but none coming to us or coming this Way to stop the Rebels, which is a melancholy Prospect for I have Accounts today both from Newcastle and Kendal that 1000 of the Rebels are left in Edinburgh to guard the Prisoners and the rest are marched to Glasgow and Dumfries to raise contributions, if so, it won't be long before they are here . . .

Derby did not share Hoghton's acute anxiety. On 30 September he wrote two letters and instructed his son to write a third, all endeavouring to calm Sir Henry's fears and to curb his desire for immediate and wholesale action. Derby saw no harm in continuing to list subscriptions, or in securing 'all the powder we can', or in 'fixing the polls' and ordering necessary arms to be made, but he turned down Sir Henry's suggestion that townships should immediately send their quotas of men to be trained. The lord lieutenant was realist enough to see that, without the support of regular troops, militiamen could only 'preserve the peace of the County, which he does not at present think in any danger', or remove all weapons and gunpowder out of the rebels' way. Sir Henry could not have enjoyed reading these letters. They authorised far too cautious and negative a policy for his liking. Nevertheless, during the next few days he did what he could to obey his lord lieutenant's orders. On 4 October he wrote to Pelham from Lancaster that he and other deputy lieutenants had been and still were busy inspecting 'the Arms Men and horses of the Militia' and arranging for 'all the Gunpowder Cannon and small Arms belonging to this Town and the Ships to be sent tomorrow to Liverpool' to be beyond the reach of the expected invaders. Once again he pointed out how difficult it was in Catholic Lancashire to give commissions 'to proper persons', and then burst out with what he considered was the right course to take:

> . . . Was in hopes we should have had Officers Arms and Cloathing sent for the private men we could raise, which would be great numbers of hearty young fellows, and as that was the terms of the Subscription I fear many will go off and not pay what they have subscribed. The next best in my poor

opinion would be if Recruiting Officers were sent down and to enlist for only 6 or 12 months. I believe we could perswade great numbers to go into the Service but I fear there won't be time for this method . . .

Throughout October 1745, Sir Henry faced one frustrating day after another. Try as he might—and the bombardment of letters never slackened—he could not persuade Derby to throw caution to the winds or the central government to recognise Lancashire's special dangers. The only consolation October offered was that the Jacobites did not appear south of the Esk. Their failure to move immediately across the border and along the traditional invasion route tarnished Sir Henry's reputation as a prophet, but gave him four weeks more than he had expected to try and convert others to his point of view. But any successes he achieved were marginal. On some days he was fairly optimistic; on others disappointment led him to the edge of despair. Yet he always managed to bounce back into action with surprising ability. In the first week of October he received two or three depressing letters from Derby—'. . . I do not see which way we can be of any great use to the Public . . .' and '. . . I pity your fatigue, and do not at all wonder at it, being myself, though at home, jaded to almost a wearyness of life'. But on 12 October, Sir Henry found sufficient spirit to write cheerfully to Pelham. After retailing the latest information from Scotland, he returned to his favourite theme of Lancashire's particular difficulties:

> . . . as for this County, our papists and those in that Interest are quiet, we have raised a handsome subscription and could raise many volunteers, but as we have none to Command them (and as you observe) its too late to do anything of that Kind in other Countys I presume the Lord Lieutenants has powers, and grants commissions to officers for their new raised men, Lord Derby can't do so here for he finds it very difficult to get Gentlemen and proper persons even to accept of Commissions in the militia, we have got our militia therowe well armed (which they was not last rebellion) and 1600 chosen men to carry them, and Lord Derby at a meeting at Wigan last Tuesday ordered a general muster, that I don't fear but we can keep this country quiet if it is thought proper to

pass an act to allow us to rise [*i.e.* mobilise the militia] for
as the Law now stands we can only be up for 4 days which
would signify nothing . . .

The main subject for discussion in the middle of the
month was the subscription. When subscribers had first
been approached, they had been told that the government
would supply arms, officers, and clothing, and that the
subscription money would be used solely to maintain the
militiamen. But in a letter to Lord Derby on 10 October,
the Duke of Newcastle ruined this plan. He promised, once
he knew the quantity required, to have arms 'sent from
the Office of Ordnance with the utmost expedition', but
doubted whether he could find any officers—'there being
very few at present on the half-pay'—and gave no hopes
at all of sending any clothing. This meant that the subscription money would now have to pay officers and buy
uniforms, and, as Sir Henry anticipated, many half-hearted
subscribers who had originally promised cash protested
against this change of purpose. Derby was ready to abandon the whole scheme, but Sir Henry, disappointed though
he was, encouraged him with new suggestions. He thought
that the government if asked might find them some *junior*
officers and sergeants, that, if the government would
guarantee no prosecution under the Test Act, a number of
Lancashire Dissenters might accept commissions, and that
the offer of an extra sixpence a day would certainly produce enough privates. He even had a scheme to solve the
problem of uniforms:

> . . . The Government should allso send down halberds
> Drums Colours and Arms, and as for Cloaths and hatts, if
> the Government cant or wont provide, let each company have
> a different Colour such as can be bought at Sadleworth or
> Elsewhere to be taken care of by the Captains the Expense of
> which to be taken out of the Subscription money . . .

The government showed little interest either in uniforms
or in the local arguments about the spending of the subscription. Instructions received by Derby on 19 October
urged him to continue to raise men, 'though it is not said
whether the Government will pay the Officers and cloth

the Men, or that it is to be done out of the Subscription
as was hinted in a former letter'. Derby was still convinced
that his militiamen would never be used as fighting troops,
but on 22 October he wrote a long letter to the Duke of
Newcastle reporting on the county's readiness for action.
'Upwards of £11,000' had been promised in subscriptions,
and this would probably finance seven companies. Officers
were still in short supply—'at this time we have few Young
Gentlemen in the Protestant Familys'. Even he, Derby, felt
obliged to decline the offer of a commission. He was
suffering from rheumatism, or slight paralysis so that 'I am
not able to walk over the Floor without dragging one leg
after me'. Five days later, he wrote less confidently to
Sir Henry. He seemed resigned to let events take their
course. He agreed with Sir Henry that Marshal Wade had
almost ensured a rebel invasion of the north-western
counties by marching his troops north through Yorkshire
and Durham, 'but what orders I or any body else can give
with regard to those matters I do not understand, nor do
I believe compulsion can be used'. The only practical
course he could see was to send all arms and gunpowder
'to Liverpoole, or somewhere farther off, that our Enemys
may not avail themselves of them'. His latest information
gave him no hope of officers being sent to Lancashire: 'the
favourite Scheme now is, that the several Countys, or at
least ours, should employ their Subscriptions to raise Men
to fill up the marching regiments, which are short of their
compliment'. Derby did not see that scheme working; in
any case, 'what occasion for subscriptions, and new Levys'
when, as Lord Strange had told him, the king's ministers
had recently stated in the House of Lords 'we had troops
enow at home already'?

An excited Sir Henry received this letter at Walton-le-
Dale on 29 October. He had spent the last few days riding
from muster to muster. Although he was impressed with
the calibre of the men, he was deeply disturbed by the
lack of adequate arms, and had been urging immediate
action:

> I was Yesterday attending the Muster at Chorley, the 2
> Companies made a good Appearance only some of the Arms

not made, I told Johnson he must make them as soon as possible, and I have sent the same Orders to Pearson for several had no arms at Kirkham, who told me on Sunday that he had 140 Swords coming down for the Ashton Division. Johnson brought some of the same to Chorley yesterday and was 7 shillings which with the belt will be 10 shillings a man and as there are 1624 foot in the County will be about £800 Charge.

Sir Henry thought it would be wise to consider equipping the men with bayonets as well as swords. To reduce the expense he suggested 'a short Sword in the Scymater kind made at Sheffield which the Army much approved of when shewed them at Doncaster'. This would cost less than 7 shillings. He offered to send for one for Derby's 'Aprobation'.

His activities of the last few days together with recent word from Pelham that 'a Bill is ordered to be brought in to enable his Majesty to raise the Militia' had convinced Sir Henry that, after all, the militiamen would go into action against the Jacobites. Half-way through the letter he acknowledged Derby's letter and news, but obviously considered that the new Bill had changed the situation. His principal concern was the equipping of his troops:

> . . . If We are to go upon Service I presume your Lordship will order Us to issue out Warrants for Trophy money, that We may have Colours drums and Halberts . . . Many of the foot are likely young fellows but poor bad Cloathes, I have spoke to several and I hope it would not be thought much of, if your Lordship thought fit to order each Man to have a Coat without lining only faced and turned up the Sleeve, if the Cloth is brown would be the cheapest your Lordship's Regiment I presume turned up with blue Lord Strange's white and mine red, and why not the Button same Colour with the facing, and if they have a Coat they should have a hat with a worsted binding and splaterdashers [gaiters] I believe all would be bought for 30 shillings and less.
>
> I believe there is not a fourth part of the Horse settled, who are to find them and very few has any Arms, We have hitherto been too busy about the foot, won't You order Us to fix the 3 Troops of Horse as soon as can be and order the Arms to be got ready.

To the end of this long letter, Sir Henry attached a feverish postscript begging the earl to allow him to begin arranging about uniforms. Would his Lordship choose the colours? Should he, Sir Henry, arrange for each regiment or each company to have its own colour, and would Derby authorise him to consult Butterworth of Saddleworth immediately, so that he should send Derby 'Patterns and what Quantities can be had of each Colour'? Would Derby order the townships to pay for the uniforms, or 'does your Lordship think We could take some of the Subscription Money and aply it in this Way'?

> I throw out these confused Thoughts please to order everything as you think proper, and if trophy money is not raised soon, no Time for making Drum Colours and Halberts, I'me in the utmost haste so please to excuse.

However the Lancashire militiamen might emerge from the battle, Sir Henry was determined they were going to enter it attired and equipped like regulars.

But the heat of Sir Henry's enthusiasm did nothing to melt the icy realism at Knowsley. Derby acknowledged the letter next day, but coldly dismissed all Hoghton's plans for making uniforms—'a great expense, and, in my opinion, at this time impracticable; for if the rebels come here at all, a fortnight at farthest will bring them, and I do not think clothing can be had in less than six weeks'. He approved of bayonets and better swords if they could be bought, and he agreed that the horse as well as the foot should be got ready, but he refused to believe that the new Militia Bill would make any real difference to the situation. Even before the Bill has passed through Parliament, 'I will venture to issue an order for raising, if there be the least prospect that they may be of use for our own defence or of service to the common Cause; but wish you would consider what they alone can be supposed to do, should the Highland Rebels get two or three days start of Mr. Wade's Army'. That day Sir Henry took to his bed, partly because Derby had so curtly punctured his excited enthusiasm, and partly because he was physically exhausted. On hearing the news Derby wrote him a kinder letter. He expressed 'sincere sorrow' for his indisposition, and comforted him with the thought 'that it is contracted

in the service of your King and Country'. But he did not
shift an inch on the matter of uniforms:

> I would not indeed burden the County with the expence of
> Clothing at present, being sensible that they may complain
> with too much reason of it, . . . but proper Arms (like a first
> principle) are never to be departed from, and therefore I
> should be glad to see the Militia both Horse and foot well
> armed with Swords, those I have seen being extremely bad

Sir Henry soon recovered: less than a week later, reports
of imminent action on the border jerked him back to full
vigour. On 5 November he sent off an urgent letter to
Lord Derby. Its news was serious and threatening, but Sir
Henry could hardly disguise a note of satisfaction:

> What I allways feard is come to pass the Rebels have
> decoyed our Army the Berwick Road, and stole a March upon
> Us the Carlisle Road I need not enlarge I inclose You a Copy
> of the Express I got this Morning, the Originals I have sent by
> flying Packet to Mr. Pelham . . . Copy of the Express is allso
> gone by Express to Manchester . . . I have sent the Account
> of the Gunpowder in Preston to Mr. Molyneux and recom-
> mended it to him and Mr. Addison to secure it and send it to
> Liverpool. I presume your Lordship will give us Orders to
> raise the Militia for 14 days or a Month and if you do We will
> send Warrants accordingly to the high Constables, what
> orders you send to me will serve for Amounderness and
> Lonsdale presume your Lordship will give Orders to the
> Deputy Lieutenants at Manchester to do the same for Salford
> and Blackburn I need not mention Derby and Leyland being
> near You. We can keep our own Country [*i.e.* county] from
> rising but can't face the Enemy except some regular Troops
> come this Road, and if they don't I suppose Your Lord-
> ship will order us to march into the South part of the County
> until we can be Joyned with more force. Tis a great Pleasure
> to me that your Lordship is in the Country in this Time of
> Confusion . . .

Derby replied the next day. He acknowledged the serious-
ness of Lancashire's position, discounted the possibility
of help from Marshal Wade—'the rebels must get at least a
weeks march of Him'—and, after consulting with advisers,
reluctantly instructed Sir Henry 'to send out orders for
your regiment to rendezvous at Preston as soon as may be,
not with any view to face the rebels, but in order to secure

the Arms'. He thought fourteen days' pay would be sufficient, and reminded Sir Henry that even now he was exceed-
ing his authority. No enabling Act had yet been passed, but
'I will take my share of the blame if any hereafter be laid
upon us'. Sir Henry, in a letter which has not survived,
apparently told Derby that he had already secured the
powder at Lancaster and Preston, but argued that the
militia should be kept in arms in order to deter the Lancashire Roman Catholics from revolting. He quoted
Pelham in his support, but his argument failed to move
Derby to further action:

> . . . it being in my opinion highly improbable the Papists
> should rise before the rebels come amongst us, and the
> Militia cannot prevent it. You say you presume no Order will
> be sent by the King for raising them till the first new Act
> is passed. Ought not then the same caution to have been
> observed by Us? But Mr. Pelham says 'He hopes it will be
> done'. If I remember his words right, He only says, He
> supposes We shall not scruple doing it for our defence, Why
> then do they scruple ordering us to do it, as they know that
> in strictness without such order it cannot be done? . . .

The events of the next few days reduced such issues to
nothing more than legal scruples. The Jacobites had begun
to move at last. On 8 November they crossed the Esk.
Carlisle offered spirited resistance, but fell a week later.
By 21 November Charles Edward had reached Penrith and
was marching rapidly south towards Kendal and Lancaster.
Yet, despite repeated promises, no regular troops arrived
in Lancashire to face the Scots. As early as 6 November
Wade advised the Mayor of Lancaster that the only way
the militia could help would be for the men to divide into
small parties 'who may fire from every Hedge to keep the
rebels from separating from their Main body to pilage and
plunder'. Hoghton relayed this advice to Derby, who dismissed it without ceremony: 'firing in small Partys at them
as they march would be to little purpose, and sure destruction to the undertakers'. Without substantial help from
regulars, the lord lieutenant had no intention of committing his militiamen to fight the enemy in any way. On
10 November he ordered Sir Henry to march his regiment

to Blackburn, Burnley, and Colne, and to arrange for the Leyland militia to assemble at Chorley with fourteen days' pay. Next day, he modified his instructions: so long as 'the rebels seem to be busied about Carlisle', Sir Henry should keep his regiment in its present quarters, and he and his senior officers should ride to Wigan on 13 November to meet Derby and discuss the situation.

This change of plan threw Sir Henry into a mild panic. He was fully occupied mustering his regiments on Preston Moor, prior to the march to the east:

> . . . We agreed to march early on Wednesday Morning [13 November] to Blackburn Burnley and Colne according to your Lordship's Orders, but as Burnley is 17 long Miles and Colne about 20, We can't possibly get to Burnley and Colne in a day from Preston, I know no Way but to march only 4 Companies to Blackburn on Wednesday as Blackburn can't contain the whole Regiment at once, and order them forward to Burnley and Colne on Thursday and order the remaining 4 Companies from Preston to Blackburn on Thursday, and when I have your Orders to march the 4 Companies from Burnley and Colne forwards I'le order the 4 Companies last at Blackburn to Burnley and Colne and to march the Regiment when and wherever your Lordship commands Us . . .

With such a weighty problem in logistics on his mind, Sir Henry wondered if Derby really needed him at Wigan. At best, his going to Wigan would mean postponing all his plans for a full day. That could be too late, for he had been informed that 600 rebels were at Keswick 'yesterday', 10 November: the rebels, he thought, might well be in Preston, before all the militia had left. Clearly, Sir Henry was getting excited again. But Derby was as practical as ever: 'I must leave the marching the men to your own discretion, only let me see you at least at Wigan tomorrow, the Captains and Subalterns may take care [for] one day . . . in half an hour We can do more by word of mouth than by 20 letters'. Derby was right. Thanks to the resistance that Carlisle was offering the rebels, the extra day did nothing to put the militia in jeopardy. On Friday, 15 November, Sir Henry wrote to one of his officers, Captain Walmsley, explaining the situation that evening:

I had an Express last night about 11 that the Rebells were returned before Carlisle, were making Scaling Ladders to get over the walls . . . I have a letter from Mr. Pelham this post that Legonier [John Ligonier, a cavalry commander] is marching down with a Large Body of Troops, and Mr. Reynolds writes me that they are 7 Flanders Regements Kerrs Dragoons and a train of artilery, and that a Battalion of Guards are ordered to be in readyness to Joyn the new raised Regiments he says there are hopes Wade may Stop them at Appleby, but I dont believe it.

I have marched this morning

Mr. Bradshay's Company to Blackburn, and tomorrow to Burnley

Mr. Stanley's to Clitherow

Captain Harrison's to Blackburn

Captain Mortons tonight to Whaley tomorrow to Coln

Captain Heskeths goes tomorrow to Blackburn

Captain Shawe's the same

Captain Sandys to Whaley

I fear you would come late to Blackburn last night, hope you are safely come to Hazlinden tonight. I intirely quitt Walton tomorrow morning, go first to Manchester, and on Sunday morning to Berry, to Lord Derby, to know whether we must be up longer than 14 days, if so, orders must go immediately for collecting the money otherwise we shall not have it before the 14 days is expired, for the men must have 2 and some of them 3 days to return home in, which must be reckoned in the first 14 days, and I propose to be with you Monday morning to bring you his Lordships resolutions . . .

If, at that time, Sir Henry felt that things were getting confused, he was soon looking back on the problems of the middle of the month as comparatively simple and straightforward. For once the men had mustered, nothing seemed to go right. The basic trouble was that the Jacobites did not keep to the time-table which Sir Henry had set for them; their unexpected dalliance round Carlisle made it most difficult for him to know how long he should keep the militia in arms. On 19 November, after his meeting at Bury with Derby, Sir Henry sent fresh orders to Captain Walmsley. The four companies from Lonsdale which were then marching to Preston were to be demobilised 'if no orders come for 14 days more pay'. The men at Haslingden and Burnley were ordered to Wigan; those at Clitheroe and Blackburn to Ormskirk. But already the fortnights' pay was running out. On Tuesday, 19 November, the same day that Sir Henry was sending his new orders from Bury, a desperate Charles Stanley was writing to him from Clitheroe:

> I should be glad to receive your advice, what is proper to be done with My Men and Arms, after the 14 Days pay is expired, which will be on Monday next, and as they are 2 Days March from Home, it will be impossible for Us to stay longer here than till Saturday. I must confess our Marching from Preston to the Quarters We now are in, was disagreable to Me, and an ill considered Scheme from the beginning, as We had no certain accounts of the Main body of the Rebells marching at that time towards us, therefore it would have been more prudent to have dismissed the Men without spending any of their pay, and they might have been called together when the danger appeared more immediate, notwithstanding it was apprehended by some that the Rebells woud be at Friergate Barrs before our Regiment coud get out of Preston . . .

Everything was at sixes and sevens. That night Sir Henry sent an urgent despatch to Derby with news that the Scots were moving towards Penrith. This shook the lord lieutenant out of his usual calm attitude, for in an uncharacteristic 'sauve qui peut' manner, he told all his deputies to solve their local problems on their own. He announced he was marching his regiment to Liverpool, and he rebuked Sir Henry for not using his own judgment 'in ordering what relates to your Regiment, without consulting me in a matter that requires the utmost despatch'. Sir Henry's regiment moved to Ormskirk as previously ordered to do, and on 22 November, in a letter from Liverpool, Sir Henry described the disorder to Pelham:

> We are in the greatest distress here upon the approach of the Rebells, and that the King's army both that comanded by Marshall Wade and General Ligonier at too great a distance to afford us any reliefe, our militia have answed as to keeping the peace of the County, but cant be of any service in stopping the progress of the Rebells, and as our first 14 days are expired, and I fear in the general Confusion we are in we cant collect the money for the other 14 days, and the men must disperse if they have not their pay, but we have Issued out our warrants, and shall see what Effect it has . . .

The confusion of this letter reflects his mental agitation, but by next day he had apparently made up his mind that he could do nothing further to halt the rebel advance. He ordered Captain Walmsley to dismiss his militiamen, and announced that after he had ridden with Derby to Man chester, he himself intended joining his wife in Yorkshire. 'I wish us a Comfortable meeting when this confusion is over'.

On the day Hoghton wrote that letter, Charles Edward entered Kendal. Two days later, 25 November, he arrived at Lancaster, proclaimed his father James III, and moved quickly south to Preston. On 29 and 30 November, he enjoyed a minor triumph in Manchester, and on 1 December crossed into Cheshire. By that time Sir Henry was far out of reach. He had put all Yorkshire's broad acres between him and the invaders, and on 1 December, in a letter from Hull, he vindicated his action to Pelham:

> We kept our Militia together until the Rebels came to Lancaster [the forward troops arrived on 24 November], then Lord Derby and such of the Deputy Lieutenants as met his Lordship at Liverpool were unanimously of Opinion for the three Regiments of Militia to be discharged as one Army was encamped at Litchfield, 60 miles from Us, and Marshal Wade then at Newcastle, I think it had been as well if We had kept together and retired into Yorkshire but near half of our Men were come to Liverpool before I came there and the Letter sent to his Grace the Duke of Newcastle Saturday Sevennight drawn up and signed by all the Gentlemen before I came, to the purpose above so I could not decline signing it as allso the Scrall I writt You by same Express. Such of our Armes as we could prevail with the Men to quit were put on board a Ship at Liverpool the rest of them the private Men took home with them promising to secure them from the Rebels and I dare say they have.
>
> We issued our Warrants for the second 14 days pay Saturday Sevennight, but the Rebels being in the Northpart of the County where my Regiment was raised, the Money could not be collected, but I hope by this Time it is collected. As Lord Derby is I presume gone for London, if the Deputy Lieutenants think it proper, I'le return and We shall rise again to keep the County quiet in Case the Rebels back again upon Us and are pursued by our Army . . .

More than a week later, Sir Henry was still at Hull: on 9 December, in another letter to Pelham, he lamented that he had no fresh news from Lancashire to give him. Apparently he had not yet heard that at Derby on 4 December the Jacobites had taken their fateful decision to retreat. At the very time Sir Henry was writing to London, the Scots were re-entering Manchester, and were finding the householders less friendly than they had appeared to be ten days earlier. On 12 December the last troops of the retreating army left Preston. The next day they cleared Lancaster. A week later the so-called Manchester Regiment, led by Colonel Francis Towneley, began its suicidal task of holding the Duke of Cumberland's army at Carlisle so that the Scots might have time to cross into Scotland and recover a little after marching 200 miles in fourteen days on 18th-century roads.

The Hoghton letters do not tell us when Sir Henry arrived back in Walton-le-Dale, but by about 20 December he was busy investigating the suspicious activities of Charles Douglas of Fishwick, Preston. On Christmas Eve he sent the Duke of Newcastle a long explanation of the case. Douglas had been 'harbouring in this neighbourhood above these 6 months'. He openly admitted himself a Roman Catholic, and in November, Sir Henry would have committed him to the house of correction as a spy had not Douglas himself claimed to be Lord Mordington, a Scottish peer. Instead, he bound 'two protestant neighbours for his appearance at our next quarter Sessions'. When the Jacobites had appeared in Preston, Douglas had joined them, accompanied them to Derby and back, worn the white cockade, but claimed that 'he never received any Pay, carryed Arms, was present at any Proclamation of the Pretender nor heard of any Contributions raised in any Town through which he passed'. 'The priviledge of Peerage being so tender a point', Sir Henry did not know what to do with the prisoner. Nor did the Duke of Newcastle. He laid the matter before George II, 'who is extremely sensible of this Instance, and of the many other Proofs you have given, on occasion of the present Rebellion, of your constant Care and Attention to His Majesty's Service'. The king ordered Douglas to be kept in custody until the attorney general could examine the evidence. Sir

Henry placed a guard over him, but on 9 January Newcastle sent specific instructions that the prisoner should be committed to gaol on a charge of high treason.

Sir Henry did not show the same scruples over other Jacobite sympathisers. For the whole of 1746 and the first three months of 1747, he was busily concerned with 'seeing justice done'. In January and February he spent most of his time interrogating suspects and recording the evidence of witnesses in Preston, Chorley, Manchester and other places. In March he reported the assizes to Derby 'all the state prisoners [162 of them] were under warrants of Detainer from the Duke of Newcastle, 32 are dead and many more dangerously ill in the Gaol feavour . . .'—and four months later he expressed satisfaction that 'such prisoners as were committed by Justices of Peace are to be tryed at Lancaster'. Later in the year, his chief concern was to have George Kenyon, the clerk of the peace, charged with failing to record the convictions of Lancashire Roman Catholics in the months both before the invasion began and since the rebels had departed. On 3 November 1746 he wrote a long letter to Lord Willoughby reciting the events of the previous year, and arguing that Lancashire had special need to watch its Roman Catholics. He pointed out how fortunate Lancashire had been in the previous November and December:

> The County is so neglected, that some say we are no part of England or that it is thought we are not able to do either good or hurt, it might be thought best (nationally considered) to let the Rebells come into this county, but it was like to have been of fatal Consequence. Mr Wade took care of Yorkshire but we had not the face of a Souldier untill the Duke's army came tis a mercy we did not suffer more, but had not his Royal Highness followed the rebells so closely upon their reateat we had been distroyed our papists would certainly have rose, and burnt and taken what we had left. I may be allowed to speak, since there are more papists than Protestants in this part of the County, there being quiet was only owing to their want of time to be otherwise . . .

Kenyon's stubbornness, Sir Henry considered, was putting the county in danger again.

Sir Henry's fight against Jacobitism was life-long, but in
1746 he was especially concerned that men who had spent
money and energy to prepare Lancashire to meet the
Jacobite invasion should be remembered and compensated.
In March and April he was busy helping Mr. Gillison to
claim from county funds his expenses for serving as
'intelligencer' and 'express messenger' during the autumn
weeks of the previous year. He explained to Lord Derby
that, through Mr. Bell, the provost of Dumfries, Gillison
had given them 'constant intelligence' of the rebels' move-
ments, 'untill the Rebells were so near us, that we were
all forced to fly for our Safety'. Gillison, Sir Henry said,
'performed this usefull piece of service with a great trouble,
he desires nothing for it only what he's out of pocket'.
Derby supported Sir Henry, but quarter sessions ruled that
it was illegal to use county funds for such a purpose. Sir
Henry tried to raise the money by voluntary subscription,
but found that everyone waited to see what everybody
else subscribed before giving their own contribution. Gillison had certainly received nothing by the end of June. But
Sir Henry did succeed in getting the lord lieutenant to
authorise the collection of trophy money, so that officers
could be reimbursed for what they had spent on 'drums
halberts sergeants or drummers pay with other reasonable
articles'.

Bringing the arms back from Liverpool to the several
townships was another of Sir Henry's worries in 1746.
He would have liked the guns entrusted to the captains
and not to the townships:

> . . . if your Lordship [Derby] would order the arms to be
> kept by the officers in such proportion as you think proper,
> with an allowance for keeping them Clean, it would prevent
> them being lost or spoiled and from being imployed in killing
> of Game which is the case at present, nay I can assure your
> Lordship in some places are used to protect Papists houses . . .

Derby agreed that Hoghton was right. The captains
would take greater care of the arms, but

> the Law says expressly, they shall be kept by the several
> posts, so that without their consent I do not see how it can
> be done; and as for a new Bill to rectify That, and many other

> things to make the Militia useful, I never expect to see it
> pass into a law, being firmly persuaded that 'tis not the design
> of any Administration to take the least step towards a thing
> that may seem to make a large standing army less necessary'.

Derby's caution and insistence upon observing the letter
of the law ever frustrated Sir Henry's enthusiastic and
demonstrably sensible plans. But at least in April 1746,
the two men found themselves of one mind. They both
rejoiced when the news of the Jacobite defeat at Culloden
reached Lancashire. Of course, Sir Henry heard first. He
received the news from at least two quarters, Barnard
Castle and Kendal, and he promptly sent it on to Lord
Derby. His letter has not survived, but from Derby's reply
it is apparent that it relayed over-optimistic rumour as
well as welcome truth. On 2 May, Derby put the record
straight in his usual measured assessment of the news:

> . . . I most heartily rejoice with you for His Royal High-
> ness's success in Scotland, which though not so great as your
> accounts from Bernard Castle make it, is yet enough to prevent
> all fear of the Rebel's return into England, for our days at
> least; and if the Legislature do not put it out of the power of
> that barren beggarly part of the Nation's disturbing the peace,
> and indangering the liberty of the whole for the future, I
> think they are justly answerable for all the evil that may befal
> their Posterity. . . . I have been told You had a letter from
> Mr. Shepherd of Kendal that the young would-be-Prince, with
> 30 of Chiefe are taken since the battel of Culloden, but I
> much doubt the News.

As on so many occasions during the previous eight months,
phlegmatic Derby was right, and excited Sir Henry had to
bear yet another disappointment.

THE LETTERS AND JOURNAL OF ELLEN WEETON, 1807-1825

[Oxford University Press published Miss Weeton: Journal of a Governess, *2 volumes, in 1936 and 1939. Both volumes were engagingly edited and annoted by Edward Hall. In 1969 David and Charles reprinted the work, adding a short introduction by J. J. Bagley and a new epilogue by Edward Hall. The letter books themselves Edward Hall presented to Wigan Public Library. They are available for consultation and study in the Reference Library.]*

But for Edward Hall's instinctive appreciation of their worth, we should never have had the pleasure of reading Ellen Weeton's letters. In 1925, rummaging in the recesses of a second-hand bookshop in Wigan, he came across a dusty letter book. It was obviously one of a series, but unfortunately had been separated from its fellows. Mr. Hall, an antiquarian bookseller from Surrey but a Lancashire man by birth, was charmed by what he bought for ninepence. He printed some of the letters in the *Wigan Examiner,* and this publicity had the luck to produce three more volumes, two almost immediately from E. A. Marshall of Southport and one much later from his brother, K. K. Marshall of the Isle of Man. Put into chronological order the four volumes turned out to be Volumes 2, 3, 5 and 7 of a series of at least seven letter books. Volumes 1, 4 and 6 have never been found, but by a happy chance E. A. Marshall had another manuscript book, in which Ellen Weeton had written what she called 'occasional reflections', and had begun to write her autobiography. These writings went a long way towards filling the gaps in her life story.

Ellen was born in Lancaster on Christmas Day 1776. Her father, Thomas Weeton, was a ship's captain in the service of the Rawlinsons of Lancaster, Quaker ship-owners

who, over two or three generations, had built a valuable
trade between the Lune and the West Indies. Her mother,
Mary, was the daughter of Richard Rawlinson, a Preston
butcher, and a distant kinsman of the Lancaster Rawlinsons. As a young woman she had served as lady's maid to
the sister of Sir Henry Hoghton, and in that capacity had
spent several months in London and the southern counties.
She was intelligent and well read. After her marriage she
settled down in Lancaster to bring up her children—
Edward, who died before he was four; Ellen, or Nelly as
she was christened; Margaret, who only lived a few days;
and Thomas Richard, who survived the perils of infancy
first to be Ellen's pride and later to be the sharpest
thorn in her flesh.

The outbreak of war between Britain and the American
colonies transformed Captain Weeton's career. Before
1775, apart from the natural hazards inherent in all
sailing, the biggest risk he ran was the possibility of a
slave revolt on the second leg of his usual triangular voyage
—from the Lune to West Africa, on to the West Indies, and
back to the Lune. But after 1775, when he took charge of
a vessel carrying a letter of marque, he became a combat-
ant and faced the dangers of war. The French and the
Dutch supported the American colonists, and made life in
West Indian waters more perilous still. Captain Weeton
gave better than he got. He returned at least twice
from very successful voyages, and in both the Indies and
Lancaster acquired a reputation as a brave fighter. But in
1782 he was killed in action. Instead of delivering the
usual letter from Weeton to his wife, 'the Jamaica packet'
brought to Lancaster news of his death and burial.

Mary Weeton faced a hard future. She was nursing a
sick mother, looking after her children, Ellen, almost six
years old, and Tom, not yet two, and helping to maintain
an orphan niece and nephew. And all Mary could rely on
was a rent of 'but £30 or £40 a year' from a small estate
at Sunderland Point together with £500 capital, which she
had managed to save. The Rawlinsons refused to pay her
the prize money which she believed her husband had won,
so that she soon had to look for ways of earning a living.

Her mother died early in 1784, and then Mary took her young family to Up Holland, four miles west of Wigan. This move had three advantages: she was close to her mother's youngest sister, Mrs. Barton; 'rents and coals were so much lower than at Lancaster'; and later, in 1788, she was able to open a school in one of the houses that stood opposite the big house called The Priory—later renamed The Abbey—which still stands on the site of the old Up Holland Priory.

Ellen grew to womanhood in Up Holland. For the most part she led a lonely life. Her mother allowed her only to play with children from 'respectable' families. Her brother, who was her favourite companion, had little time to spare for her. Until he was fourteen he was a pupil at Up Holland Academy, a select boarding school run by the Rev. John Braithwaite, who lived at The Priory. From school Tom went straight to Preston to serve an apprenticeship with a solicitor: 'I was entirely bereft of the companion of my girlish days; the promoter of mirth and frolic; the stimulator of my studies'. Occasionally, Ellen spent an hour or two with the daughters of Richard Prescott, 'the galloping parson' at Up Holland, or with the Misses Braithwaites, but most days she spent at home helping her mother in the house and school, meeting no one but the pupils, and relying upon books and her lively imagination for entertainment. She had no fear of solitude, but she grew up to be shy and awkward in company. She could write fluently and expressively, but sat tongue-tied when visitors came to the house or she went on one of her rare visits to a neighbour. But if her tongue was still, her mind was very active. She listened carefully, observed keenly, and often chuckled inwardly. Later, in the quietness of her room, she had great fun putting her impressions on paper, or storing them in her retentive memory.

After months of indifferent health, Mary Weeton died in December 1797. Ellen, almost 21, was left to continue running the school. The next few years were not at all happy. Tom's expenses in Preston could only be met by practising strict economy at home: Mary had deprived herself of food and clothes, and, after 1797, Ellen had to do the same. All the Sunderland rent went to Tom, and out of her meagre earnings, about 10s. 0d. a week, Ellen had to keep herself, pay off her mother's debts and funeral expenses, and send all she could possibly spare to her brother. She made herself ill with worry and lack of nourishment, but she endured in the hope that once Tom qualified, his earnings would banish her poverty for ever. Tom was the apple of her eye. In her day-dreams she romanticised their childhood, and convinced herself that once he had returned to Up Holland he and she would live together, indifferent to the rest of the world and with sufficient money to enjoy long leisure hours in each other's company. It never crossed her mind that her brother might not want to live the life of a bachelor recluse.

Tom Weeton completed his articles in January 1802. After spending three extravagant months in London, he 'staid with me at Holland a few weeks'—a happy, peaceful interlude for Ellen—'and then went to settle at Wigan, coming every Saturday to see me, and returning either that evening or the next'. Such arrangements hardly ever last long. Within a few months Tom had 'formed an attachment' to Jane Scott, the daughter of a Wigan cotton master, and, in October 1803, 'hastily and imprudently married'. In the life she had planned ahead, Ellen had not reserved a place for a sister-in-law. Consequently, any wife Tom chose would have had to be exceptionally talented, patient, and long-suffering ever to have won affection and approval from Ellen. And, according to the evidence derived from Ellen's letters, Jane Scott had none of these virtues.

For the first month of their married life, before Mrs. Scott had 'been persuaded to notice her daughter after her imprudent wedding', Tom and Jane went to live with Ellen at Up Holland. Ellen's verdict then was that Jane 'was too indolent, too slow, and too little used to household work'. Three or four years later, when Tom, helped by Scott money, was busy establishing himself as an attorney in Leigh, Ellen paid the family two or three visits. She disapproved of their way of life, said so in

her blunt, elder-sister fashion, and was then surprised that
she provoked anger and resentment. To her correspondents, she schooled herself to portray her sister-in-law in a
kind light. In August 1808, she wrote this indulgent description to her friend, Miss Bolton:

> Since I left Up Holland, I have spent between four or five
> weeks at my brother's as agreeably as I could wish. Mrs. W.
> [Jane] is a little oddish, but I did not care, so we did not
> quarrel. My brother does seem so fond of her, and his
> children, that seriously it was a most exquisite pleasure to me
> to witness his happiness. He is not content with kissing and
> cuddling by moonlight, but he must do it by sunlight too.
> Every day, after dinner and supper, instead of a desert on his
> table, came his wife upon his knee, and her lips to his mouth,
> sweeter I dare say in his opinion than the finest garden fruit,
> and more grateful to his heart. And his son Tom [born
> November 1804] is one of the *sweetest* lads that ever God
> sent upon earth to be a blessing to his parents! His two little
> sisters [Catherine, born August 1806 and Jane born December
> 1807] are fine children, but they are such infantile buds that
> it is not easy at present to say what kind of flower will blow.

But, to Tom and Jane, Ellen expressed her displeasure
far more directly. She read them lecture after lecture about
time-wasting and unhealthiness involved in 'indulging [in
bed] so late every morning: but should your days be
shortened by self indulgence—which I almost fear they
will—think how many, my dear Tom, must suffer with
you; and suffer more, much more than you, because their
sufferings may be protracted to a much longer period than
yours'. After meals she rose and bustled about in pointed
protest against their habit of lingering and talking, and, to
draw attention to her sister-in-law's reluctance to tackle
dirty jobs, began 'to do what Mrs. W. considered as the
most disagreeable kind of work she had'. In all these matters Ellen acted with the best intentions and out of deep
love for her brother, but she incensed Jane. Nor was Jane
pleased when, in polite company, Ellen spoke plainly about
what she could and could not afford. Jane had social
ambitions, and she felt these were not being fostered by
her sister-in-law giving the impression, however true it
might be, that she had to be careful how she spent her
money.

Once Tom was earning, Ellen, by her mother's will, received half the Sunderland rent, and, with school fees and her minute personal expenditure, she was soon far better off than she had ever been. In 1808 she closed her school, moved to Liverpool first to stay for a while with the pretentious Chorley family in Dale Street, and then to go into river-side lodgings at Kirkdale. Ellen anticipated that leaving Up Holland for Liverpool would be a thrilling adventure. From the stories she had heard about the busy, rapidly-growing borough, she thought she was exchanging her place in a backward, ignorant rural community for a life among knowledgeable, intelligent men and women, who would make her ashamed of her own short-comings. She was quickly disillusioned. Before she lived in Liverpool, she suspected there would be certain disadvantages: as early as February 1808 she had written to Miss Chorley,

> The intelligent beings I meet with in a large society delight me beyond measure, but the noise of the crowd distracts me. The beautiful buildings, fine open streets, and elegant equipages excite admiration; yet, when the novelty wears off, I wish for a more frequent sight of fields, groves, hills, and vales; and would sooner go into a hay meadow than the most crowded rout I could be invited to . . .

But, after living in Liverpool and Kirkdale for a few months, she confessed in her *Journal* that she had encountered far more fundamental disappointments than the loss of rural quietness:

> When I came to Liverpool I expected to have found it filled with intelligent beings, imagining knowledge to be so generally diffused. I begin to discover that it contains as much proportionate ignorance as any little village in England, where perhaps the curate is the only intelligent man in it. How astonished am I daily to find so many more ignorant than myself, so few more knowing . . . Here, not one in ten can speak their native language tolerably; not more than one in twenty correctly; and of these last, scarce one tenth can boast any greater literary acquirement than that of their grammar. I thought myself very ignorant when I came here, expecting to find so many wise, so many learned—I find them not . . . The people here do not seize the opportunities of improvement that so frequently occur—which they must almost wilfully reject—Their ignorance is astonishing! It would almost appear

as if ignorance was taught, as if it were something to boast
of . . .

Ellen was censorious by nature. She condemned Up
Holland as 'licentious' and 'scandalous', and few of her
friends and acquaintances lived up to the high standard
she set for them. Those whom she loved she chided
most, so that, not surprisingly, her lack of tolerance and
her sharp tongue made difficulties for her throughout her
life.

Ellen's stay in Liverpool lasted less than eighteen
months. After years of endless chores, she had looked
forward to the pleasures of rest, self-indulgence and
uninterrupted reading: 'I have been almost wild with joy
to think that I had broken loose, and commenced eternal
holiday'. But Ellen and idleness proved uneasy bedfellows.
The inaction and stuffy, airless atmosphere of the Chorley
household soon made her restless. She found lodgings with
Edward and Betty Smith at Beacon's Gutter—'fine romantic name to utter'—on the shore at Kirkdale, about two
miles from Liverpool's town hall. The site offered river
bathing and invigorating air instead of the noise and bustle
of Dale Street, and threw in the traffic on the river as an
additional attraction—'ships are going out or coming in
every day; and brigs and boats are continually on the
river'. Ellen was thrilled with the novelty of her new
home. Within the first fortnight she witnessed a daring
rescue just opposite the house. Strong winds had blown a
ship 'setting sail for the Brasils' onto the rocks off shore.
The crew cut away the masts, and the lifeboatmen only
reached the ship with great difficulty. Luckily, most of
the cargo was salvaged, and, during the next few days,
Ellen watched it being auctioned on the shore; 'today two
fields adjoining this house are almost covered with Irish
linen'. In the following March, thieves used Smith's outhouses for storing hides and tallow taken, Ellen believed,
from a wreck near Hoylake, and rowed by night across
the mouth of the river. The owners discovered what had
happened, and, in a manner reminiscent of a children's
television serial, arrived one evening at Beacon's Gutter
to recover the stolen property. By ill chance for Ellen, the

Smiths were not at home. Apprehensive of what might happen, Ellen barred herself inside the house: 'at twelve, I went to bed, but you may suppose I did not sleep. I heard the men about all night, for the hides stunk so intolerably, there was no existing in the barn with them . . .'. It was a nerve-racking experience, but it was splendid copy for a long, exciting letter to Brother Tom.

For most days of the year, the Kirkdale shore was a pleasant, isolated stretch of sand. The very spot on which Jesse Hartley, Liverpool's outstanding dock engineer, was destined to build the Wellington, Sandon and Huskisson docks forty years later, Ellen Weeton, in 1808, described as 'a very retired situation, pleasant and clean'. It offered good bathing: 'you might undress in the house and walk into the water'. Ellen's generation held salt-water bathing in high regard both as a recreation and as a healthy exercise. She had tried the baths—a fenced-off section of the river—at Liverpool, but she much preferred the almost private site at Kirkdale or the shore at Southport. The new bathing centre at South Hawes, which was rapidly growing in popularity as *Southport,* had the added attraction of being increasingly fashionable. In May 1808, just before she left Up Holland, Ellen spoke of it 'as becoming a famous bathing place . . . a fine open sea, spacious shore to walk upon . . .'. Exactly a year later, she reported more houses and a new inn (now the Prince of Wales), and obviously preened herself for having associated there with 'many people of some consequence and fashion'. But in 1825, bathing at Southport had become far too popular for fastidious folk. Ellen wrote in her *Journal:*

> I have seldom bathed but at Southport, and there it is sadly exposing, as all who resort there well know, and the modest complain much, gentlemen's and ladies' machines standing promiscuously in the water! Besides, at spring tides, it is hardly possible to have a machine for only one person, such crowds resort there to bathe; and as there are no dressing rooms, time is positively not allowed for any one to dress in the machine before quitting it. Perpetual rappings at the door, and, 'oh, do come out', 'Do make haste', reiterated until we are thrown into a trepidation, so as not to be able to finish dressing; and probably, on issuing forth, 2 or 3

> *gentlemen,* to your utter confusion, at the door, ready to
> jump in! The bustle, hurry, and confusion, are most extremely
> disagreeable; the only comfort is, that amongst such a crowd
> we may pass unnoticed perhaps.

Ellen enjoyed her months of leisure on Merseyside. The
letters she wrote from there are gay and witty, and even
her brother professed that he noticed she was less strained.
He paid her the back-handed, brotherly compliment of
saying that she had 'lost something of that tarnish' and
had 'less old-maidenly notions'—'in short, she had come
to be like other people in the more pleasant parts of their
character'. Obviously Ellen was recovering from the tread-
mill years at Up Holland, doing new things and meeting
interesting people. She found pleasure in occasionally
visiting Liverpool from Kirkdale and, in the early summer
of 1809, in going back to Up Holland to stay a few days
with her aunt. In July 1809 her cousin, Henry Latham,
visited her at Beacon's Gutter, and together they walked to
Liverpool to see Sarah Siddons play Lady Macbeth at the
Theatre Royal in Williamson Square. 'Much as I expected,
my expectations were exceeded; particularly in that scene
where Lady Macbeth is represented as walking in her
sleep'. But the witches—'such a merry set', the ghosts—'so
substantial', and the thunder—'not loud enough', all caused
her to laugh when the rest of the audience was sitting awe-
struck. She was for ever seeing the comic side of things and
enjoying quiet, private chuckles. When she returned to
Kirkdale from her visit to Up Holland, she walked to
Appley Bridge, and then took the canal barge to Liverpool.
The 'thank-you' letter which she wrote to Aunt Barton is
full of amusing, telling observations upon her fellow
travellers:

> . . . most people who go in the tail end of the packet
> [second-class seats] seem to think that eating and drinking is
> the most delightful amusement of travelling. The generality
> of those who sail in the upper end seem to have very different
> ideas. They appear as if ashamed of such a piece of vulgarity
> as the indulging a propensity to eat . . . Some very odd faces
> are to be seen at times. Two old ladies got in a few miles
> from Liverpool. The very moment they could squat them-
> selves on the cushion, they began to knit. One had a good

hardly look, as if she had been stewed to make her keep. She looked more like a coddled gooseberry than anything else . . . A very nice old lady got in much about the same time, accompanied by almost as nice a young one; both of respectable appearance. The old one had rather an ill-tempered look, but fortunately she was very deaf, so she could not often be put out of her way by what she heard. A clergyman sailed with us five or six miles; he had that wolf-like keenness in his eyes, as if he knew which was the best method of taking tithe.

Ellen stayed at Beacon's Gutter exactly a year. She then went to live as a paying guest with the Winkley family in Princes Street, off Dale Street, Liverpool. But in little more than a month, she had accepted a post as 'Governess to superintend the Education of a Young Lady'. It was an unusual assignment. Edward Pedder, a member of a well-to-do Preston family of bankers, had recently married a second time. By his first wife he had had a daughter, who was ten years old in 1809. She required a governess. But Ellen's chief task was to educate the second Mrs. Pedder and fit her for the social life she now had to lead, for, in a rush of blood, thirty-four-year-old Edward had carried off his seventeen-year-old dairy-maid, Mary, and married her over the anvil at Gretna Green. Bringing the young mistress up to scratch could hardly be accomplished in the family home in Preston. Pedder, therefore, took a lease on 'Dove's Nest', a newish house at Low-wood, near Ambleside, and in that comparatively isolated spot, hoped that Ellen Weeton would be able to instruct his new wife in the habits of gentlefolk and teach her sufficient to enable her to hold her own among the ladies of Preston. Ellen priced her services at thirty guineas a year. Pedder accepted immediately, and, excited and eager, Ellen, now thirty-three years of age, began to pack her trunk and prepare for the adventure ahead. She told Tom exactly what she had agreed to do, but she gave most of her friends the impression that she was going to stay in Lancaster with an old friend of her mother. This she did as a precaution against failure, for, as she wrote to her brother, 'should I find the situation uncomfortable, and be obliged to return soon, I should not wish anyone to know where I

had been, or for why'. All went very successfully at first.
Ellen found 'Dove's Nest' pleasant and its situation over-
looking Windermere most charming. She delighted in the
unaccustomed luxury of the household—'five servants (two
men and three maids), a curricle, four or five horses, five
or six dogs, a cow, two pigs, and a whole host of rats, too
many to be counted'—and she had a tolerable regard for
both Edward and Mary Pedder. She described Mr. Pedder
as 'a good looking man . . . good natured, liberal, hospit-
able and unsuspicious . . . and a good husband—he would
be a better if he were less fond of the bottle'. Mrs. Pedder
was pleasanter company still—'a most sweet tempered
woman, and of a disposition upright and amiable in the
extreme'. The only snags were that the child, Gertrude,
had frequent epileptic fits, and that the noise of the rats
in the rafters sometimes made sleep impossible. The rest
of the household would not believe that rats could be
responsible for such loud and frequent 'bumps in the
night'. They blamed the restless spirit of old miser
Benson, the builder of the house. But practical Ellen
proved her point. Armed with a candle, 'accompanied by
Mrs. P., and *followed* by the tittering domestics', she
carried a ladder upstairs, climbed into the cock-loft, and
found heaps of rat-droppings and a number of floor-boards
loose and disarrayed.

Two months after Ellen's arrival, the Pedder household
suffered a terrible calamity. Gertrude, left alone for a few
moments, stood so close to the parlour fire that her
clothes caught fire, and, despite Ellen's best endeavours,
the demented child died of her burns. This disaster changed
the whole atmosphere of 'Dove's Nest'. Edward Pedder
took to drink more resolutely than before: 'he is scarcely
ever sober, and often out of temper, except when drinking
and singing with workmen and servants'. Mary Pedder
wearied of her studies: 'her common lessons she submits
to as a task, with very great reluctance, and were I to say
much on the subject, I am afraid she would reject them
altogether'. She preferred to play cards, and Ellen, who
longed to enjoy 'the feast of books' in the library, found

herself obliged to waste day after day amusing her young
mistress at the card table.

Ellen's two compensations were the solitude of her
room, and the occasional delight of an excursion into the
neighbouring countryside. She took every opportunity to
row on the lake, and in July 1810 wrote enthusiastically
about the regatta she had attended at Bowness. But probably the outing she enjoyed best was the assault on Fair-
field. The party, fifteen in number not counting the four
men who carried the picnic baskets, breakfasted in
Ambleside, and soon after six o'clock set out as if they
were about to penetrate the fastnesses of Kashmir. The
ladies rode in a cart as far as 'the extremity of Scandale',
and then, 'after labouring up the steep for an hour or two',
everyone managed to puff and blow their way to the
summit. Out came the 'veal, ham, chicken, gooseberry
pies, bread, cheese, butter, hung leg of mutton, wine,
porter, rum, brandy, and bitters', and 'when our hunger
was appeased', the more energetic strolled about enjoying
'the extensive prospect'. Going down proved as difficult
as climbing up: 'one or two of the party who had not
provided nails in the soles of their shoes . . . were obliged
to sit down frequently, and descend by sliding'. But Ellen
could not have been better pleased. She later told Bessy
Winkley that she had never in her life enjoyed a more
'agreeable excursion'. Later that year, she scrambled to the
top of the Langdale Pikes—'the ruggedness and steepness
of the ascent and descent were to me one half of the
inducement'—and in June 1812, she battled against a gale
to reach the cairn on the summit of Snaefell in the Isle of
Man—'determined that the wind should not entirely
conquer me, I crept over on my hands and knees, though
with great difficulty, and then added my mite to the heap
of stones'. Much later in life, in her fiftieth year, she
climbed Snowdon. As usual she went on her own. She
fully appreciated how daring and unconventional it was
for a woman to go mountaineering without an escort, but
to have engaged a guide to take her up Snowdon would
have ruined the whole adventure. 'Here I stood, perched
on a ridge like a crow on the point of a pinnacle; not a

human creature could I see anywhere; for aught I knew,
I had the whole mountain to myself . . . I was higher than
ever I had been in the world before'.

Life at 'Dove's Nest' became intolerable for Ellen early
in 1811. Pedder grew more offensive and fitful than ever,
and Ellen decided to leave. But she did not go further
away than Ambleside. For the whole of the spring and the
summer, she stayed as a paying guest at the house of
William Green, the Lakeland painter and engraver, and
became so friendly that she stood as godmother for one
of the children. Ambleside won her heart: she seriously
contemplated opening a school in the village 'for there
is not *one* decent one in the place'. In the end, she changed
her mind, and as winter approached returned to Lancashire.
At first, she moved restlessly about—Lancaster, Liverpool,
Leigh, Up Holland—until she came temporarily to rest
again at her old lodgings in Princes Street, Liverpool. With
her brother's help, she managed to put her finances in
order, but, after much questioning and mental anguish, she
discovered that the reason her aunt, uncle, cousin, and
several of her friends had met her with stern faces and
cold words was that Tom of all people had explained her
departure from Liverpool by saying that she had 'gone
off with a gentleman'. The Winkley household had changed
for the worse too. Young Ann, Ellen's favourite, had left
home to become a governess in Ireland, and Bessy was
about to marry a Mr. Price and move to a 'pretty-looking,
small new house' on the top of Copperas Hill, looking
down on the ever-expanding Liverpool. Ellen could not
settle: in March 1812, she confessed to Ann Winkley that
she could not 'bear this inactive life' and that she was
'on the point of engaging to instruct the children of a
lady in Yorkshire'. But first she spent May and June
exploring the Isle of Man—she enjoyed everything but the
sea voyages there and back—and did not begin work in
Yorkshire until the middle of July.

To move to 'High Royd' in Honley, four miles south of
Huddersfield, and in the summer of 1812 to take up resi-
dence in the house of Joseph Armitage, the son of Sir
George, notorious millowner and justice of the peace, was

to land right in the middle of the Luddite battlefield. Machine-breaking, arson, and shooting had left the whole region angry, resentful, and full of fear for the future. The manufacturers seemed to value profits more than men— 'the people in this part of Yorkshire appear to be all a money-getting, but not a money-spending people' wrote Ellen. The bewildered operatives fought an endless battle against poverty, and all wondered with concern what would happen at the next York assizes when many suspected Luddites were due to appear before the king's judges. The new governess could hardly have been unaware of the tension in the air, and of the strain under which Joseph Armitage and his wife were constantly living. She recognised this in a letter written during the assizes in January 1813:

> Though Mr. and Mrs. A. are extremely cautious of what they say on the subject, I can discover that they feel very serious uneasiness respecting the Luddites: and, they may well! having been fired at in their bed [in the previous April], and an intimate acquaintance (Mr. Horsfall) murdered, their terror will be some time ere it subsides. Even since the assizes commenced, Mr. Radcliffe's house has been fired into, I have just heard, by some unknown hand. He has been a most active magistrate, and by his means, principally, have the ringleaders been discovered and apprehended. He received, a short time ago, several anonymous letters, threatening his life if the men then in York were executed . . .

But however much Luddite activities dominated the thoughts of the district and permeated conversation at the Armitage dining table, they do not seem to have disturbed Ellen's peace of mind. Her chief concerns were far more personal. The continued estrangement from her aunt and her brother worried her deeply, but her governess duties, which began no later than 7.00 a.m. and continued virtually unbroken until 7.30 or 8.00 p.m. seven days a week, kept her continually busy and left her little energy for anything else—even for letter-writing. At times she felt herself to be nothing more than an imprisoned slave: she wrote to Mrs. Green at Ambleside that much as she admired 'the pretty and romantic' countryside and the 'extensive, and in some points, fine view from the front

windows', the 'confined life' which she led made her
almost hate the district in which she was so 'imprisoned'.
The children were her chief consolation. At times, they
pushed her beyond the limits of her patience—in one or
two letters she bemoaned their 'perverse and violent tem-
pers', 'screaming and shouting', and 'everlasting quarrelling'
—but in time she managed to win their affection and
obedience. Both they and she were reduced to tears, when
in July 1814, at the end of two years' service, she returned
to Lancashire.

Less than two months after leaving 'High Royd', Ellen
Weeton married Aaron Stock, the owner-manager of a
small cotton-spinning mill in Wigan. How Ellen met Stock,
and how she at thirty-seven came to accept his offer so
quickly is not at all clear. Tom seems to have encouraged
the match, but that hardly explains why Ellen, hitherto so
independent and so protective of her money, should
surrender her liberty and her precious savings in order to
become mistress of the household of a virtual stranger. All
the ingredients of a disastrous marriage crowded into that
cheerless home at the rear of the factory in Chapel Lane
—two jealous, adult daughters of Stock's first wife; a
spirited, touchy step-mother, and a dominating, violent-
tempered husband and father used to having his own way.
In June 1815, Ellen gave birth to a daughter, Mary, but
the child, upon whom Ellen doted and Aaron smiled with
fond indulgence, failed to hold husband and wife together.
There was a perpetual conflict of wills, Aaron ordering and
Ellen defying. Aaron tried to bring his wife to heel by
keeping her short of money, yet somehow or another
Ellen escaped to Liverpool with her child and stayed there
until debts and lack of cash forced her to return home 'to
avoid starvation'.

Because Volume 6 of the letter-books is missing, we can
only see the years 1819-1822 darkly through Ellen's later
recollections. In 1819 Aaron took Mary from her mother's
care and sent her to a boarding school at Parr Hall, near
the growing industrial town of St. Helens. He then began
a deliberate campaign—at least, so Ellen thought—to drive
his wife to suicide, the asylum or the gallows. In an

exceptionally long letter to her brother written early in
1823, she bitterly reminded him of those forlorn, despair-
ing days:

> Repeatedly turned out destitute; twice imprisoned . . .
> several times obliged to flee for my life, the time when I broke
> the windows, if I had not by that means forced my way in, I
> must have been out all night, on the cold and wet pavement of
> a dark November night. I had then been turned out only for
> complaining, whilst enduring exceedingly unkind treatment. I
> was threatened with being sent to a Lunatic Asylum, only for
> asking for food. Cloaths I could not procure until I got them
> on credit . . .

Tom Weeton was no help at all. To mollify his wife, who
had no love for Ellen, and to avoid upsetting influential
friends, he refused to take his sister's side. Indeed, in the
end, he agreed to act as one of Aaron's legal advisers. And
yet, Ellen had sufficient spirit and energy eventually to
secure a legal separation from Aaron. The terms were hard,
especially the clause which restricted her to three visits a
year to see Mary, but they could have been much worse.
With her allowance of £70 a year, she was at least financially independent again.

In 1822 Ellen returned to Up Holland. She took lodgings
in a 'poky parlour' in a farmhouse, and there slowly but
steadily recovered her health and much of her former
confidence and poise. Volume 7 contains friendly letters
to Mrs. Price, Miss Braithwaite, Miss Hawarden of Wigan,
and Miss Dannett, an old Up Holland neighbour; motherly
letters to Mary, with careful covering letters to her
schoolmistress; formal, business letters to her husband, and
the long, last, blasting letter to Tom. But in this volume
Ellen devoted more and more space to journal entries as
death or changed circumstances deprived her of several of
her old correspondents and as she retreated within herself.
But at least she did not allow her room to become a
prison. In the Spring of 1823, she began regularly to
attend Hope Chapel in Wigan. July and August she spent
partly in Southport and partly in Flintshire. The following
year she took two holidays, an Easter visit to her favourite
Southport and then, from 12 May to 30 July, a never-to-

be-forgotten stay in London, crowding in as much sight-
seeing and exploring as time and physical endurance
would allow. On her return to Lancashire, she moved from
Up Holland to Prescot, half-way between her friends in
Liverpool and her daughter in Parr Hall. In the following
summer she toured North Wales, and the last we see of her
is at Caernarvon, restricted by the rain from doing more
than a comparatively short turn along the Pwllheli road.

Ellen was an enthusiastic walker all her life. She regarded
it as routine that she should walk from Up Holland to
Wigan or Parr Hall, or from Prescot to Liverpool, and
after her tour of London she calculated she had walked
538¾ miles on her many excursions. But, of course, she
could not travel everywhere on 'shank's pony', however
much she enjoyed it. Her husband took her to Southport
in the gig; on her own, she usually travelled by canal from
Liverpool or Appley Bridge to the Red Lion at Scaris-
brick, and finished the remaining five miles by 'the cart' or
by landau. In 1817 she sailed from Birkenhead to Runcorn
on the new paddle-steamer, and was most amused to watch
it 'puffing and blowing and beating its sides, and labouring
along with all its might'. In 1825 she rode more than once
in the crowded Sothern's 'caravan' or public conveyance
from Liverpool to Prescot, and the clouds of dust which
the horses kicked up moved her to comment that 'if Mr.
Mc.Adam could lay the dust as *well* as the roads, he would
be a clever fellow'. But Ellen's most exciting and exacting
journeys were all on the top of a stage-coach. Riding
inside was not only more expensive, but, like sailing, it
made her travel sick. She therefore braved the rigours of
outside travel, perched high above the road, clutching the
rail or the sides of the seat, scanning the countryside, and
enduring whatever weather the elements had fashioned for
the day. In August 1823 she had a stormy ride on the
Eclipse from Southport via Ormskirk to Liverpool:

> The wind blew so furiously, no umbrella could be opened
> or carried. The coachman was very attentive and kind to me;
> he gave me a stout horse rug to cover my shoulders, and
> another to cover my knees, and in this elegant costume I rode
> . . . as heedless and contented as possible, the rain soaking
> through all the way, driving in at a little crevice between my

hood and my neck, and trickling in little streams down my
back . . . when I descended from my elevated situation, my
cloaths were so entirely wet, that I found I was a woman of
much greater weight in Liverpool than I had been at
Southport.

It took a full day to travel by coach from 'High Royd' to
Liverpool, but the journey between Liverpool and London
was a much greater test of stamina. Horses were changed,
different drivers took charge, but, day and night, the
passengers rode on with only brief stops at inns for necessary refreshment. Ellen left Prescot at 2 p.m. on 13 May
and reached her London lodgings at 5.30 p.m. the next
day. She mounted the return coach in Piccadilly at
5.45 a.m. on 29 July, travelled by way of Windsor, Oxford
and Leamington, and reached Birmingham just as it was
going dark. There she had to change coaches, and rode
through the night 'on a very dangerous outside seat' facing
backwards with the head of a large, snoring Irishman press-
ing on her shoulder. She never got a wink of sleep, but,
characteristically she could laugh about it later: 'I extracted
sweets from bitters, and enjoyed the ride and the prospects,
arriving in Liverpool at 11 o'clock on the morning of the
30th June'.

Fortunately for us, Edward Hall was not content to
leave Ellen Stock stranded in North Wales. He could not
find more letter books or more journal entries, but by dint
of much searching he managed to establish that Ellen eventually returned to Wigan. In 1827 she was admitted a
member of Hope Chapel, and five years later was of some
consequence in chapel circles. Ellen would find satisfaction
in being a respected member of such a gathering, but
undoubtedly the departure of Aaron to become a coal-
owner in Ashton-in-Makerfield, and Mary's decision to live
with her mother rather than her father would please her
far more. We can assume with confidence that the last
dozen years of Ellen's life—she died in 1844 or 1845—were
happy, but whether they were entirely calm and unruffled
is very doubtful. Many readers of her letters will close the
book suspecting that, like Samuel Johnson, Ellen Weeton
found a measure of delight in the 'conflict of opinions
and sentiments'.

THE AUTOBIOGRAPHIES OF SAMUEL BAMFORD OF MIDDLETON, WEAVER, 1788-1872, AND OF JOHN RUSHTON OF WALKDEN, COALMINER, 1833-c. 1914

[Samuel Bamford published Passages in the Life of a Radical *in parts from 1839 to 1841 and* Early Days *from 1848 to 1849. The two works were reprinted by Frank Cass and Company in 1967 under the title* The Autobiography of Samuel Bamford. *To this edition Dr. W. H. Chaloner contributed a valuable explanatory introduction. John Rushton's* Autobiography *has not been published. With the permission of James Edward Rushton, John's son, Frank Mullineux of Walkden made a copy of it in 1953 and has kindly allowed me to quote from it in this chapter.]*

If a Lancastrian knows anything at all about the history of his county, he is bound to have heard the story of Peterloo. He may be hazy about the events which preceded this notorious occasion and be unsure why so many men and women crowded into St. Peter's Field, Manchester, on that particular Monday in August 1819, but he will surely know sufficient to relate how the magistrates ordered the yeomanry to arrest the platform speakers, how the horsemen slashed their way through the crowd, and how sabre cuts and trampling, fleeing feet killed several and injured hundreds of panic-stricken people. It is also almost certain that he will hold the magistrates fully responsible for the tragedy, and dismiss with impatience any attempt to justify either the arrest of Orator Hunt and his fellows or the use of the yeomanry to execute the order. The reason is that, directly or indirectly, most Lancastrians have gained their impression of Peterloo from Samuel Bamford's detailed and graphic account in *Passages in the Life of a Radical.*

Peterloo is the climax of Bamford's most celebrated book. *Passages in the Life of a Radical* begins with the end of the Napoleonic War and the enactment of the Corn Law. It traces the growth of the reform movement in South Lancashire, describes the hopes and disappointments of four melancholy years, and then launches into the detail of the fateful 16 August 1819. As Bamford himself says, the book is not 'a strict record, but a narrative only of events, in most of which I was personally concerned', so that, following his description of 'the massacre', he is content to finish the book with an account of what happened to him in the months after he had escaped from the crowded Field.

Bamford led the Middleton contingent to St. Peter's Field. He describes the procession that left home soon after 8 a.m. 'Twelve of the most comely and decent-looking youths, who were placed in two rows of six each, with each a branch of laurel held presented in his hand, as a token of amity and peace' led the way. A band, 'an excellent one', enlivened the route, and two silk banners, one blue and one green, and 'a cap of liberty' held high on a pole explained the purpose of the demonstration. Bamford's fast-moving narrative carries the reader along so well that he senses the initial expectation and excitement of the Middleton men and women, falls in step with the drum beats, hears the cheering as the procession passes through Blackley, Harpurhey, Collyhurst, and the Irish district of Newton, and feels the rising tension as the Middleton contingent is absorbed into an ever-increasing flow of people moving resolutely towards the meeting. By the time Bamford and his followers reach the Field itself, the reader has become one of the demonstrators. He appreciates the effort that the local leaders have been making to keep this huge assembly orderly and peaceful. He shares the natural impatience of the crowd at being kept waiting a full hour for Hunt to arrive, and, finally, experiences the horror of the stampede and the need to escape as quickly as possible.

> On the first rush of the crowd, I called to our men to break their flag-staves, and secure their banners ... He with the blue banner saved it—the cap of liberty was dropped and left behind—indeed woe to him who stooped, he would never have risen again—and Thomas Redford, who carried the green

banner, held it aloft until the staff was cut in his hand, and his shoulder was divided by the sabre of one of the Manchester yeomanry. . . .

On the first advance of the yeomanry, one of the horses, plunging at the crowd, sent his fore-feet into the head of our big drum . . . Thus booted on both legs at once, the horse rolled over, and the drum was kicked to pieces in the mellee. . . . In my retreat from the field, a well-dressed woman dropped on her knees a little on my left: I put out my hand to pluck her up, but she missed it, and I left her. I could not stop; and God knows what became of her. Two of the yeomanry were next in our way, and I expected a broken head having laurel [the sign of leadership] in my hat, but one was striking on one side, and the other on the other, and at that moment, I stepped betwixt them and escaped.

Peterloo occurred in 1819, in the deepest part of the post-war depression. The Radicals had advertised and arranged the processions and rally in defiance of the magistrate's ban. They were determined to demonstrate the strength of popular support for Parliamentary Reform, and possibly to choose for unrepresented Manchester a 'legislatorial attorney' such as Birmingham had appointed two or three weeks earlier. But the authorities, fed on reports of hidden arms and of cottagers drilling in Pennine valleys, were fearful that such a large gathering—estimates vary from less than 60,000 to over 150,000—would get out of control and cause havoc in the narrow streets of Manchester. The magistrates, Lord Liverpool's Tory government, and most members of the opposition, all believed Parliamentary Reform to be the thin edge of a revolutionary wedge: to them, Radicals and Jacobins were hardly distinguishable.

But twenty years later, when Bamford began to write his account of Peterloo, the political atmosphere was very different. To be a moderate parliamentary reformer—and, in retrospect, that is what the Lancashire Radicals of 1819 then appeared to have been—was considered quite respectable. The left-wing agitators of 1839 and 1840 were the Chartists, whom Bamford strongly opposed, and, in Lancashire especially, the Anti-Corn-Law League, with which Bamford expressed sympathy but had not joined, was establishing itself as the new political dragon-slayer. In 1819

Bamford had been a marked man, whom the Lancashire establishment looked upon as a trouble-maker and rabble-rouser: by 1840, when the first parts of *Passages* were published, he was something of an establishment figure himself. From the end of the 1820s he had ceased to be regarded as an extremist; in 1839 he even enlisted as a special constable to help control the Chartist disorders. It was not so much that he changed his political views and moved to the right as that, during the 'twenties and 'thirties, public opinion moved further to the left. All his life Bamford claimed to be Radical in his political thought, but, like most men, as he grew older, he found himself less and less in sympathy with extremism.

In the last chapter of the original version of *Passages* published in 1842, he listed the political aims he still hoped to achieve—'a suffrage coextensive with direct taxation'; annual parliaments; cheap food, clothing and rents; 'cheap education for every one'; a 'vanity-shunning priesthood' and an 'open-handed aristocracy'. But, unlike 'the O'Connorites' or Chartists, he would not insist upon having all these things at once, but 'would take any part, and think well of it, and get the others as soon as I could'. He also warned his fellow reformers that nothing was permanent. However right it was to fight the Corn Laws, cheap bread would not put an end to social injustice, and Lancashire's manufacturers would be foolish to assume that they would always be 'spinners and weavers for the world; and if we could, I do not see that it is desirable we should'.

> We cannot, any more than we can still the ocean, prevent our manufactures from being set up in other nations. We have read them too profound a lesson for that. We have exhibited the spectacle of a small community combatting the world, and buying, or beating it all round. We have shown the secret of our strength, of all our warlike strength—and they will act upon it.

In his youth Bamford had earned his living in several different ways including warehouse-keeping, weaving, and sea-faring, but at the time of Peterloo he and his wife, Mima, were handloom weavers. When the police knocked him up in the early hours of 26 August 1819 to arrest

him, Bamford bade them enter the house but 'not soil the
silk work in the looms'. In *Early Days,* chronologically the
first volume of his autobiography but written second, he
describes a typical handloom weaver's cottage in Middleton:

> My uncle's domicile, like all others, consisted of one
> principal room called 'the house'; on the same floor with this
> was a loom-shop capable of containing four looms, and in the
> rear of the house on the same floor, were a small kitchen
> and a buttery. Over the house and loom-shop were chambers;
> and over the kitchen and buttery was another small apartment,
> and a flight of stairs. The whole of the rooms were lighted by
> windows of small square panes, framed in lead . . .

During the 1820s it became progressively harder for hand-
loom weavers to compete against the power looms, and
this pressure, combined with desire and ambition, eventually drove Bamford into journalism. Writing had attracted
him for many years. In 1817 he published a political
pamphlet, 'An Account of the Arrest and Imprisonment
of Samuel Bamford on suspicion of High Treason'. He was
taken to London and examined by Lord Sidmouth concerning the part he had played in a treasonable plot to
burn Manchester to the ground. Nothing could be proved
against him—indeed, Bamford maintained that he had dis-
couraged the plotters from the beginning—but the pamphlet, with its several insertions of 'rustic poetry', draws a
convincing and tolerant picture of the ordeal which Bamford endured. Just before Peterloo, Bamford published *The
Weaver Boy,* a very slim volume of verses, and two years
later, after his release from Lincoln gaol, a hundred-page
volume entitled *Miscellaneous Poetry.* Writing for the
London *Morning Herald* and the *Manchester Guardian,*
therefore, was to Bamford a congenial way of earning a
living. The many boisterous political meetings during the
months preceding the passing of the Reform Bill of 1832
kept him and his pen exceptionally busy, and gave him
useful practice and greater ability as a writer.

For reasons that are still obscure, Bamford ceased to be
a full-time journalist before the end of the 1830s. Apparently he returned to weaving for a short time, but in 1839
moved from Middleton to Blackley and began to earn a

living as an author. In imitation of Dickens and other
contemporaries, he arranged to publish his writing in
instalments. In 1843 he gathered together the instalments
he had already published, and produced the first edition
of *Passages*. The following year he brought out an enlarged
edition, in the extra four chapters of which he explains
why he wrote the book:

> During many years, it had often been impressed on my
> mind, that to write a narrative such as I have presented to
> the reader . . . was a duty plainly marked down for my perfor-
> mance . . . There were facts with which I alone was
> acquainted; truths which I alone could enunciate; faults which
> I had the disposition candidly to admit, and palliations on
> behalf of enemies, as well as of friends, which had never been
> made known; and if I—God having given me the power—left
> this thing undone, then I should pass out of life without
> having fulfilled my duty to my country . . .

He also used these additional chapters to quote and
comment upon the reviews which *Passages* had earned in
the press, and to print letters of approval which he had
received from such notables as Lord Francis Egerton, Lord
Lonsdale, and, above all, Lord Abinger, who as Mr. Scarlet
had presented the case for the prosecution at the trial of
the Radical leaders, including Bamford, after Peterloo.

Originally, Bamford had tried but failed to interest a
publisher in his *Passages* project. He then determined to
publish the work himself and, in November 1839, he had
500 copies of the first instalment printed. He sold them
among his friends and acquaintances. The second part
appeared in January 1840, and the others followed every
three or four weeks. Sales improved, so that in the summer
of 1840 he had to reprint the early parts and increase his
order for future instalments from 500 to 1200 copies.
Being author, binder, publisher and retailer all in one was
exacting, and, at times, wearisome. But it was also exhila-
rating. And, although the reader gains the impression that
nothing short of complete disaster would have deterred
Bamford, *Passages* brought him enough profit to encourage
him to go on writing. In 1844, he produced *Walks in South
Lancashire*, which is a miscellaneous collection of writings

as much concerned with reminiscence, political opinions and local stories as with topographical descriptions of town and countryside, and in 1848-9, he published in parts *Early Days,* in which he tells the story of his life up to the year 1813.

In *Early Days* Bamford is less concerned with politics than he is in *Passages,* but he seems constitutionally unable to avoid writing about political matters for long. His earliest recollections were of the stormy days of the 1790s, when the French Revolution and Tom Paine's *Rights of Man* inspired many British reformers, and caused Pitt's government to adopt a repressive policy. Middleton had 'a small band only of readers and enquirers after Truth' but they included young Samuel's father and uncle. The members of the group met in each other's houses to read political pamphlets and discuss Parliamentary Reform. From time to time they had to face abuse from thoughtless ruffians, who, ever ready for excitement, were easily goaded into rampaging through village after village on an anti-reform or anti-Painite spree. In April 1794, such a hostile crowd broke up a reform meeting in Royton with exceptional violence. They smashed windows, doors, and furniture, and looted houses and cellars. Arrests followed, but the local authorities treated the Reformers more harshly than 'the Church and King mob', who had attacked them. This incident—or, more likely, his parents' frequent re-telling of the story—made a deep impression upon six-year-old Samuel. It was his political baptism.

Among other matters of interest to the political historian, Bamford describes the naval press gangs in action, gives us details of the Luddite attack on the power looms of Messrs. Burton and Sons, Middleton, and tells us how he became a regular reader of Cobbett's *Political Register.* But most of the politics in the book appear in the form of political sermons: the views expressed, therefore, are those of Bamford in his maturity and not necessarily those he held in his youth. He follows the story of the Royton riot of 1794, for example, with a denunciation of the system of grand juries, and the account of a recruiting drive for 'the army of reserves' in the 'invasion days' of 1804 with a tirade against the dictatorial power of the magistrates. He uses an imaginary conversation between a weaver and his master as a means of stating his opinions concerning the ethics of buying and selling; expresses directly and dogmatically his views upon the bringing up of children, and several times warns the country and those in authority against the folly of not 'cultivating the masses', of underrating 'the horny hand and the dewy forehead':

> The hardest workers will always be the hardest and best fighters . . . Let us then cherish our workers. Let them be anxiously cared for—they are the strength and the defence of the country, and of every thing within it which is worth defending. Let them never have less than plenty of all comfortable requisites, whatever other class is stinted. Let them be accepted with respect, so long as that respect is merited. . . . Cherish then these elements of giant power for the sake of their inestimable results, which are the guarantees of untold blessing of all. Promote honest labour. Honour it wherever or however found.

This was one of Bamford's favourite themes. He had already developed it in *Walks in South Lancashire,* where he had reassured the doubters that English workers would never behave like a French mob. They had far too 'aristocratic a spirit' for that: 'they are as regularly stratified as are the rocks of our island'.

Bamford freely acknowledges that as a young man he was too fond of strong drink, and in his later years he acquired an undesirable reputation for occasional bouts of drunkenness. But words and phrases could intoxicate him too. As he looked back on his youth from his fifties, he tended to see the past in idealised form and to describe it in the vocabulary of romantic fiction. Admittedly in his generation the steam-engines had polluted and transformed much of South Lancashire. Without too much exaggeration he spoke of 'the green banks of the Irk' between which in his boyhood the stream 'like crystal rippled and dimpled'. Justifiably he deplored the cutting down of trees in 'all the cloughs and hollows in the neighbourhood of Middleton', and lovingly described the area to the north of

Manchester 'before the hill-streams were poisoned dye-vats, and the valleys were studded with smoke funnels'. But, as his hero Cobbett tended to do, Bamford painted the pre-industrial picture in colours too rosy and flattering to be true. At Lower Broughton, for example, he recalled 'six or eight small farm houses, many of them with low thatched roofs, and peeping out with cowsheds and barns from amidst gardens and orchards—trailing shrubs festooning the clear blinking windows and climbing rose bushes garlanding the quaint old gables'. This picture postcard hamlet which his words created caused him to forget, or at least fail to describe, how hard life undoubtedly was in 'these plenteous little steadings'. His enthusiasm for the past led him to think that in contrast with Victorian times 'gentlemen then lived as they ought to live . . . in kindliness with their tenants, in open-handed charity towards the poor', and that relations between masters and men had 'greatly altered for the worse since the days which could be spoken of from remembrance'. It even persuaded him that there was more merit in eating a 'mess-pot of water-porridge' scooped 'from a brown earthen dish placed on a low beaufet near the middle of the floor' than in the manners 'which now prevail around fashionable boards, where, if a person cannot, or will not, both gabble and gobble at the same time, he is looked upon as vulgar'. In Bamford's remembrance, oaten cakes, barm dumplings, and drink porridge became delectable dishes; in reality, they had been the staple foods of his childhood simply because working-class families could afford nothing better.

For the general reader as well as the historian, the most interesting parts of *Early Days* are those where the author makes no attempt to justify and convince but is content to describe and relate. Such stories as the tragedy of Ailse o' Bharla's soldier lover and the comedy of Richard Hall, who 'tasted' a roast duck so comprehensively that he left nothing but the pickings for his guest, were obviously among the yarns that were often repeated in the Bamford family circle or when a group of Middleton neighbours sat together in the evenings. Doubtless, like all such tales, they became trim and smooth with much telling. The portrait of Jeffrey Battersby, Samuel's maternal grandfather who had supported the Jacobites in 1745, is particularly well drawn, but of more general local interest are Bamford's descriptions of Middleton customs, especially the annual rushbearing ceremony and the week of intemperance which followed, his stories about people's fear of 'boggarts, fyerin, witches, fairees, clap-cans, and such like beings of terror', and the topographical details he gives about Middleton and Manchester at the end of the 18th century. Among other places no longer standing or visible, he remembered Middleton Hall 'built of plaster and frame works, with panels, carvings, and massy beams of black oak, strong enough for a mill floor', and the scanty remains of the Roman fort in Manchester—'a level plot of ground almost of a circular form . . . the centre of the plot was lower than the circuit, along which, here and there might be seen grey stones, and lumps of mortar'. By the time Bamford was writing *Early Days,* the cleared site of Middleton Hall had been 'let for the erection of a cotton-mill', and 'the small remains of the old "Mancastle", hoary in tradition of untold years', had disappeared under industrial development.

Of wider interest still are a number of incidental descriptions which form the background of the autobiographical story which Bamford is relating in *Early Days.* There are, for example, lively impressions of the workhouse at Strangeways, where Samuel's father was governor during the 1790s, of the Methodist Sunday School and Free Grammar School at Middleton, and of the lower school of Manchester Grammar School, all three of which Samuel attended for short periods. In a single paragraph he perpetuates the atmosphere of that small Methodist schoolroom crowded with scholars on Sunday mornings, 'girls in the gallery above, and boys below', with desks ranged round the sides for the writers, and reading groups standing and intoning their lesson in the middle of the floor. He destroys any illusions about the academic superiority of the nearby grammar school with the stark statement that he did 'not recollect that the rudiments of the classics were at that time taught to anyone', and his picture of the lower school at Manchester, Dickensian in

style, can only make every 20th-century schoolboy
thankful that he had not to endure such monotonous and
unimaginitive instruction. But probably the most enter-
taining period piece is the story of Bamford's wedding at
'the Old Church', or Manchester Cathedral as it is now.
The great day began badly, for Samuel mistook the time
by one hour and was late for his appointment with the
bridal party at Harpurhey. Then, in the middle of the
service, at which half a dozen couples were married,
Samuel and the priest had a private row about the ring,
which refused to go over the joint of Mima's finger:

> 'Let the ring go over', he said. 'It can't go further', I replied,
> 'her finger is swelled'. 'It can go further, and it shall go
> further', said the irritable little being, and I, almost as irritable,
> said quickly, 'It shant go further'. 'Oh! very well', then ob-
> served he, 'stand down, you are not man and wife until I
> have bestowed the benediction'.

But Samuel and Mima knelt with the other couples for the
benediction, and thus entered upon their happy married
life.

Several of Bamford's descriptions concern the textile
trade. Not only do we see the members of a weaver's
family busily engaged in their cottage with their allotted
tasks, but we also help the weaver stuff the finished work
into his 'poke' or 'bearing home wallet' and carry the heavy
load to the warehouse in Manchester. After he has
collected his pay at 'the counting-house' and lunched on
'bread and cheese or cold meat and bread with ale' at the
public house, we return with him to Middleton by way of
The Queen Anne in Long Millgate, The Flower Pot on Red
Bank, and either The White or The Golden Lion at Blackley. We share the twelve-hour activity of a Manchester
warehouse on market day, and we hear of success stories,
such as that of the bleacher, Hulme, who came from
Belmont, near Bolton.

> He first came round with a one-horse cart collecting calicoes,
> and as he was a steady industrious man, he got on fast and
> his employment increased. He next appeared in the street
> with a cart drawn by two stout horses; soon after he had a
> waggon, and in a short time he had as many waggons as his

business required, with men to drive them and collect pieces
for him.

Bamford claimed that when Hulme had been 'striving for
a living with his horse and cart' he had 'put thousands of
pieces in his way'. But when Hulme became rich, 'he just
condescended to let me know that he remembered having
seen me before; and he seemed to think that was quite
sufficient'.

For his autobiographical books Bamford said he relied
upon 'a tolerable good memory assisted by some ineffaceable impressions'. He does not mention using diaries,
although in later years, 1858-61, he kept a diary which is
preserved in manuscript in Manchester Public Library.
No doubt Peterloo and its immediate consequences stood
out as the most vivid of the 'ineffaceable impressions', and
as Thomas Carlyle wrote to Bamford in a letter quoted
by Dr. W. H. Chaloner in his introduction to the 1967
edition of *Early Days,* 'All men are interested in any
man if he will speak the facts of his life for them, *his*
authentic experience, which corresponds, as face with face,
to that of all other sons of Adam'. Yet it has to be admitted
that the longer the time between event and narration, the
more likely it is that even 'ineffaceable impressions' become
blurred or acquire significance and meaning that they
did not have originally. Dr. Chaloner has already drawn
attention to the difference between Bamford's account of
his first arrest in 1817 and 'the somewhat tailored account'
of the same events published over twenty years later in
Passages, and we have always to keep in mind that
Bamford's overriding need was to entertain his readers so
that he could continue selling his work.

This does not mean, however, that Bamford's books are
useless as historical records, any more than the Gospels
are not to be trusted because they were written a generation after the events they describe. *Early Days* and *Passages*
have a different kind of value from that possessed by a
diary or a collection of contemporary letters. Bamford
purposefully set out to convey to his readers his impressions of the people, events, and quality of life of days
gone by. He took pains to choose the most appropriate

words, polish his phrases, revise his sentences, and create as good a literary work as he could. The result is, of course, a very subjective picture: all the events have been chosen and described by the author who experienced and witnessed them. A couple of Bamford's diaries or a bundle of his contemporary letters would have been less contrived and would have conveyed a more immediate impression, but to make them historically meaningful either the historian or the reader would have had to evaluate their contents and select from them those facts which appeared to him to be most significant. And because no historian or reader is without partiality or bias of some kind, it is beyond human skill to write completely objectively. Objective history would probably be dull stuff anyway, and the outstanding merit of such history as Bamford wrote is that it is entertaining to read.

John Rushton's *Autobiography* is a slender work compared with Samuel Bamford's two volumes. Rushton wrote it in 1908 in his 76th year. His first attempt, written in a school exercise book, apparently did not satisfy him, so he tried again and almost filled a second exercise book with reminiscences chiefly of the 1830s and 1840s when he was a boy and youth. Both versions are straightforward accounts of people, events, and social conditions as he remembered them. They were not written for publication, but simply to satisfy himself and interest his descendants.

Unlike Bamford, Rushton did not romanticise the past. Remembrance of his early years was clear enough for him to recognise that in most ways life in Worsley and district had improved considerably by the beginning of the 20th century. Yet he never bemoans that he had the ill-luck to be born in 1833. He gives the impression that he had enjoyed his life, however much he recognised that South Lancashire had much more to offer lads of his class born after Victoria's reign than it had offered him and his friends, who were born a few years before Victoria came to the throne.

Rushton's two exercise books have three main interests —details of topographical changes in the Worsley and Walkden areas; facilities for education in that district in early Victorian days, and mining conditions during the middle years of the 19th century. To appreciate the topographical changes, it is necessary either to know the district intimately or to be armed with copies of the first and subsequent editions of the appropriate sheets of the ordnance survey map. And the bigger the scale the better, for the author makes no concessions to the comparative stranger! He lists the inns, houses, smithies, and other buildings that had been pulled down in his life time, speaks of the encroachment of house-building on the countryside, praises the changes that had put Worsley 'in the front rank of places worthy of a visit by tourists, picnic parties and pleasure excursionists', and comments upon the one-time primitive state of several local roads, which by the beginning of the 20th century had become main thoroughfares.

> The roads in my youth were in wretched condition. The Manchester Rd., Bolton, and Shaving Lanes were paved with cobbles. They did not seem to have any special construction or level, but [were] made just as the ground varied in level. From Howarth's Smithy to opposite the Church it descended as into a trough or valley when it began to rise until the top of Shaving Lane was reached. It was an awful time in Winter for the poor horses. Where a carter was in charge of two horses and two carts, it was usual for him to take one horse out of one of the carts and, by means of chains hooked to the shafts, this horse assisted the other in drawing the cart up the steep hill, after which he unharnessed and went for the other cart in like manner . . . The names of those great road-makers Telford and Macadam were unknown in Walkden in those days, and it was only at the close of the last century and during the present that Macadam's methods have been fully adopted. During the last half century, things have gradually and wonderfully improved.

No doubt old men living in other parts of industrial Lancashire in the first years of this century had similar observations to make about the roads in their home district. Probably too their recollections of schooldays were similar to John Rushton's, although Worsley had the advantage that the Countess of Ellesmere was interested in the welfare of the villagers. Her husband, Lord Francis

Egerton, succeeded to the Bridgewater estates in 1833.
Shortly afterwards he moved to Worsley, and he and his
wife set about improving what Lord Francis called 'the
religious and educational destitution' of the whole area.
Rushton tells us that in 1838 he was one of the children,
who attended the new infants' school which the Countess,
or Lady Egerton as she still was until 1846, had opened
in the nave of 'Walkden chapel', which she and her husband
had just had built. Next year, the Egertons opened a
purpose-built school room, but this was too small almost
immediately. The overflow of children had to be taught
in the Bull's Head Inn, until in 1844 the Egertons provided
yet another school building. Rushton remembers his
teachers—Susannah Cooke the local girl; James Mc.Leod
the patient Scot; William Crawford irritable and violent;
Henry Norris the veteran soldier who drilled the boys; and
the musical Ezekiel Wilkinson, who 'taught Hullah's
system of music, which he illustrated by large sheets
progressively arranged'. Lady Francis encouraged Wilkinson
by occasionally calling in the school to hear his pupils
sing. But the main teaching was in the Three Rs, and
Wilkinson used the traditional method of class-placings,
which Bamford had enjoyed or endured in the Lower
School at Manchester.

> Every branch [of instruction] was competitive. The best
> [pupil] was at the top of the class, so long as he could keep
> it. Any failure in his lesson, if more correctly rendered by
> another, displaced him and his rival took his place. Absent
> without leave displaced one, though at the top, to the
> bottom. These were exciting times.

John's father died while John was still at school, so that
his family needed him to earn as soon as possible. He went
down the pit when he was thirteen. A little while later,
the Countess offered him a chance of becoming a pupil
teacher in the village school, but he could not take it.
The family so 'felt and appreciated' his small wages that,
even at so young an age, he could not afford even a
temporary reduction in pay. He continued as a collier.
But, in 1868, his last year in the mine, he helped to
found a Mutual Improvement Class among the people who

attended St. Paul's Sunday School. The Class devoted half
its time to group-reading of 'the classics'; its first choice was
the works of William Cowper, so no doubt in rehearsal
ardent students proclaimed John Gilpin's fame in many a
Walkden kitchen that year. The other half of its time the
Class gave to papers written and read by members. The
papers Rushton best remembered were all concerned with
the speakers' daily work. He himself spoke on 'Gas in Coal
Mines' and obviously, forty years later, was still proud of
what he had written and said. He had preserved—and
quoted in full the short report which the *Farnworth
Weekly Observer* published of that meeting. Unfortunately,
the Class did not last long. Members dropped out partly
because they could not bear criticisms of their read-
ings, and partly, one suspects, because the prospect of
having to write and then read a paper frightened them to
death.

The section of Rushton's *Autobiography* which will
interest most readers is that in which he describes mining
conditions when he first began to work underground. The
Mines Act of 1842 had recently prohibited the employment of women and girls in the mines—in the Worsley
area many of the displaced women took up the doomed
trade of hand-loom weaving—but it still allowed boys
over ten years of age to drag tubs from the coal face to the
bottom of the shaft. Young John first worked with his
uncle in the Cinder Field mine off what is now Manchester
Road, Walkden. He climbed into 'the basket'—in reality an
iron-shod wooden tub—and once the signal was given, the
beam engine rattled him down the narrow shaft into the
'appalling' darkness below. From the bottom of the shaft,
he crouched his way through the tunnel and along the
'upbrow' which led to his allotted place at the coal face.
His uncle tested for gas and then began digging out the
coal; John shovelled the coal into the waiting basket. When
his uncle had cut sufficient coal for the day, he buckled on
belt and chain and drew

> the basket filled with coal, I myself pushing with all my might
> behind. When two baskets had been filled and drawn they
> were placed on a sledge and pushed along to the pit shaft.

Empty tubs having been procured we proceeded again to the
working place, filled again and continued in like manner until
the number of tubs for the day's work was accomplished.

Rushton describes the sledge—a low, four-wheeled waggon
fitted at each end with 'curved iron stays' to prevent the
tubs from falling off. The miners pushed the sledges along
'a tramway of angle iron'; 'the wheels were low, flat and of
thin edge and were called pancake wheels', but despite the
low centre of gravity the bad state of the track made it
necessary for the waggoner constantly to watch that the
baskets were not jolted off the sledge.

George Birkbeck, a Scot, improved matters when he
became underlooker. He sank a new shaft, fitted it with
cages instead of baskets, replaced hemp ropes with wire
ropes, and powered the winding gear with a bigger engine.
Down below he increased the height of the passage-ways
from the bottom of the shaft to the coal face. He replaced
baskets and sledges with 'corves or box-waggons', each of
which held six hundredweights of coal, and he took ponies
into the pit to pull corves along the tramways. Rushton
cannot praise his work too much: 'were there any saint
worthy of the patronage of the collier lads of Worsley and
adjacent townships it would be St. George of the North'.

The behaviour of gas in coal mines seems to have
fascinated Rushton. Like every collier he respected its
potential as a killer. He was strict in his precautions, yet
he remembered with awe how 'terribly grand' it was 'to see
the flames roll along the roof of the working level', and
sixty years later, he still shuddered to think what risks
colliers habitually ran in his earlier years in the pit:

> . . . our getters worked with candles, although we, the
> drawers used lamps. . . . one of our men, observing his candle,
> noticed the presence of gas. He immediately cried out, 'Candles
> out, gas is upon us' as loudly as possible, which was heard by
> the other men and instantly obeyed. With all possible haste
> we secured our clothing and not waiting to dress hurried to the
> shaft in darkness, candles and lamps extinguished.

The fear of losing wages led to desperate devices to disperse
the gas as quickly as possible. Rushton mentions 'brattic-
ing'—'a system of directing the air by means of boards'—

and batting the air with jackets 'to drive out the gas and make way for fresh air to enter', and he describes the danger of accidentally setting fire to an accumulation of gas above a working place by raising a candle or lamp too high:

> Another time, when drawing, along with another youth, for a man named William Taylor . . . the working place was an upbrow or narrow bay about 240 yards from the pit shaft, and about 4 ranks or 80 yards up to the working face. . . . our master returned to the face to re-commence work, having left it for a few minutes to get dinner. In a playful mood he was getting hold of me as if to wrestle, when on lifting his candle upwards, a sharp explosion took place. It was a mere flash but sufficient to cause a shock and a smarting as if he had received a stroke from a birch rod. As for me, I threw myself down on the floor alongside of my basket . . . On recovering our position, he [the master or getter] enquired if I had escaped. 'Yes I got none of it', I replied. He asked me if I perceived any skin burnt or singed. I said it had singed his hair a little and there was a slight redness along his back. He said he smarted dreadfully. He did not commence work again for that day. . . .

It was a happy release for John Rushton when he was able to leave mining. In 1869 he was appointed a porter in the office of the Bridgewater Company, and he stayed there until he was pensioned off at the age of seventy. As far as he was able, he played a helpful part in local activities. For many years he was a prominent member of the local lodge of the Ancient Order of Foresters. He helped to found St. Paul's Sick and Burial Society, and in 1908 claimed to be 'the only surviving member of the Walkden and Little Hulton Burial Society'. Before the days of National Health Insurance such societies solved many a working-class family's financial problems. For twenty years, he served as a deacon of Walkden Congregational Church, and in middle age he frequently contributed articles to the local papers. Had he been able as a boy to take advantage of Lady Ellesmere's offer to train as a teacher, it is possible that today he would be as well known as Samuel Bamford as a Lancashire author.

TWO 19TH-CENTURY DIARIES KEPT BY JOHN O'NEIL, A WEAVER FROM CLITHEROE, AND WILLIAM FISHER, A LOW FURNESS YEOMAN FARMER

[The middle third of O'Neil's Diary, *covering the years 1860-64, has been edited by R. S. France and published by the Historic Society of Lancashire and Cheshire, Vol. 105, under the title* The Diary of John Ward. *The other two thirds, covering 1856-60 and 1872-75, have not yet been published. The owners, Mr. R. and Mr. H. Davies, have kindly deposited the manuscripts in the Lancashire Record Office.*

Mary Brigg has published Life in East Lancashire, 1856-60: a newly discovered Diary of John O'Neil (John Ward), Weaver, of Clitheroe *in Vol. 120 of the Transactions of the Historic Society, and Owen Ashmore has written a two-part article,* The Diary of James Garnett of Low Moor, Clitheroe, 1858-65 *(Historic Society, Vols. 121 and 123), which enriches our knowledge of O'Neil's social and industrial background. Mr. Ashmore's* Low Moor, Clitheroe: a nineteenth-century factory community, *published in Vols. 73 and 74 of the Transactions of the Lancashire and Cheshire Antiquarian Society, is equally informative about the mill where O'Neil worked. These three articles have completed the partial picture of O'Neil revealed in his* Diary.

William Fisher's Diary *has not been published, but with the kind co-operation of the owner, Mr. R. Rowlandson of Ulverston, a duplicated copy is available to readers in Barrow Public Library. William Rollinson has written* The Diary and Farm Accounts of William Fisher, a Low Furness yeoman farmer, 1811-59. *This is published in Vol. 66 of the Transactions of the Cumberland and Westmorland Antiquarian and Archaeological Society.]*

Samuel Bamford would have expected his writings to be included in such a Lancashire miscellany as this, and would have been quite caustic if they had been omitted. But John O'Neil would have been astonished to find that his daily jottings interested anyone but himself, and that he was as well known today as he was in his lifetime. On New Years Day 1872 he began a new volume of his *Diary* with the comment, 'I have got this book on purpose to note down anything that may occur during the year as far as lies in my power'. He did just that—nothing less and nothing more—throughout the three diary volumes that have survived. At the end of each day, or during some months at the end of each week, he wrote a brief account of what had affected or interested him in his restricted world at Low Moor, near Clitheroe. He never attempted to revise: his entries constitute a true diary, untarnished by hindsight and free of literary aspirations.

A number of people have had a hand in discovering and identifying O'Neil's *Diary*. In 1947 an unknown labourer rescued the first volume from being shovelled into the destructor at Clitheroe. He passed it on to Arthur Langshaw, the local historian, who deposited it for safe keeping in the Lancashire Record Office. The county archivist, R. Sharpe France, thought so highly of the *Diary's* historical value that he immediately made a copy of it, and in 1954 published an edited version in Volume 105 of the *Transactions of the Historic Society of Lancashire and Cheshire*. The *Diary* had no author's name on it, but beginning from the entry of 4 January 1862—'My daughter was married today at the old church in Clitheroe' —Mr. France discovered that the diarist's name must be John Ward. Consequently, it was published under the title of *The Diary of John Ward of Clitheroe, Weaver, 1860-64*. It gained a lot of attention, not least because it covered the years of the Lancashire Cotton Famine.

In December 1966, Reginald Davies of Clitheroe sent Mary Brigg a similar diary covering the period January 1856 to February 1860. This was a surprise result of Mrs. Brigg drawing *John Ward* to the attention of her adult classes in Blackburn and district. There was no doubt that the 'new' diary was an earlier volume of *John Ward,* but by carefully following fresh clues Mrs. Brigg revealed that *Ward* was wrong. The diarist's name was O'Neil. 'Jane Ward' had indeed married Bernard Knowles on 4 January 1862, but the Roman Catholic register at Carlisle shows that in 1836 she was baptised 'Jane, daughter of Margaret Ward and John O'Neil'. This is a

real mystery and not one of the many skeletons that crowd
the cupboards of respectable Victorian families. Although
the census returns of 1841 list John O'Neil—but no
Margaret or Jane—as a member of his mother's household,
yet Margaret, who died in 1855, was buried as Margaret
O'Neil. The record of the wedding between John and
Margaret has not yet been found—it could be in the
Manchester area as likely as not—but there is no doubt
that they were man and wife and that Jane's name was
Jane O'Neil. Mr. Davies and his brother Harry are great-
grandsons of John O'Neil, and the 1856-60 diary, together
with a third volume covering the years January 1872 to
May 1875, they have kindly deposited alongside the
original *John Ward's Diary* in the Lancashire Record
Office.

Meantime, Owen Ashmore of Manchester University
was studying another Low Moor diary of the same period.
This had been kept by James Garnett, the younger son of
Thomas, who in 1858 became head of Thomas Garnett
and Sons, cotton manufacturers, the very firm for which
O'Neil worked as a weaver. Before 1858 Thomas had
managed Low Moor Mill for his uncle, Jeremiah Garnett.
The deaths of Jeremiah and his only son left Thomas in
complete command, and in May 1858 he brought his two
sons, William and James, into the new partnership. To
O'Neil, then aged 47, James, aged 29, thus became one
of 'the young masters'.

From 1858 to 1865 the two diaries make it possible
to compare two accounts of the same local events, and
see them through the eyes first of a manager and then
of a worker on the shop floor. Both diarists always comment on the weather: the one supports the other about
such things as severe frosts, exceptional periods of drought
or heavy rainfall, and dark, gloomy skies which made it
necessary to keep the mill's gas-lighting on all day. They
both tell us when the Ribble was too low or too full to
turn the mill-wheel properly, and when, in consequence, it
was necessary to cease spinning and weaving for a time.
But naturally enough they do not take the same view of
industrial disputes. In January and February 1860, for

example, O'Neil wrote exceptionally long daily entries about the strike and negotiations to increase wages at Low Moor. The weavers brought the union secretary, Abraham Pinder, to speak for them, and after a few days 'struggle' they reached agreement with the employers. O'Neil recorded that all the weavers 'seemed to be very well pleased' with the increase of 'one halfpenny per cut', but a fortnight later, James Garnett was complaining that everybody was 'clamouring for an advance of wages and even then dissatisfied', and that 'the insubordination of work people is now beyond all bounds'. At the end of that year, both men were reasonably happy with the results of the year's work. O'Neil considered that 'if I am anything changed it is for the better', for he and his daughter had 'better clothes, better furniture and better bedding': with 'good health and plenty of work we will do well enough'. Garnett confessed that despite some moderate increase of wages, 'trade on the whole has been pretty good', but he was troubled about the 'hands', who, because trade had been brisk had been 'almost unmanageable'.

During the next year, 1861, cotton suffered a very severe blow. War between the northern and southern states in U.S.A. began in April. By midsummer the North's blockade of the southern ports was becoming effective, and rapidly stocks of raw cotton in Lancashire began to dwindle. In 1860 the masters had feared a glut with consequent falling prices: at the end of 1861 they faced increasing shortages and the inevitability of rising prices. O'Neil's *Diary* traces the progress of the creeping paralysis:

31 August (1861). . . . We got notice at our mill this morning to run four days per week until further notice . . .

12 September [Thursday]. We are stopped again for this week . . .

27 September [Friday]. We had a stop this afternoon for want of weft and not start again till Monday . . .

30 September [Monday]. . . . We commenced work at half past seven this morning and gave over at five this afternoon, and stop an hour for dinner, to be the same all week until Friday, when we stop at four o'clock and does not start again till Monday.

16 November. . . . There is great distress all through the manu-

facturing districts; they are all running short time through the
scarcity of cotton.

1 January (1862). We are beginning the New Year under very poor
prospects. Bad trade, short time, and a prospect of war with
America, which, if it should take place, will be worse than
ever, as we will get no cotton from it . . .

8 January. . . . owing to the scarcity of cotton we are working such
rubbish [Surat cotton] as I never saw in my life. We cannot
do the half work that we used to do.

17 January. Dark weather, bad yarn and short time answers very
badly. A great number of weavers have given up their odd
looms, as they cannot keep it on, the yarn is so bad.*

During these same months James Garnett's chief worries
were constantly rising prices and increasingly short supplies of American cotton. By the autumn of 1861 his
family was buying Surat or Indian cotton to eke out the
insufficient American supplies. Each month the percentage
of Surat increased, and since it was dirty and much shorter
in staple than the American cotton, it pleased neither masters, workmen, nor customers. In such circumstances the
masters felt it necessary to cut expenses by reducing both
wage-rates and hours of work. As early as the autumn of
1861, Garnett admitted that a strike against reduced
wages would play into their hands 'as it would suit us very
well to stop altogether'. In the winters of 1862-63 and
1863-64, Low Moor Mill, like most Lancashire mills,
worked very short hours indeed, and many of their workmen were idle for weeks on end.

The Garnetts were not indifferent to the suffering caused
by unemployment. They contributed to relief funds, and
in imitation of similar schemes in other cotton towns,
opened a sewing school for girls. They were probably more
considerate employers than most, but James Garnett obviously felt that there were serious dangers in relief schemes.
He wrote of 'large grants' and 'enormous sums' given to
relieve the plight of out-of-work operatives, and feared
their effect upon the future morale of cotton workers.
He was convinced that many unemployed preferred 'relief
to working' and spoke scornfully of those who 'played'

*O'Neil uses very little punctuation in his *Diary*, so for the sake of
clarity I have followed R. S. France's precedent and inserted some.
The spelling is O'Neil's.

instead of 'working Surat'. Garnett could never have numbered O'Neil among his 'careless idle weavers'. Idleness and poverty so depressed O'Neil that he had not the heart to keep his *Diary* from June 1862 to April 1864. When he did take up his pen again, he put on record that during the winter of 1863-64 the relief committee had allowed him 3s. 0d. a week 'which barely kept me alive', and that, working with Surat cotton, he had 'not earned a shilling a day this last month and there are many like me'. In these dire days he had seen one of his own prophecies fulfilled. In June 1856 the newspapers had talked about possible war between Britain and U.S.A. O'Neil had been excited and jingoistic enough to think that Britain could give 'the Yankees' 'a good thrashing', but he recognised that 'the consequences would be disastrous to both nations. The cotton trade would be stopped altogether in this country, and the Americans would get nothing exported from their country'. Fortunately, Britain did not go to war with America either then or in the 1860s, but the curtailment of exports from the southern states had the calamitous effect upon the cotton industry that O'Neil had foreseen.

The independent researches of Mrs. Brigg and Mr. Ashmore proved mutually helpful. Together they revealed sufficient information to outline O'Neil's career and sketch an adequate background to his life in Low Moor. John O'Neil was born in Carlisle in 1810. According to his *Diary* he 'lived many years as a boy and young man' in Hyde and Newton Moor to the south-east of Manchester, but it appears that he spent most of his early years in his native city. He first earned his living as a hand-loom weaver, but an inborn intellectual curiosity led him to become far better educated than most of his fellow weavers. At 18 years of age, he was using his spare time teaching weavers' children how to read and write, and by the time he was 40 he was prominent among the Liberals in Carlisle and was secretary of a Working Men's Reading Room. Unfortunately for him and his many friends, the increasing difficulty of making a living by hand-loom weaving eventually compelled him, in June 1854, to sell 'some

books and other little things' and go 'on tramp' looking
for work. He found it in Bentham, Yorkshire, weaving
linen on power looms. He sent for 'the wife and daughter',
but he was soon in difficulties again. The outbreak of the
Crimean War made trade very slack, the winter proved
unusually hard, and in February 1855 his wife, Margaret,
died. Before the end of that month, O'Neil and Jane left
Bentham, and found new work at Low Moor Mill. They
set up house in one of the mill cottages, 15 St. Ann's
Square, and John lived there for the rest of his life. He died
in August 1876, within a few days of his 66th birthday
and about fifteen months after making the last extant
entry in his *Diary*.

O'Neil's *Diary* can be quarried for a variety of historical
facts. Any meteorologist interested in weather patterns
will find the daily comments on weather invaluable: a
cursory reading quickly demolishes the widely-held theory
that Lancashire weather was more reliable and 'seasonable'
before atomic bombs, aircraft, and moon rockets began
'interfering with Nature'. In a similar way, O'Neil's
frequent comments on the many murders and robberies
reported in the press show that previous generations as well
as our own suffered from lawlessness and in exasperation
wondered 'what we should come to'. Mr. Ashmore found
the *Diary* most useful when writing the industrial history of
Low Moor, and both he and Mrs. Brigg used O'Neil's
evidence as a foundation on which to build their accounts
of trade union activity in North-east Lancashire in the
mid-19th century.

O'Neil was a second Bamford in that his ability to
read and to 'calculate', together with his reputation for
being well informed, made him a natural leader among
his fellow weavers. He joined the Clitheroe Power-loom
Weavers' Union in February 1859. He did not attend his
first meeting until September, but by the following January
he was deeply involved in union activity. On 19 January
1860 the Low Moor weavers 'turned against the stuff that
they are using for dressing with. It is a mixture of soda
and sand and something else which is very injurious to
health'. The next day they sent a deputation 'to wait upon

the Masters'. O'Neil was one of the deputies, and on 23 January the weavers appointed him their leader. For the next two years—years of acute industrial unrest and trade union activity—O'Neil spent most of his spare time on union business. His activities brought him no material gain and cost him much patient labour. As early as April 1860, he experienced how pig-headed and unthinking some of his fellow workers could be. The Low Moor weavers had set the Blackburn standard list of payments as their goal. O'Neil and Pinder negotiated a different, but overall more generous, list. The weavers rejected this and 'by a large majority carried the Blackburn standard list'. Naturally, Thomas Garnett did not complain, and next day the weavers realised what they had done. 'They feel disappointed', wrote O'Neil, 'and I am not sorry for it'.

By this time, April 1860, O'Neil was so enmeshed in union affairs that, angry though he might be, he could not easily resign. Leading the Low Moor weavers to the reasonably satisfactory settlement of January 1860 had brought him into local prominence. On 23 February, the Clitheroe weavers had appointed him treasurer of a fund 'to enable us to remove any family of weavers who wishes to go away and have not the means', and on 4 April 1860 they had elected him president for the year ahead. This 'very high honour', as O'Neil regarded it, entailed ceaseless activity, because it meant taking charge of the Clitheroe weavers, and also representing Clitheroe on the executive committee of the East Lancashire Association of Power-loom Workers, which was endeavouring to co-ordinate the work of the local weavers' unions. Unions which were at work pledged themselves to help unions that were on strike. Members usually contributed 2d. a loom. Every week union officials collected the cash and sent it to be distributed among the strikers. In this way, each Low Moor striker had received 7s. 0d. during their short strike of January 1860.

Hardly had O'Neil become their president than the Clitheroe weavers were called upon to contribute to a strike fund to support the Bolton weavers, but they were soon having to sustain a far more serious strike. The

executive committee of the East Lancashire Association
instructed the Colne weavers to give notice that they
would strike if the masters continued to refuse to pay the
Blackburn rate of wages. The Colne masters stuck to their
argument that 'local disadvantages' prevented them from
paying Blackburn wages, and so, on the expiration of their
notice, the weavers walked out.

The Colne strike lasted eleven months. The weavers
could never have defied the masters so long had not other
local weavers' unions faithfully sent them weekly dona-
tions. O'Neil acted as secretary of the strike committee
at Clitheroe. He posted a weekly report to Colne, and
almost every week put down in his *Diary* the sum of
money collected. At first it varied between £26 and £28,
but in the winter, when Clitheroe weavers were on short
time, it sometimes fell as low as £20. A couple of delegates
took this money to Colne each Sunday. O'Neil went at
least nine times. He describes how he got up no later than
5 a.m., met his 'colleague' in Clitheroe, and walked cross-
country over the flanks of Pendle to Colne: 'it is 12 miles
to Colne and one of the worst roads I ever travelled in
my life, over mountain and moor, over bog and mire,
through byways and on highways'. O'Neil and the other
Clitheroe delegates travelled on foot to save expenses,
but on 8 October, after a particularly wet tramp the day
before, the committee resolved 'that there be no more
walking to Colne but that we go by railway on Saturday
nights for the future'.

From the beginning, delegates had returned from Colne
to Clitheroe by rail on the Sunday evening. It was a
roundabout route through Accrington and Blackburn.
Normally, it took two and a half hours, but was not
entirely free of hazards. The journey on 23 December
1860 developed into a most fatiguing ordeal: indeed,
nothing seemed to go right during the whole weekend.
Timetable alterations forced O'Neil to stay in Accrington
on the outward journey on the Saturday night. The meeting on Sunday proved particularly unpleasant: the committee felt impelled to dismiss the secretary because the
auditors' report 'showed a great deal of dishonesty' on

his part. The consequent long discussion threw O'Neil so late that he had to race for his train through thick snow. As it turned out, he could well have saved his breath, for the train was running ninety minutes late. It took another two hours to reach Blackburn, and by that time the Clitheroe connection had gone. The station master was no help at all: 'he only laughed at us and made game of us'. Eventually, the stranded travellers began to look for lodgings in Blackburn, but because one man 'was obliged to go home as he had his work to go to in the morning or lose it altogether', O'Neil volunteered to walk with him the dozen miles to Clitheroe:

> We set off and I never had such a journey in all my life. We got to Clitheroe at three o'clock in the morning and had to wade all the road nearly knee-deep in snow and one of the hardest and coldest frosts that ever I was out in. When I got home my shoes was frozen to my feet and I was a long time before I could get them off. My trowsers were frozen like two iron pipes. I got into bed as soon as I could. I was fairly done up.

By Boxing Day, O'Neil was busy trying to recover from the railway board compensation for those Clitheroe passengers who had been forced to stay overnight in Blackburn. On the advice of the Clitheroe station master, he wrote to the railway superintendent at Accrington, but unfortunately he does not record the outcome in his *Diary*.

The last three months of O'Neil's presidential year were the most strenuous of all. By the beginning of 1861 the fear of civil war in U.S.A. was already beginning to have a serious effect upon the cotton industry. As early as 24 January, three months before the war began, O'Neil wrote:

> Thawing all day and we have got a notice put up in our mill today giving us notice of a reduction of wages. It is upon account of the disturbances in America. The cotton market has risen on speculation that there will be no crop next year if civil war should happen in the United States.

The masters' first defensive action was to reduce wages. The unions accepted that hard times were ahead, but hoped to persuade employers to agree to work short-time instead of reducing piece rates. They were particularly anxious to maintain the principle that all East Lancashire weavers were paid the same rates, and so struggled against the masters re-introducing the argument of 'local advantages' as a means of compensating themselves for extra transport costs when their mills were at some distance from a main railway line or the nearest coal pit.

The conflict lasted all through February and March. The masters' notice expired on 20 February, and on the previous evening a mass meeting of weavers in Clitheroe offered 'to work four days a week at five per cent reduction', but determined 'not to go on full time without full price'. The employers refused the offer: they closed down their factories and locked the men out. Garnett's *Diary* shows that the cotton masters of North-east Lancashire were just as well organised as the local unions, and, of course, they had far bigger resources to help them live through the weeks of inaction. The Clitheroe weavers soon discovered that outside help was difficult to get because so many other local unions were locked out too. They sent delegates here and there to plead their cause: O'Neil went to Preston three times, and on 12 and 13 March and again a week later, he was in Haslingden, Great Harwood, and the little village of Henfield explaining why the Clitheroe weavers were on strike and asking for urgent help. He spoke to mass meetings, and attended several committee meetings.

The weavers' determination was strong, but the decisive argument was the impossibility of keeping their families for long on strike pay that averaged about 1s. 6d. per week. James Garnett was quite right when, on 21 March, he judged that the 'hands' were 'nearly at the end of the strike'. On 25 March the Clitheroe weavers accepted the principle of arbitration. Three days later they reluctantly agreed to the masters' terms that they should go back to work before the arbitrators met. The mills re-opened on Easter Monday, 1 April, and on 11 April the deadlocked arbitrators, three from each side, decided to call in the umpire, the incumbent of St. James's Church, Clitheroe. He upheld the employers' argument of 'local disadvantage', but did not see why the workmen should pay the whole of the extra cost. To the anger of the Garnetts and other Clitheroe employers he awarded the masters 1½ per cent. instead of the expected 5 per cent. A week later the Clitheroe weavers held their annual general meeting. They pressed O'Neil to accept office for a second time. After such an exhausting year it is not surprising that he insisted upon resigning the presidency, but he did agree to serve on the committee for a further six months.

Throughout his life O'Neil derived considerable pleasure from newspaper reading. He never records buying a paper, but before he joined the Liberal Club in January 1872 and was able to read the news in the club room, he spent many fascinating evenings in a corner of the Castle Inn, Clitheroe, with a glass of beer and the newspaper. He followed the progress of such events as the Indian Mutiny, the Austrian-Italian War of 1859, and the debate on the Ballot Bill in 1872 as avidly as a boy might follow the instalments of an adventure serial. The details of the campaign reports from America helped him temporarily to forget the despondency of the Cotton Famine years, and in 1872 and 1873, the long-drawn-out Tichborne trial, especially when it was concerned with the Stonyhurst evidence, added considerable excitement to his life. Occasionally O'Neil found the newspaper disappointing and uninteresting—'very little news' or, as in June 1873, 'the papers were all filled with the Shah's visit to London and Windsor but as I cared little about it I did not read it'. Usually, however, he found some item worthy to be devoured and later commented upon in his *Diary*. International affairs, party politics, the details of the *Alabama* claim and settlement, the prospects for gold diggers in Australia and emigrants sailing to New Zealand, descriptions of exhibitions or news of the royal family—all interested this self-educated man. He held his own opinions too. As a life-long Liberal he dutifully condemned most Tory policies and actions—in April 1872, for example, he 'thought nothing of Disraeli's speech' in the Free Trade Hall, Manchester, and he damned the Queen's speech with 'like all Tory speeches there is nothing in it for the benefit

of the working man'—but he was no 'Little Englander'.
Cobden might have worked miracles for the cotton
industry, but O'Neil did not agree with his disparaging
attitude towards the colonies. The newspaper reports of
the Indian Mutiny shocked and angered him, and he
registered no more disapproval of the cruel revenge taken
by the British army than he did of British gunboats bom-
barding defenceless Canton, simply because the Chinese
had sent Admiral Sir Michael Seymour 'nothing but
insolent replies' to his demands. Had O'Neil lived a
decade longer, the Conservatives' new enthusiasm for a
strong imperialist policy might have won them an unexpected voter in Clitheroe.

Newspapers and books provided vicarious satisfaction
for O'Neil's intellectual curiosity, but he also took full
advantage of his limited opportunities to enjoy new
experiences and to find out things for himself. When he
first arrived at Low Moor he began slowly to explore the
country round about. He had not much free time—fine
Sundays and Bank Holidays were all he could rely on—
but when he did manage to move outside the immediate
vicinity of Low Moor and Clitheroe, he usually put down
his impressions in his *Diary*. On 27 January 1856, for
example, 'Marmaduke Coates and me' spent a sunny winter
Sunday walking about 12 miles through Waddington and
Grindleton to Sawley and returning through Chatburn and
Clitheroe. The highlight of the walk was their inspection
of the ruins of Sawley Abbey;

> . . . it had been a fine plce in its time. There were several
> gravestones some of them with inscriptions on them, which
> was translated to us by the woman who has the care of it.
> We gave her twopence apiece.

In June 1856 and again in July 1857, O'Neil visited
Clitheroe Castle, then in private hands. He enjoyed viewing
the countryside through 'the large telescope' on 'the top
of the tower or keep', but his most impressive experience
of that kind was from Pendle:

> . . . there was a party there with a large telescope which we
> got looking through. We could very well see Twiston, Colne,

Sawley, and Gisburn with the naked eye, but when we looked
through the telescope we could [see] the people walking the
streets in all them places, and then we could see Skipton,
Long Preston, Giggleswick and Settle, and all the country
round. We staid about three hours on the hill . . .

O'Neil liked to visit towns that were new to him. Preston
attracted him—he particularly approved of St. Walbergh's
church: 'it is a very fine place, but not quite finished yet
[April 1857]'—but his first visit to Blackburn, in October
1856, disappointed him. He grudgingly admitted that the
market had a wider variety of goods than Clitheroe market
had, but goods were no cheaper unless you were buying in
bulk to sell again. And, for O'Neil, the only Blackburn
'building of any importance' was the new town hall.
Manchester, however, was quite another matter. He spent
a very full day there on Whit Tuesday 1859. He arrived
about 8.30 a.m., spent a couple of hours in the morning
watching his brother, Daniel, weaving—'they are all fancy
ginghams and Jacquard looms and as I had never seen any
before I was much interested in them'—and then visited
the museum in Peel Park. In the afternoon he took his
sister-in-law to hear 'a great fife and drum band contest'
at Belle Vue:

> . . . I am no judge of music so I could not tell which played
> best but the Royal Sovereign Mill of Preston got the head
> prize. We went all through the gardens. There was a great
> deal to be seen and it was very throng. There was about
> 12,000 persons in the place. . . .

He stayed at Belle Vue until 9 p.m., said goodbye to Dan
at Salford station, and got back to Clitheroe at 2.30 next
morning. On the Wednesday, also a holiday, he justifiably
'lay in bed nearly all forenoon'.

The *Diary* mentions two other day excursions that fall
little short of this Manchester trip as endurance tests. They
both occurred in 1872. On Whit Tuesday, a favourite day
for excursions, O'Neil visited Keswick for the first time
since 1840. He travelled by train, was there by 10 a.m.,
and back home again at midnight. He made an equally
early start on 21 July, to spend a day in Southport:

> . . . we left Clitheroe at 5 o'clock and got into Southport 10
> minutes before 7 in the morning. We spent a very pleasant
> day. The weather was all that could be desired. I had never
> been there before and I think it is the prettiest place I ever
> was in, such fine wide streets and so very clean. We left
> shortly after 8 o'clock and got home by 10, everything right
> and safe and everyone satisfied.

Despite such occasional treats, no one could say
that John O'Neil's life was an exciting one. His grandchildren's generation, and certainly the generation of their
children, would condemn it as too work-ridden, too near
the edge of real poverty, and too lacking in opportunities
for relaxation and pleasure. The Nine Hours Act came
into force on 1 January 1875, too late to give O'Neil much
benefit: it granted him, for the last twenty months of his
life, half an hour longer in bed every morning. Before 1875
O'Neil began work at 6 a.m. and finished at 6 p.m., with
breaks for breakfast and dinner. Necessity drove him to
work when he was too ill to go: in the early weeks of 1856
and again in January 1859, for example, he suffered from
acute neuralgia in his face and neck—*tic doloreux* was his
name for it—but he struggled to the factory more often
than he stayed at home. In December 1857 he dislocated
his shoulder. The doctor reduced the dislocation next day,
and left him 'laid up like an old invalid with only one arm
to do anything with'. Four days later, 'the Manager sent
me word that if I could not come to my work or find a
weaver to work for me, he would shop my looms'. O'Neil
protested, and promised to go to work on the following
Monday morning. He kept his promise despite his black-
and-blue painful arm:

> . . . had a very miserable day. I could only use one hand to
> start and stop the looms. I could not pull a cutt off and
> shuttling cops was very painfull all day. It was a very dark
> day and I got on very badly when I had any yarn to tie. I
> had to lift my hand over the healds with my right hand as it
> could not lift by itself . . .

O'Neil never mentions the wages he took home, but for
a sixty-hour week, working three looms, he probably earned
about 12s. 0d. before the Famine. Apart from the black

days of Surat cotton and short time, he expressed no
bitterness. Indeed, he considered he was not badly off,
but it is obvious that he and his daughter lived a Spartan
life. The *Diary's* obsession with the price of potatoes
indicates their staple diet: a 'Cumberland breakfast' of
bacon and egg was a rare enough treat to be sure of a
line or two at the end of the day. The purchase of a
new pair of boots or of 'a working waistcoat' was an
achievement worth singing about, and it required a
prolonged financial campaign to save sufficient cash for a
new suit. The O'Neil cottage, 'whitewashed and scoured'
every Spring, had the minimum of furniture, and, by
20th-century standards especially, little or no comfort.
In the winter O'Neil's chief problem was to keep warm,
even in bed. Just before Christmas 1856, he bought 'a pair
of very large blankets to be paid at a shilling a week'. One
evening in March 1858 he carried back from Clitheroe
'two sacks of chaff to fill a bed with and it gave me a
sweating to get it home', and he took every opportunity
to gather bundles of sticks for winter burning. But despite
all reasonable endeavours to keep the house warm, O'Neil
and Jane often shivered and ached with cold in their beds.
The relative warmth of the factory must have been welcome on many a dark, freezing morning. And yet John
O'Neil was appalled when he saw the poverty in which his
brother Dan was living in Pendleton. Dan had 'six lodgers
who pay very well', but he drank too heavily ever to have
money in his pocket. In Dan's wife's opinion, John was
'both decent and respectable and a credit to the family'.

Against such a drab background, simple delights such
as the Christmas tea-party at the Catholic church, a procession of friendly societies through the streets of
Clitheroe, 'the grand procession of the Sacred Host' during
the Corpus Christi service at Stonyhurst, and the visits
of the 'American circus' and the Agricultural Show shone
with welcome colour and brightness. And O'Neil's intelligence and imagination gave him a sense of occasion too.
He felt he was privileged, for example, to be in Blackburn
on 24 May 1858 when the foundation stone of the Infirmary was laid, and, during the summer of 1874, to watch

the progress of the railway being built from Chatburn to
Settle. He fully realised the political significance of the
election of Alderman Trapper, a Roman Catholic, as
mayor of Clitheroe in 1874, and of the bye-election at
Preston in September 1872, the first Lancashire parliamentary election held by secret ballot. He puckered his forehead at the irregularity which 'somehow or other' allowed
the Preston authorities 'to tell the state of the poll every
hour'. Astronomical phenomena fascinated him, and therefore he appreciated his luck to see the comet in 1858
and, on three or four occasions, to gaze at fine displays of
the Aurora Borealis, 'blood red' in December 1858 and
'very brilliant' a year later. Our own generation no doubt
feels that it has witnessed more memorable historic occasions than the firework celebrations that marked the end
of the Crimea War, and has enjoyed more technical
triumphs than the completion of the transatlantic telegraph
cable that O'Neil recorded in August 1858. We have little
to envy O'Neil for, but I for one would have liked to have
been with him at the 'grand tea-party' which the Clitheroe
Liberal Club arranged in October 1874, if only to see that
remarkable pioneer educationalist, Sir James Kay-Shuttle-
worth, take the chair, and hear the speech of Lord Fred-
erick Cavendish, who soon afterwards was assassinated in
Phoenix Park, Dublin. Even more than that, I would
willingly have walked with O'Neil from Low Moor to
Clitheroe on the cold night of 25 January 1875 to hear
Edwin Waugh read some of his poems and sketches.
O'Neil records, 'I was very well pleased with him'. I
wonder if Waugh's programme included 'Come, Mary,
Link thi Arm i' Mine' and 'The Pig and the Purse'. I hope
it did, for both in quite different ways would have given
John O'Neil cause to smile as he trudged back to his cold
and lonely home in St. Ann's Square, Low Moor.

One of the fascinations of diaries is that they reveal
more clearly than most documents the personality of the
author. The diarist need not express a single opinion or
write directly about himself, his interests, or his feelings;
his very choice of what news to include in his entries

helps the reader to assess him, and, however sparse, his record of what he is doing and where he is going helps to define the picture of the man and his particular world. William Fisher's *Diary* is not so eloquent a record as John O'Neil's, and is far from being so regularly kept. In some months Fisher contented himself with a single entry, or, occasionally, no entry at all. But he kept his *Diary* over a long span of years, 1811-59, and at least a sketch of his personality gradually emerges from its pages.

William Fisher lived all his life, from 1775 to 1861, in what became the county borough of Barrow-in-Furness. During his boyhood and young manhood, the place was no more than a hamlet. Half a dozen yeoman farmers, together with their families and labourers, constituted the community. William inherited the Fisher farm of about 85 acres, and settled down to farming the land as his father and grandfather had done before him. But William belonged to that generation in Low Furness that was destined to see big changes, and although William did not know it when he became head of the family, Barrow hamlet was destined to be at the centre of the coming upheaval.

From the first page to the last, Fisher used his *Diary* as a record of births, marriages, and deaths of relations, neighbours, friends, and acquaintances throughout Furness and Cartmel and on occasions much further afield. Deaths claimed most space, and the more gruesome or unusual a death the more detail Fisher gave about it. Suicides were just sufficiently uncommon to be sensational, but a woman or a girl burned to death by her clothes catching fire at the kitchen hearth is an unexpectedly frequent entry. And of course the Duddon Sands and the sands route across the mouth of the Leven inevitably claimed victims from time to time.

19 January (1837). Fatal Accident on Duddon Sands. William Clark of Barfield and Robert James a neighbour wear coming to Ulverston Market the Morning beeing verry dark the[y] got lost on the sands the[y] Shouted and the[y] wear heard to Marchgraings [Marsh Grange] a man rode down and found Clark and his Horse fast in the Quick sand and tide flowing the[y] could not get too him the[y] got a Boat he

was got off home but he died soon after the horse was ded
under him Robert James was found in the same place the
next day it is suposed that he had falen from his horse at
the time it went into the hole the Horse got out alive.

5 February (1840). Bengiman Kirkby of Ulverston Shoe Maker with
his Son and Daughter and Mrs. Parker there loger went on an
excursion to the Chaple Island and wandred down to a place
called elwood Scare [Elwood Scar] and was surrounded by the
tide and in atempting to wade through his Son and Daughter
with Mrs. Parker wear Drowned but he suceed in getting on to
Chaple Island where he was taken of by a person in a boat.
Mrs. Parker and his Daughter was found near the place after
the tide returned but his son has not been found at the time I
wright this February 23.

Even the crossing from Barrow Island to Walney—since
1908 spanned by a wide bridge—demanded care and
constant attention:

27 January (1848). John Kimsh b[l]acksmith and Farmer at North-
s[c]ale Isle of Walney was Comming from the Market and set
to cross before it was tide he had a Horse and Cart with two
young Piggs in it the[y] wear all Drowned he had partaken
rather too frely of John barly corn the[y] wear all found the
next morning not fare off he was 45 years of age.

Shipwrecks chiefly on Walney's western shore occurred
from time to time. Fisher records four in 1833 and three
in 1839, but these were years of exceptional storms.

Next to births, marriages, and deaths, the most regular
items in Fisher's *Diary* concern the progress of the farming
year. He recorded any exceptional or extreme weather,
and entered the dates when he sowed oats, wheat, and
barley or planted his potatoes. So conscientious was he
to make a note of the dates of his harvests that his
entries have enabled William Rollinson to construct a
chart showing the spread in time of all his harvests from
1811 to 1856. On average he began to reap—he uses the
term *shear*—during the second or third week in August
and had finished comfortably before mid-September. But
in the half century covered by the *Diary* there were some
remarkable exceptions. The years 1831 and 1852 were
good years in that harvesting began in the last week of
July and 'all was safely gathered in' four weeks later, but

they were outclassed by 1862 when Fisher could happily write, 'began to Shear on the 22 July Shore out August 18'. By contrast, in 1817 and 1823 Fisher could not send his reapers into the fields before 1 September and 30 August respectively, and in 1817 and 1835 the harvest continued until the first and second weeks of October. But the worst harvesting he ever experienced was in 1816: 'September 16 began to Shear: October 23 Shore out'. He made no further comment. The two dates told their own sad story of a wet, cold summer followed by an autumn of frustration and despair for all Furness farmers.

Omissions from diaries can be as eloquent as the entries in them. Fisher opened his *Diary* in 1811, when Britain was at war with Napoleon. He kept it through the gloom of the post-war depression, the politically exciting days, especially for Lancashire, of the Reform Act, the Chartists, and the Anti-Corn-Law League, and into the 1850s with its two crises of the Crimean War and the Indian Mutiny. Yet none of these events Fisher thought worth recording. Like Ellen Weeton he was immune apparently to national or international issues. In 1816, when Samuel Bamford was actively agitating for reform and deeply concerned with the suspension of the Habeas Corpus Act and the effect of the Corn Law, William Fisher's whole attention was taken up with farming and family matters. The excitement of the year was that his brother-in-law arrived from America on a visit, and to judge from his *Diary,* Fisher's only serious concern was the bad summer weather and the consequent late harvest. Again in the 1850s, John O'Neil spent hours with the newspapers anxiously following the development of the Crimean War and in shocked outrage reading reports of the horrors of the Indian Mutiny, but William Fisher makes no mention of either happening except that, immediately after recording on successive days the deaths of William Fell of Rampside and his married daughter Margaret, he startles his reader with:

2 *March* (1855). Died at St. Petersburgh Nicholas Emperor of Russia aged 60. It was during the War in Crimea with Turkey France and England.

Very rarely did Fisher allow news items like this to intrude upon his record of Furness events. The word *Victoria* never graced his pages, but he did note the death of William IV, and the christening of the Prince of Wales, the future Edward VII. The unusual circumstances of Huskisson's death merited four lines, but the *Diary* makes no mention of any other British statesman. It is clear that politics and international affairs left William Fisher stone cold.

Yet even isolated Furness could not always ignore the rest of the country or avoid all contacts with a wider world. Political contagions such as radicalism or chartism were easier to keep at bay than epidemic diseases. Just as in previous centuries Furness had suffered its fair share of plague and pestilence, so in the 1830s it could not completely avoid the cholera that at that time was taking a cruel toll in the growing towns of South Lancashire. In December 1834 Fisher put on record that in the previous October cholera had almost wiped out a neighbouring family, the Fishers of Little Mill Stile. Father, mother, and granddaughter died; only the daughter recovered. The parish authorities burnt every article in the house—'the Clock alone was saved'—to prevent the disease from spreading, and, so far as Fisher's evidence goes, the desperate remedy was successful.

Farming in Low Furness might have satisfied William Fisher, but it did not attract everyone who was born there. Many boys and young men yearned to seek their living in other places. Some satisfied their longing for new horizons by becoming sailors. Others moved south into busier parts of England, and the most adventurous emigrated. John, William's third son, was one who left home. When he was twenty-two he found work in Liverpool, but two years later, he sailed for the United States and joined his uncle, William Cock of Kendal, in Pennsylvania. He must have prospered, for he came back to Furness for a holiday in the winter of 1856-57, and then returned to his work in Pennsylvania again. Towards the end of the *Diary* half a dozen scattered entries speak of Furness men and women dying abroad. In January 1854 Thomas Fenton of Kendal died in 'Vandiemans Land Aged about

70 years': it took three months or so for this news to travel
from Tasmania for Fisher recorded the item in between an
Ulverston death on 15 April and 10 May, when John Bragg
of Whitehaven, a sailor who had just finished a voyage
from Jamaica, died in London. William Cock died in
Pennsylvania in March 1856; in 1857 Mary Alice, 'daughter
of Henry Casson late of Holme', died in Illinois, and Joseph
Lesh, formerly of Newbarns, died in Melbourne. In the
next year, Mary Parker of Ulverston died 'on her homeward
voyage from Australia'.

However, the most insistent factor which was breaking
down the isolation of Furness and changing its traditional
way of life was the growth of industry. Industry was no
stranger there. In the Middle Ages, the monks of Furness
Abbey had developed an iron smelting industry in the district, and much longer than Fisher's generation could
recall iron ore had been regularly mined in Low Furness
and slate had been cut in quarries, particularly at Kirkby
Ireleth. But Furness industry had remained both small in
scale and primitive in method. From young manhood,
Fisher had seen an increasing number of piers built at Barrow for the shipping of iron ore to other parts of Britain,
but the ore, raised from shallow pits by a horse gin, travelled the half-dozen miles from Lindal and Whitriggs slowly
and precariously in horse-drawn carts along execrable
roads. Rapidly-developing industrial Britain was needing
the ore faster than the Furness miners could produce it.
At first, pressure of demand simply produced more
miners and more carts. From the middle of the 1820s,
however, there was considerable talk about constructing
horse-tramways from Lindal and Kirkby to the piers at
Barrow, but nothing was done until the '40s. Then the
first part of the Furness Railway was constructed from
Kirkby to Roa Island, with branch lines running to Barrow
piers and to Lindal. This belated but successful venture
only partly laid the foundations for big-scale industrial
development. There still remained the need to link the
Furness Railway with the main network of national
railways. This was eventually achieved in 1857 when the
line from Barrow at last reached Carnforth.

Fisher's constant interest in recording tragedies reflects the successive chapters of this industrial story. Throughout the *Diary* there are occasional entries about mine disasters, and some of them reveal how simple and unguarded were the mining methods. In 1833, for example, two men died in the Kirkby slate quarries through 'a Quantity of rubish falling on them'. In 1838 two miners suffocated because the smoke from a surface fire poured down the shaft, and two years later, at Lindal, the ground fell in and buried two miners three yards deep. As late as 1850 a bucket falling down a shaft killed a miner at Whitriggs, and in 1854 five men were lost in an iron ore mine at Park, near Dalton, by 'the bursting in of a pond of water'. A grim sign of industrial progress was that a boy was dragged into a machine at Orgrave Mill Iron works in November 1848, and gradually from 1845 railway fatalities creep into the record. In July 1845 a railway worker was trapped between two waggons. The collision fractured his knee, the wound turned septic, and he died a week later. Another railway man was killed on 'the Dalton Railway' in 1847, and in 1851, on 'the Furness Railway', two labourers were 'crushed to Death' by an engine and its twelve waggons. Later, in November 1855, when the Company was extending the line to Ulverston, blasting in Lindal Tunnel killed one man and wounded another. But Fisher does not confine himself to the sad occasions, for he also records, respectively in February 1853 and June 1857, the marriages of William Walker, 'Surveyor on the Furness Railway', at Ulverston, and, of James Hoggarth, engine driver, at Dalton.

Sprinkled among the lists of births, marriages, and deaths are a few items that make more direct reference to the changes that industry was making in the Barrow area. In February 1841, Fisher tells us that 'the Harbour Master entered his situation at Barrow'. In August 1845 he thought it important to write 'the Railway from Roa to Dalton was opened for Passangers', and, next year, that 'on the 30th April the locomotive engin belonging to the Furness Railway was for the first time driven up to Kirby Ireleth'. With some local pride he recorded, on

15 September 1852, the launching of the *Jane Roper*, 180 tons, 'the first New Ship Built at Barrow', and, in November 1859, the opening of the new Iron Works at Hindpool. In July 1854, he was excited to think that, on the very morning it was installed, the telegraph from Barrow to Ulverston had been successfully used to catch a thief. It is also not without industrial significance that on 4 February 1844 the first place of worship in Barrow town was opened:

> The new Chapel at three lanes end Barrow [Newbarns] was Opened by the Reverend John Baldwin of Dalton [curate] the congregation was so large that many wear Obliged to stand at the out side.

Hitherto, local families had worshipped at Dalton parish church or the old chapel of St. Michael at Rampside, but Barrow's increasing population was now beginning to justify a church of its own. Unknown to William Fisher, this dual purpose chapel and school at Newbarns was to be followed by many places of worship of all denominations built in the growing town during the next half century.

INDEX

CENTRAL LANCASHIRE